Understanding Islamic Doctrines

Table of Contents

Understanding Islamic Doctrines: Unraveling the Differences in Islamic Sect Belief and Practice

A.A. Castor

Dedication

To my beloved family,

Your unconditional love, unwavering support, and endless encouragement have been my greatest blessings. From the earliest days of dreaming to the challenging moments of writing, you have stood by me with patience and belief. This book is as much yours as it is mine, a reflection of the values you've instilled and the faith you've shown in me. Thank you for being my rock and my inspiration.

To my dear friends,

Your friendship has illuminated my path with laughter, shared moments, and invaluable support. You've cheered me on through every triumph and lifted me up through every challenge. Your belief in my endeavors has been a source of strength and motivation. This book is a testament to the power of friendship, and I am grateful for each of you who has walked this journey by my side.

To God,

Your grace and guidance have been my constant companions. In moments of doubt, you've shown me the way; in moments of joy, you've multiplied my gratitude. This book is a testament to your faithfulness and the blessings you've bestowed upon me. May it serve as a reflection of your love and the lessons you continue to teach me.

With heartfelt gratitude and love,

A.A. Castor

Copyright © 2024 by A.A. Castor

TABLE OF CONTENTS

Why I Am Writing This Book

The motivation behind writing this book stems from the desire to offer a comprehensive, respectful, and insightful exploration of the diverse **Islamic doctrines** that have shaped the faith and practices of Muslims across the world. In an era where misunderstandings and misrepresentations about Islam are prevalent, it is crucial to provide a well-researched, balanced, and informative account that delves into the historical, theological, and jurisprudential differences between the various Islamic sects.

I believe that by understanding the nuanced beliefs and practices of **Sunni, Shia, Ibadi, Ahmadi,** and other Muslim communities, we can foster greater empathy and appreciation for the diversity within Islam. The differences in doctrine, while sometimes a source of division, also reflect the richness and intellectual depth of the Islamic tradition. This book aims to explore these differences with integrity and respect, focusing on the contributions of each sect to the broader Islamic discourse.

Another key reason for writing this book is to provide a resource for those who seek clarity on often complex theological and legal debates within Islam. By examining the **foundational texts**, key figures, and historical contexts of these sects, I hope to offer readers a deeper understanding of how Islamic thought has evolved and how it continues to shape the lives of millions of people today.

Moreover, I wish to emphasize the **conservative values** held by various Islamic communities, which have preserved the **core teachings** of the **Quran** and **Sunnah** through centuries of social and political change. Highlighting these values not only underscores the continuity of the faith but also offers insight into how Muslims have upheld their beliefs in the face of modern challenges.

Ultimately, this book is a journey into the heart of Islamic doctrines, written with the hope that it will educate, inspire, and contribute to a more informed and nuanced understanding of Islam's rich theological landscape. By unraveling the differences in belief and practice, I aim to build bridges of knowledge and foster a more thoughtful dialogue on the role of religion in our world today.

Warning and Disclaimer

The content of this book is intended for informational and educational purposes only. While every effort has been made to ensure the accuracy and reliability of the information provided, the author and publisher make no guarantees or representations as to the completeness, accuracy, or timeliness of the material presented.

The views and interpretations expressed in this book are those of the author and do not necessarily reflect the opinions of any religious, legal, or scholarly institution. Readers are encouraged to consult with qualified scholars, religious authorities, or legal professionals for specific advice or guidance related to the topics discussed in this book.

Neither the author nor the publisher shall be held liable or responsible for any damages, losses, or claims arising out of the use, reliance on, or interpretation of the information contained in this book. This includes, but is not limited to, any legal, religious, or personal consequences resulting from the use of this material.

By reading this book, you acknowledge and agree that the author and publisher are not responsible for any actions you may take based on the content herein and that you accept full responsibility for any decisions made in relation to the material presented.

This book is provided "as is," with no warranties, express or implied, and the reader assumes full responsibility for the use of the information contained in the book.

About the Author

A.A. Castor is a dedicated writer and researcher with a passion for exploring religious doctrines, history, and cultural diversity. With a particular interest in Islamic theology, Castor has spent years studying the intricate differences between various Islamic sects and how they have evolved throughout history. His work seeks to provide a deeper understanding of the rich theological landscape of Islam and to present complex religious concepts in an accessible and respectful manner.

In addition to his work on Islamic studies, A.A. Castor has written extensively on political strategy, relationship dynamics, and religious history. His books reflect a commitment to thorough research, balanced perspectives, and a desire to foster understanding and dialogue between different communities.

Driven by a belief in the power of knowledge to build bridges and break down barriers, A.A. Castor continues to write on topics that challenge conventional thinking and encourage readers to explore new ideas.

Introduction

Islam, a faith embraced by over a billion people across the globe, is built upon the foundational teachings of the oneness of Allah, the final prophethood of Muhammad (peace be upon him), and the divine guidance of the Quran. These core beliefs have provided a firm, unshakable foundation for Muslims throughout history. However, as with any great tradition, the complexities of human experience and history have led to differences in interpretation, giving rise to a variety of sects and schools within Islam. These differences, while important to understand, all revolve around a shared commitment to the submission to Allah and the adherence to His commandments.

The death of Prophet Muhammad (peace be upon him) marked a critical juncture for the nascent Muslim community. The question of who should lead the believers after him—whether through familial lineage or chosen companions—was not merely a political issue but one with deep spiritual significance. This question gave rise to the major sects of Islam, primarily **Sunni** and **Shia**, each with a conservative commitment to the teachings of the Prophet (peace be upon him) but differing in their understanding of leadership.

Sunni Muslims, who form the majority of the global Muslim population, believe in the caliphate as a political institution and place emphasis on following the example (Sunnah) of the Prophet (peace be upon him) through his rightly guided companions. **Shia Muslims**, by contrast, view the leadership of the Muslim community as a divinely appointed position that should have remained within the family of the Prophet (peace be upon him), specifically with his cousin and son-in-law, Ali (may Allah be pleased with him), and his descendants. These distinctions have shaped the way each group approaches Islamic law, theology, and community leadership, but both remain steadfast in their devotion to Allah and the Prophet's teachings (peace be upon him).

Beyond Sunni and Shia, other significant conservative traditions within Islam, such as **Wahhabism** and **Salafism**, arose as reform movements, calling for a return to the purity of the faith as practiced by the early generations of Muslims (the Salaf). These movements reject innovations (**bid'ah**) in religious practice and emphasize a strict adherence to monotheism (**Tawhid**). Their influence can be seen today in many Muslim-majority countries, where calls for a conservative interpretation of Sharia (Islamic law) guide both personal and public life.

The rise of **Sufism**, the mystical dimension of Islam, also contributed to a deeper, more spiritual practice for many conservative Muslims. Sufism focuses on purifying the heart and drawing closer to Allah through inner devotion, remembrance (**Dhikr**), and spiritual discipline. While there are differing views on Sufi practices within the wider Muslim world, many see it as an extension of the Prophet's example (peace be upon him) of inner reflection and humility before Allah.

Despite these differences, what remains constant in all sects and schools of thought is a conservative adherence to the **Sharia**, the divine law that governs every aspect of a believer's life. Whether in matters of prayer, fasting, or personal conduct, Muslims around the world turn to the Quran and the Sunnah for guidance, seeking to live a life that is pleasing to Allah. The core values of modesty, family, and community are upheld with great reverence in all sects, reflecting the conservative nature of Islamic practice throughout history.

This book aims to explore the rich doctrinal differences that have emerged within Islam, always with a deep respect for the conservative principles that guide the life of every true believer. By understanding these differences, one gains a clearer picture of the various paths within Islam that, despite their divergences, all lead back to the same source: the worship of Allah and the following of the noble example set by His Prophet Muhammad (peace be upon him).

Overview of Islam's Core Beliefs and Practices

AT THE HEART OF ISLAM lies a profound commitment to the oneness of Allah and the guidance provided through His final prophet, Muhammad (peace be upon him). This faith, practiced by Muslims across the world, is built on clear and well-defined principles that shape both belief and daily life. These beliefs and practices are grounded in the **Six Articles of Faith** and the **Five Pillars of Islam**, providing a comprehensive framework for how Muslims relate to Allah, their fellow humans, and the world around them.

The Six Articles of Faith (Iman)

THE FOUNDATION OF A Muslim's belief system is encapsulated in the Six Articles of Faith, which represent core theological principles:

1. Belief in Allah:

○ Central to Islam is the belief in **Tawhid**, the oneness of Allah. Allah is unique, incomparable, and has no partners or equals. This strict monotheism emphasizes that Allah alone is the creator, sustainer, and ruler of all things, and nothing occurs without His will.

2. Belief in the Angels:

○ Muslims believe in the existence of **angels**, spiritual beings created by Allah to perform various duties. Angels, such as **Gabriel (Jibril, peace be upon him)**, who revealed the Quran to the Prophet Muhammad (peace be upon him), play an essential role in delivering Allah's messages and maintaining the divine order.

3. Belief in the Divine Books:

○ Muslims are required to believe in all the holy books revealed by Allah to various prophets throughout history. These include the **Torah** (given to Moses, peace be upon him), the **Psalms** (given to David, peace be upon him), the **Gospel** (given to Jesus, peace be upon him), and the final and complete revelation, the **Quran** (given to Muhammad, peace be upon him). The Quran is regarded as the ultimate and unaltered word of Allah.

4. Belief in the Prophets:

○ Muslims believe in all of Allah's prophets, from **Adam** to **Muhammad** (peace be upon them all). The Prophet Muhammad (peace be upon him) is considered the final messenger, sent to confirm the teachings of previous prophets and deliver the final message to humanity. Every prophet was chosen to guide their people to the worship of Allah alone.

5. Belief in the Day of Judgment:

○ Central to Islamic belief is the conviction that there will be a **Day of Judgment**, where all humans will be resurrected and held accountable for their deeds. Allah will judge with absolute justice, rewarding the righteous with **Paradise (Jannah)** and punishing the wicked in **Hell (Jahannam)**.

6. Belief in Divine Decree (Qadr):

o Muslims believe in **Qadr**, or divine predestination. This means that everything that happens, both good and bad, is within Allah's knowledge and decree. While humans have free will and are responsible for their actions, nothing occurs outside of Allah's will.

The Five Pillars of Islam

THE FIVE PILLARS OF Islam form the essential framework of a Muslim's life, representing the practical acts of worship and devotion to Allah. These pillars are obligatory for all Muslims and reflect their submission to Allah's will.

1. Shahada (Testimony of Faith):

o The declaration of faith, **"La ilaha illallah, Muhammadur rasulullah"** ("There is no god but Allah, and Muhammad is His messenger"), is the most fundamental expression of Islamic belief. Uttering the **Shahada** with sincerity is the entry point into Islam and confirms a Muslim's commitment to the worship of Allah alone and the acceptance of Muhammad (peace be upon him) as His final prophet.

2. Salah (Prayer):

o **Salah**, or ritual prayer, is performed five times a day at prescribed times: **Fajr** (before dawn), **Dhuhr** (midday), **Asr** (afternoon), **Maghrib** (after sunset), and **Isha** (night). Salah serves as a direct link between the worshipper and Allah, offering Muslims regular opportunities to seek forgiveness, guidance, and spiritual nourishment. Before each prayer, Muslims perform a purification ritual called **Wudu** (ablution), which symbolizes physical and spiritual cleanliness.

3. Zakat (Charity):

○ **Zakat** is an obligatory charity, requiring Muslims to give a fixed percentage (usually 2.5%) of their wealth to the needy. Zakat purifies wealth and ensures the well-being of the Muslim community by redistributing resources to support the poor, widows, orphans, and others in need. It is not just a financial transaction but a form of worship that fosters social responsibility and compassion.

4. Sawm (Fasting during Ramadan):

○ During the month of **Ramadan**, Muslims fast from dawn until sunset, refraining from food, drink, and other physical needs. The fast is a means of purifying the soul, increasing piety, and developing empathy for those who are less fortunate. Ramadan is a time of heightened devotion, with increased prayer, Quran recitation, and charitable activities.

5. Hajj (Pilgrimage to Mecca):

○ **Hajj**, the pilgrimage to **Mecca**, is required once in a lifetime for every Muslim who is physically and financially able. Hajj occurs annually during the Islamic month of **Dhu al-Hijjah** and involves a series of rituals that commemorate the trials of **Prophet Ibrahim** (peace be upon him) and his family. The pilgrimage fosters a sense of unity and equality, as Muslims from all walks of life come together to worship Allah in the holiest place in Islam.

Islamic Law (Sharia)

ISLAMIC LAW, OR **Sharia**, is a comprehensive system that governs all aspects of a Muslim's life, from daily rituals to family life, economic dealings, and criminal justice. Sharia is derived from two primary sources:

- The **Quran**: The literal word of Allah and the ultimate source of guidance for all matters of faith and life.

- The **Sunnah**: The sayings, actions, and approvals of the Prophet Muhammad (peace be upon him), preserved in collections of **Hadith**.

Sharia ensures that every aspect of a believer's life is aligned with Allah's will. Its principles emphasize justice, fairness, and compassion, and the application of Sharia varies depending on the school of thought a Muslim follows. The main schools of jurisprudence include **Hanafi**, **Maliki**, **Shafi'i**, and **Hanbali**, each offering unique interpretations on various legal matters.

Unity in Faith, Diversity in Practice

WHILE THE CORE BELIEFS and practices of Islam remain consistent across the Muslim world, there are variations in interpretation and application depending on the sect and cultural context. The Sunni, Shia, and other sects uphold these pillars and articles but may differ in their theological views and legal rulings.

Despite these differences, all Muslims share a commitment to the worship of Allah alone and strive to follow the example set by the

Prophet Muhammad (peace be upon him). Through the fulfillment of the Five Pillars and the adherence to the Six Articles of Faith, Muslims maintain a strong connection to Allah and seek to lead lives of devotion, righteousness, and compassion.

This overview of Islam's core beliefs and practices lays the foundation for understanding the diverse ways in which these principles are expressed across different Islamic traditions.

Importance of Understanding Sectarian Differences in Islam

ISLAM, AS A GLOBAL faith, is united by its belief in the oneness of Allah, the finality of the prophethood of Muhammad (peace be upon him), and the divine guidance provided through the Quran. However, throughout its history, Islam has witnessed the development of various sects and schools of thought. These differences, while rooted in a shared foundation, reflect the diverse interpretations of religious, legal, and political matters that have emerged over centuries. Understanding these sectarian differences is essential for several key reasons:

1. Preserving the Historical Context of Islam

THE DIVISION BETWEEN sects such as **Sunni** and **Shia** traces back to the earliest days of Islam, immediately following the death of the Prophet Muhammad (peace be upon him). Understanding the origins of these sects provides vital insight into how different groups of Muslims approached key questions of leadership and authority.

- **Sunni-Shia Divide:** The primary difference arose from a dispute over who should lead the Muslim community after the Prophet's death. Sunni Muslims, believing in the legitimacy of the Rashidun caliphs, see leadership as a matter of consensus among the Prophet's companions (peace be upon them). In contrast, Shia Muslims believe that the leadership should have remained within the Prophet's family, particularly through Ali (may Allah be pleased with him) and his descendants.

By understanding this historical context, one can better appreciate the theological, political, and cultural factors that shaped the development of different sects and their perspectives on Islamic governance and law.

2. Promoting Unity and Reducing Sectarian Conflict

WHILE THE DIFFERENCES between sects are important to acknowledge, it is crucial to recognize the shared beliefs that unite all Muslims. An informed understanding of sectarian differences can help reduce unnecessary conflict and foster a sense of unity within the global Muslim **Ummah**.

- **Common Faith in Allah and the Prophet (peace be upon him)**: Regardless of sect, all Muslims believe in the oneness of Allah and the prophethood of Muhammad (peace be upon him). This common ground is a powerful unifying force that transcends sectarian divisions.

- **Intra-Muslim Dialogue**: Understanding the nuances of various sects encourages respectful dialogue and cooperation between Sunni, Shia, and other Muslim communities. By focusing on shared values and avoiding misconceptions, Muslims can build stronger bonds within their community.

Recognizing these differences while promoting a spirit of mutual respect is essential for fostering harmony and unity among Muslims, particularly in regions where sectarian tensions have led to conflict.

3. Countering Misconceptions and Stereotypes

SECTARIAN DIFFERENCES are often misunderstood, not only within the Muslim community but also by those outside of it. Lack of understanding can lead to harmful stereotypes, misrepresentations, and even sectarian prejudice.

- **Clarifying the Sunni-Shia Divide**: For many, the Sunni and Shia sects are seen as irreconcilably different, but a deeper understanding reveals that their core beliefs in Allah, the Quran, and the Prophet (peace be upon him) are the same. The differences largely lie in issues of leadership, historical events, and certain legal interpretations.

- **Avoiding Generalizations**: By studying the distinctions between Islamic sects, one can avoid viewing Islam as a monolithic faith. Understanding these differences allows for a more nuanced appreciation of the diversity within the Muslim world, countering simplistic or biased views.

This knowledge helps in promoting a more accurate and respectful understanding of Islam, both within Muslim-majority societies and in non-Muslim contexts.

4. Understanding Modern Political and Social Implications

SECTARIAN DIFFERENCES, particularly between Sunni and Shia Muslims, have profound political and social implications in today's world. These differences are often intertwined with national, ethnic, and political identities, influencing the dynamics of power and governance in many Muslim-majority countries.

● **Political Divides in the Middle East**: The Sunni-Shia divide plays a significant role in the geopolitics of the Middle East, particularly in countries like **Iran**, **Iraq**, **Saudi Arabia**, and **Yemen**. Understanding the religious and historical roots of these divisions is crucial for analyzing contemporary political alliances and conflicts.

● **Sectarian Conflicts**: In certain regions, sectarian divisions have unfortunately been a source of violence and conflict. Recognizing the underlying theological and historical differences can help in developing strategies for peacebuilding and conflict resolution, particularly in countries like **Syria** and **Lebanon** where sectarianism plays a central role in ongoing struggles.

Having an informed perspective on how sectarian differences intersect with modern politics allows for a better understanding of the challenges facing Muslim societies today.

5. Theological and Legal Diversity in Practice

WHILE THE SIX ARTICLES of Faith and the Five Pillars of Islam provide a common foundation, the interpretation and application of Islamic law (**Sharia**) vary significantly between sects and schools of thought. Understanding these differences is key to appreciating the richness of Islamic jurisprudence and its practical implications.

● **Sunni Schools of Law**: Sunni Islam has four major schools of jurisprudence — **Hanafi**, **Maliki**, **Shafi'i**, and **Hanbali** — each with its own interpretation of legal matters, including prayer, fasting, and personal conduct.

- **Shia Jurisprudence**: Shia Islam, particularly **Twelver Shia**, follows the **Jafari** school of jurisprudence, which differs from Sunni schools in areas such as inheritance, temporary marriage, and leadership.

By understanding these legal distinctions, one gains insight into the diversity of practice within Islam and how different sects navigate issues of religious law and daily worship.

6. Appreciating Cultural and Regional Diversity

ISLAMIC SECTS HAVE often developed alongside distinct cultural and regional traditions. Understanding these sectarian differences also sheds light on the rich cultural diversity that exists within the Muslim world.

- **Sufi Mysticism**: While Sufi practices focus on spirituality and personal devotion, they differ in their expression across regions and sects. Sufism plays an important role in the cultural and spiritual life of many Muslim communities, particularly in regions like North Africa, South Asia, and Turkey.

- **Religious Festivals and Rituals**: Shia Muslims, for example, commemorate the **Day of Ashura** to honor the martyrdom of **Husayn** (peace be upon him), while Sunni Muslims generally view Ashura as a day of fasting. These differences highlight the unique ways in which Islamic history and beliefs are celebrated across cultures.

Recognizing these distinctions helps foster a greater appreciation for the diversity of religious practice within Islam, enriching one's understanding of how faith is lived in different contexts.

7. The Role of Reform Movements

IN RECENT CENTURIES, movements like **Salafism** and **Wahhabism** have sought to reform and purify Islam by returning to what they view as the original practices of the early Muslim community (Salaf). Understanding the conservative outlook of these movements is crucial for grasping their influence on contemporary Islamic thought.

- **Salafi Ideology**: Salafis emphasize strict adherence to the Quran and Sunnah, rejecting later innovations (**bid'ah**) in religious practice. This movement has had a significant impact on conservative interpretations of Islam, particularly in countries like Saudi Arabia.

- **Wahhabism**: A specific strand of Salafism, Wahhabism originated in 18th-century Arabia and calls for a return to the pure monotheism (**Tawhid**) of the early Muslims. Its influence is seen today in the conservative religious landscape of the Arabian Peninsula.

Understanding these movements provides insight into modern conservative Islamic thought and its role in shaping religious and political discourse.

Conclusion

Understanding sectarian differences in Islam is essential for appreciating the complexity and diversity within the faith. While these differences have led to various theological, legal, and political interpretations, they all stem from a shared belief in the oneness of Allah and the prophethood of Muhammad (peace be upon him). By exploring these distinctions, a clearer picture of Islam emerges—one that respects its diversity while acknowledging the core principles that unite all Muslims.

A Brief History of Islam's Development Post-Prophet Muhammad (peace be upon him)

THE DEATH OF THE PROPHET Muhammad (peace be upon him) in 632 CE marked a significant turning point in the history of Islam. His passing left the Muslim community, or **Ummah**, without its beloved leader, leading to crucial decisions about the future of Islamic leadership. What followed was the development of Islamic political, theological, and legal traditions, which shaped the faith as it expanded beyond the Arabian Peninsula.

1. The Rashidun Caliphate (632–661 CE)

AFTER THE DEATH OF the Prophet Muhammad (peace be upon him), the Muslim community had to decide on his successor, leading to the establishment of the **caliphate**, a system of leadership that would govern the Muslims and protect the faith.

- **Abu Bakr (may Allah be pleased with him)**: Chosen as the first caliph, Abu Bakr (may Allah be pleased with him) was a close companion of the Prophet (peace be upon him). His brief rule (632–634 CE) saw the consolidation of the Muslim state and the suppression of tribal revolts (the **Ridda wars**), solidifying the unity of the Muslim Ummah.

- **Umar ibn al-Khattab (may Allah be pleased with him)**: The second caliph (634–644 CE), Umar (may Allah be pleased with him) was known for his administrative skills and military conquests. Under his leadership, Islam expanded rapidly into the Byzantine and

 A.A. CASTOR

Sassanid empires, bringing much of the Middle East, Persia, and North Africa under Muslim control.

- **Uthman ibn Affan (may Allah be pleased with him):** The third caliph (644–656 CE), Uthman (may Allah be pleased with him) is best known for commissioning the compilation of the Quran into a single, standardized text, ensuring the preservation of Allah's message. His rule, however, was marked by internal dissent and accusations of nepotism, which led to his assassination.

- **Ali ibn Abi Talib (may Allah be pleased with him):** The fourth caliph (656–661 CE), Ali (may Allah be pleased with him), who was both the cousin and son-in-law of the Prophet Muhammad (peace be upon him), faced significant opposition, including the first major civil war among Muslims, the **First Fitna**. His assassination in 661 CE marked the end of the Rashidun Caliphate and deepened the division between those who supported him (the **Shia**) and those who opposed him (the **Sunnis**).

---

2. The Emergence of the Sunni-Shia Split

THE LEADERSHIP OF ALI (may Allah be pleased with him) and the events surrounding his caliphate laid the groundwork for the most significant division in Islam: the split between **Sunni** and **Shia** Muslims.

- **Sunni Islam:** Sunni Muslims believe that the leadership of the Muslim community should be based on consensus, as demonstrated by the election of the first four caliphs.

Sunnis regard these caliphs, known as the **Rashidun (Rightly Guided Caliphs)**, as legitimate successors of the Prophet Muhammad (peace be upon him).

• **Shia Islam**: Shia Muslims, on the other hand, hold that the leadership should have remained within the Prophet's family, specifically with Ali (may Allah be pleased with him) and his descendants. This belief in the divinely appointed leadership of the **Imams** forms the core of Shia theology.

The Sunni-Shia split is both theological and political, with Shia Muslims focusing on the martyrdom of **Husayn ibn Ali** (peace be upon him), the grandson of the Prophet Muhammad (peace be upon him), at the Battle of Karbala in 680 CE, as a defining moment in their history.

3. The Umayyad Caliphate (661–750 CE)

AFTER ALI'S ASSASSINATION, the **Umayyad Dynasty** was established under **Muawiya** (may Allah be pleased with him), marking the transition from a caliphate based on election to one that was hereditary. The Umayyad Caliphate, with its capital in **Damascus**, saw the further expansion of the Islamic empire, stretching from Spain in the west to Central Asia in the east.

• **Expansion of Islam**: The Umayyads were successful in expanding Islamic rule across vast territories, including the conquest of North Africa and Spain, where Islam would flourish for centuries.

• **Arabic as the Administrative Language**: The Umayyads made Arabic the official language of the

Islamic empire, facilitating greater unity and cultural development within the vast territories under Muslim rule.

- **Opposition and Dissent**: Despite their successes, the Umayyads faced internal opposition from both non-Arab Muslims (the **mawali**) and Shia Muslims, who rejected the legitimacy of the Umayyad rulers. This opposition eventually contributed to the Umayyad downfall.

---

4. The Abbasid Caliphate (750–1258 CE)

THE **Abbasid Revolution** in 750 CE overthrew the Umayyad dynasty, establishing the **Abbasid Caliphate** with its capital in **Baghdad**. The Abbasid period is often considered a **Golden Age** of Islamic civilization, marked by significant advancements in science, philosophy, medicine, and culture.

- **Cultural Flourishing**: The Abbasid Caliphate became a center for intellectual and cultural development, with scholars translating Greek, Persian, and Indian texts into Arabic. This period also saw the growth of Islamic theology (**Kalam**), legal thought, and the development of the major schools of jurisprudence.

- **Development of Islamic Law**: Under the Abbasids, Islamic jurisprudence was formalized into the **four major Sunni schools of law** (Hanafi, Maliki, Shafi'i, and Hanbali). The Abbasid period also saw the crystallization of **Shia law** through the **Jafari school**.

- **Fragmentation and Decline**: Despite its cultural achievements, the Abbasid Caliphate weakened over time as regional powers asserted their independence. The caliphate was eventually weakened by internal strife and the rise of local dynasties, leading to its downfall when the **Mongols** sacked Baghdad in 1258 CE.

---

5. The Rise of Islamic Empires: Ottoman, Safavid, and Mughal Dynasties

FOLLOWING THE FRAGMENTATION of the Abbasid Caliphate, new Islamic empires rose to prominence, each playing a crucial role in shaping the Muslim world.

- **The Ottoman Empire (1299–1922 CE)**: A Sunni Muslim empire based in **Anatolia**, the Ottomans were known for their military conquests and vast territorial control. The Ottomans captured **Constantinople** in 1453 CE, transforming it into the capital of their empire and a center of Islamic culture. The Ottoman sultans claimed the title of **Caliph**, positioning themselves as protectors of Sunni Islam and its holy sites.

- **The Safavid Empire (1501–1736 CE)**: Based in **Persia**, the Safavid Empire established **Twelver Shia Islam** as the state religion, marking a major turning point in the history of Shia Islam. The Safavid rulers played a key role in shaping Shia theology and culture, contributing to the Shia-Sunni divide that continues to influence the region today.

- **The Mughal Empire (1526–1857 CE)**: The Mughals ruled much of the **Indian subcontinent**, spreading Islam through their patronage of art, architecture, and culture. Their most famous contribution, the **Taj Mahal**, remains a symbol of Islamic art and devotion.

---

6. The Modern Period and Islamic Reform Movements

THE 19TH AND 20TH CENTURIES saw significant changes in the Muslim world, driven by European colonialism, the fall of the Ottoman Empire, and the rise of modern nation-states. In response to these changes, various Islamic reform movements emerged, each seeking to reinterpret or return to Islamic principles.

- **Salafism and Wahhabism**: These movements advocated for a return to the practices of the **early Muslims (Salaf)** and emphasized a strict adherence to **Tawhid** (the oneness of Allah). **Wahhabism**, in particular, gained prominence in the Arabian Peninsula and continues to influence the religious landscape in the region.

- **Political Islam**: The 20th century saw the rise of **political movements** such as the **Muslim Brotherhood**, which sought to establish governance based on Islamic principles. The 1979 **Iranian Revolution** also marked the establishment of a Shia theocratic state.

Conclusion

The development of Islam after the death of the Prophet Muhammad (peace be upon him) is a story of both unity and diversity. While the core beliefs of Islam remained intact, the question of leadership, political realities, and cultural influences led to the emergence of different sects, dynasties, and interpretations of the faith. From the Rashidun Caliphate to the rise of modern Islamic movements, the history of Islam's development reflects a dynamic and ever-evolving tradition, deeply rooted in the teachings of the Quran and the example of the Prophet Muhammad (peace be upon him).

Chapter 1: The Foundations of Sunni Orthodoxy

Sunni Islam, the largest branch of Islam, represents a tradition that traces its theological and legal foundations back to the teachings of the Prophet Muhammad (peace be upon him) and his closest companions (may Allah be pleased with them). It is built upon the belief that leadership of the Muslim community, following the Prophet's death, should be based on the consensus of the community and the example set by the Prophet's companions, rather than being limited to his family alone.

At the heart of Sunni orthodoxy is the reverence for the **Quran** as the direct word of Allah and the **Sunnah** (the sayings, actions, and approvals of the Prophet, peace be upon him) as a guiding source for understanding the practical application of faith. These two sources form the foundation upon which Sunni legal and theological thought is based, giving rise to a rich tradition of jurisprudence, theology, and scholarly inquiry.

The Sunni tradition is not monolithic, but it is united in its emphasis on preserving the continuity of the Prophet's teachings (peace be upon him) through the scholarly consensus of the early generations of Muslims, known as the **Salaf**. Over time, Sunni Islam developed four main schools of jurisprudence: **Hanafi**, **Maliki**, **Shafi'i**, and **Hanbali**, each contributing to the diversity of thought within the Sunni framework while maintaining a commitment to the core tenets of Islam.

Sunni orthodoxy is marked by its adherence to a balanced approach to faith and practice, emphasizing both the importance of ritual worship and the pursuit of justice, fairness, and social harmony within the Muslim community. It is this commitment to maintaining the purity of the original teachings while adapting to changing circumstances that has allowed Sunni Islam to flourish across various cultures and regions, from the heart of the Arabian Peninsula to the far reaches of Asia, Africa, and Europe.

This chapter delves into the foundations of Sunni orthodoxy, exploring its historical development, key beliefs, and the role of jurisprudence in shaping the everyday lives of its adherents. By understanding the roots of Sunni thought, a deeper appreciation of its enduring influence and adaptability can be gained, reflecting the strength and coherence of this central tradition in Islam.

Historical Evolution of Sunni Islam

THE ORIGINS OF **Sunni Islam** can be traced back to the earliest days following the death of the Prophet Muhammad (peace be upon him) in 632 CE. The term "Sunni" itself is derived from the word **Sunnah**, meaning the tradition or practice of the Prophet (peace be upon him). Sunni Islam emphasizes the importance of adhering to both the Quran and the Sunnah as guiding sources for faith and practice. The historical evolution of Sunni Islam is deeply intertwined with the development of the Muslim community's leadership, legal thought, and theological principles.

1. The Rashidun Caliphate (632–661 CE)

THE ROOTS OF SUNNI Islam lie in the establishment of the **caliphate** immediately following the death of the Prophet Muhammad (peace be upon him). The **Rashidun Caliphs**—Abu Bakr, Umar, Uthman, and Ali (may Allah be pleased with them)—were chosen to lead the Muslim community, and their leadership set the foundation for the Sunni understanding of governance.

- **Abu Bakr (may Allah be pleased with him)**: As the first caliph, Abu Bakr (may Allah be pleased with him) was elected by the companions of the Prophet (peace be upon him), establishing the principle that leadership should be chosen by the community's consensus, rather than being determined by familial ties.

- **Umar (may Allah be pleased with him)**: Under the second caliph, Umar (may Allah be pleased with him), the Islamic empire expanded significantly, spreading into the Byzantine and Sassanid territories. His rule is remembered for justice and administrative reforms, laying the groundwork for future governance.

- **Uthman (may Allah be pleased with him)**: Uthman (may Allah be pleased with him) standardized the **Quran** by compiling it into a single, authoritative text. His assassination in 656 CE contributed to growing internal dissent, eventually leading to civil conflict.

- **Ali (may Allah be pleased with him)**: The leadership of Ali (may Allah be pleased with him), though contested by some factions, reinforced the need for a just and capable leader. His assassination marked the end of the Rashidun Caliphate and the beginning of significant internal divisions.

This early period established the Sunni belief that the community's leader (the caliph) should be selected through **Shura** (consultation) and consensus, rather than through hereditary succession.

2. The Umayyad Caliphate (661–750 CE)

FOLLOWING THE DEATH of Ali (may Allah be pleased with him), the **Umayyad Dynasty** was established under **Muawiya** (may Allah be pleased with him), marking the first major transition in Islamic leadership. The Umayyads shifted the caliphate to a hereditary system, with their capital in **Damascus**.

- **Expansion and Consolidation**: Under the Umayyads, the Islamic empire reached its largest territorial extent, spreading from Spain to Central Asia. This period saw the consolidation of political power and the spread of Islam into new regions.

- **Sunni Identity Formation**: During the Umayyad period, the majority of the Muslim community began to coalesce around what would become the **Sunni** interpretation of Islam. Sunni scholars emphasized the importance of the **Quran** and **Sunnah** as the central sources of Islamic law, distancing themselves from the political and theological claims of the Shia minority.

- **Dissent and Conflict**: Despite their expansion, the Umayyads faced opposition from various groups, including the Shia, who rejected their leadership. This opposition would later contribute to the fall of the Umayyads and the rise of the Abbasid Caliphate.

---

3. The Abbasid Caliphate (750–1258 CE)

THE **Abbasid Caliphate**, which replaced the Umayyads, moved the political center of the Muslim world to **Baghdad** and presided over what is often referred to as the **Golden Age of Islam**. This period was crucial in the development of Sunni theology, law, and intellectual culture.

- **Sunni Legal Schools**: It was during the Abbasid period that the four major **Sunni schools of law** (Madhahib) were formalized:

  - **Hanafi**: Founded by **Imam Abu Hanifa** (may Allah have mercy on him), this school emphasized reason and analogy in deriving legal rulings. It became widely practiced in areas such as Iraq, Turkey, and South Asia.

o **Maliki**: Founded by **Imam Malik** (may Allah have mercy on him), this school focused on the practices of the people of Medina as a source of law. It is predominantly followed in North and West Africa.

o **Shafi'i**: Founded by **Imam al-Shafi'i** (may Allah have mercy on him), this school systematized the use of the Quran, Hadith, consensus, and analogy in legal reasoning. It is widespread in Southeast Asia and East Africa.

o **Hanbali**: Founded by **Imam Ahmad ibn Hanbal** (may Allah have mercy on him), this school stressed the literal interpretation of the Quran and Hadith, with limited reliance on reasoning. It is the dominant school in Saudi Arabia.

• **Theological Development**: The Abbasid period also saw the rise of Sunni theology through the works of scholars like **Imam al-Ash'ari** and **Imam al-Maturidi**. These scholars sought to reconcile reason with revelation, developing orthodox Sunni theology that emphasized the attributes of Allah, the nature of divine decree (**Qadr**), and the role of the prophets (peace be upon them all).

• **Intellectual Flourishing**: The Abbasid Caliphate fostered advancements in various fields, including philosophy, medicine, mathematics, and astronomy. The translation of Greek philosophical works into Arabic sparked a period of intellectual growth, and Sunni scholars played a crucial role in developing Islamic sciences.

---

4. The Rise of Regional Powers

BY THE 10TH CENTURY, the Abbasid Caliphate began to fragment, leading to the rise of regional powers that shaped the development of Sunni Islam in different ways.

- **The Ottoman Empire**: The **Ottoman Empire** (1299–1922 CE) became a powerful Sunni state, with its sultans claiming the title of **Caliph** and protector of the Muslim world. The Ottomans played a central role in preserving Sunni orthodoxy and established themselves as the custodians of the Islamic holy cities of Mecca and Medina.

- **Sunni Rule in South Asia**: In South Asia, the **Mughal Empire** (1526–1857 CE) promoted Sunni Islam, contributing to the spread of the Hanafi school of law. The Mughals also patronized Islamic arts, architecture, and culture, leaving a lasting legacy on the region.

---

5. The Development of Sunni Orthodoxy in Modern Times

THE MODERN PERIOD BROUGHT new challenges and opportunities for Sunni Islam, as Muslim societies encountered colonialism, nationalism, and the rise of secularism.

- **Wahhabism**: In the 18th century, **Muhammad ibn Abd al-Wahhab** (may Allah have mercy on him) sought to purify Sunni Islam from what he viewed as un-Islamic innovations. His teachings emphasized strict adherence to the Quran and Sunnah and rejected practices such as the veneration of saints. This movement gained prominence in the Arabian Peninsula and had a lasting influence on the religious practices of Sunni Muslims, particularly in Saudi Arabia.

- **Salafism**: A broader movement within Sunni Islam, **Salafism** advocates a return to the practices of the early generations of Muslims (the Salaf) and calls for a rejection of later innovations in religious practice. Salafism has become a significant force in the global Sunni world, influencing conservative interpretations of Sunni theology and law.

In the modern era, Sunni Islam has continued to evolve, responding to the challenges of modernity while maintaining its core commitment to the Quran, Sunnah, and the consensus of the early Muslim community.

Conclusion

The historical evolution of Sunni Islam reflects its adaptability and resilience in the face of changing political and social conditions. From its roots in the Rashidun Caliphate to its flourishing during the Abbasid period and its continued influence in the modern world, Sunni Islam has remained grounded in the belief that the Quran and Sunnah form the foundation of faith and practice. Through its development of jurisprudence, theology, and governance, Sunni Islam has provided a coherent framework that has guided the lives of countless Muslims across the globe for over a millennium.

The Role of the Rashidun Caliphs in Shaping Sunni Doctrine

THE PERIOD OF THE **Rashidun Caliphs** (632–661 CE) holds a special significance in Sunni Islam, as these four caliphs—Abu Bakr, Umar, Uthman, and Ali (may Allah be pleased with them)—are regarded as the **Rightly Guided** successors of the Prophet Muhammad (peace be upon him). Their leadership, characterized by a deep commitment to the teachings of the Quran and the Sunnah, played a crucial role in shaping Sunni doctrine, law, and governance. Sunni Muslims view the Rashidun period as a golden age of Islamic leadership, where the community was governed in accordance with the values and principles established by the Prophet (peace be upon him).

1. Abu Bakr (may Allah be pleased with him) – Consolidation of the Ummah

AS THE FIRST CALIPH, **Abu Bakr** (may Allah be pleased with him) was instrumental in consolidating the Muslim community after the death of the Prophet Muhammad (peace be upon him). His election by the companions of the Prophet (peace be upon him) set the precedent for the Sunni belief that leadership of the Muslim Ummah should be determined by **Shura** (consultation) and consensus, rather than by hereditary succession.

- **Unity and Authority**: During his brief rule (632–634 CE), Abu Bakr (may Allah be pleased with him) unified the Muslim community through the **Ridda Wars**, which suppressed tribal rebellions and reaffirmed the authority of the central Islamic state. This act of consolidation was seen as crucial in maintaining the unity of the Ummah, a key value in Sunni thought.

● **Preservation of the Quran**: Abu Bakr (may Allah be pleased with him) also initiated the collection and preservation of the **Quran** in written form, after many of the memorizers of the Quran were martyred in battle. This ensured that the divine revelation would be safeguarded for future generations, reinforcing the Sunni commitment to the Quran as the ultimate source of guidance.

---

2. Umar ibn al-Khattab (may Allah be pleased with him) – Expansion and Legal Foundations

THE SECOND CALIPH, **Umar ibn al-Khattab** (may Allah be pleased with him), is widely respected for his strong leadership, administrative reforms, and military conquests that expanded the Muslim state into the Byzantine and Sassanid empires. His rule (634–644 CE) was pivotal in shaping both the political and legal structures of the growing Islamic empire.

● **Institution of Shura**: Umar (may Allah be pleased with him) further institutionalized **Shura** as a method of governance, establishing councils that would consult on important matters. This reinforced the Sunni principle that leadership should involve consultation and community participation, a key aspect of Sunni political thought.

● **Expansion of the Islamic State**: Under his leadership, the Islamic state expanded into new territories, including

Syria, **Persia**, **Egypt**, and **Jerusalem**, spreading the message of Islam far beyond the Arabian Peninsula. This expansion laid the foundation for the widespread influence of Sunni Islam in these regions.

- **Establishment of Islamic Legal Principles**: Umar (may Allah be pleased with him) is also remembered for his contributions to the development of Islamic law (**Sharia**). He appointed judges (**Qadis**) to administer justice according to Islamic principles, ensuring that the laws of the state were grounded in the Quran and Sunnah. His legal reforms became a model for future Sunni jurisprudence, influencing how Islamic law would be applied in various contexts.

---

3. Uthman ibn Affan (may Allah be pleased with him) – Standardization of the Quran

THE THIRD CALIPH, **Uthman ibn Affan** (may Allah be pleased with him), is perhaps best known for his role in preserving the integrity of the Quran. His reign (644–656 CE) was marked by internal dissent, but his most significant contribution to Sunni doctrine was the **standardization of the Quran.**

- **Compilation of the Quran**: As Islam spread to new regions, differences in Quranic recitation began to emerge. To preserve the uniformity of Allah's word, Uthman (may Allah be pleased with him) ordered the compilation and distribution of a single, standardized text of the Quran. This act ensured that the Quran remained consistent and unchanged, a belief that is central to Sunni doctrine.

- **The Unity of the Ummah**: Uthman's (may Allah be pleased with him) efforts to standardize the Quran were also aimed at preserving the unity of the Muslim Ummah, a key goal for Sunni leaders. Despite facing internal criticism and opposition, his commitment to safeguarding the integrity of the Quran had a lasting impact on Sunni thought, reinforcing the Quran as the primary source of law and guidance.

---

4. Ali ibn Abi Talib (may Allah be pleased with him) – Leadership Amidst Conflict

THE FOURTH CALIPH, **Ali ibn Abi Talib** (may Allah be pleased with him), was both the cousin and son-in-law of the Prophet Muhammad (peace be upon him). His leadership (656–661 CE) was marked by significant internal conflict, including the **First Fitna** (civil war), which pitted various factions against one another. Despite these challenges, Ali's (may Allah be pleased with him) commitment to justice, piety, and the teachings of the Prophet (peace be upon him) made him a revered figure in Sunni and Shia Islam alike.

- **Emphasis on Justice**: Ali (may Allah be pleased with him) was known for his emphasis on justice and fairness, even in the face of widespread unrest. His leadership during a time of deep division highlighted the importance of ethical governance in Sunni Islam.

- **Shura and Leadership**: While his caliphate was contested by figures such as Muawiya (may Allah be pleased with him), Ali (may Allah be pleased with him) upheld the principle of **Shura** and sought to maintain unity within the Muslim community. His assassination in 661 CE marked the end of the Rashidun Caliphate and led to the rise of the **Umayyad Dynasty**.

- **Legacy in Sunni Doctrine**: Although Ali (may Allah be pleased with him) is particularly revered in Shia Islam, Sunni Muslims also hold him in high regard for his piety and adherence to the teachings of the Prophet Muhammad (peace be upon him). His legacy contributes to the Sunni belief that leadership should be based on justice, piety, and service to the Muslim community.

---

5. The Rashidun Legacy in Sunni Doctrine

THE RASHIDUN CALIPHS are viewed by Sunni Muslims as the **ideal model of leadership** after the Prophet Muhammad (peace be upon him). Their collective example is considered a golden age of Islamic governance, and their actions continue to influence Sunni thought on leadership, law, and governance.

- **Shura and Consensus**: The Rashidun Caliphs demonstrated that leadership in Islam should be based on **Shura** and consensus, rather than familial ties or hereditary succession. This principle is central to Sunni political doctrine, which emphasizes the importance of consultation and community involvement in decision-making.

- **Adherence to the Quran and Sunnah**: The Rashidun Caliphs ruled according to the Quran and the Sunnah of the Prophet Muhammad (peace be upon him), setting a precedent for future generations. Their emphasis on justice, fairness, and adherence to Islamic principles laid the groundwork for the development of Sunni jurisprudence (**Fiqh**).

● **Unity of the Ummah**: Despite the challenges they faced, the Rashidun Caliphs sought to maintain the unity of the Muslim Ummah. Their efforts to consolidate the community and prevent division remain a guiding principle for Sunni Muslims, who emphasize the importance of unity and cooperation within the Muslim world.

Conclusion

The Rashidun Caliphs played a pivotal role in shaping Sunni doctrine and practice. Their leadership established key principles of governance, law, and religious adherence that continue to influence Sunni thought to this day. Through their commitment to the Quran, the Sunnah, and the unity of the Ummah, the Rashidun Caliphs provided a model of Islamic leadership that serves as an enduring example for Sunni Muslims around the world.

The Quran and Hadith in Sunni Theology

IN SUNNI ISLAM, **the Quran** and **the Hadith** are the two primary sources of theological guidance, shaping every aspect of religious belief and practice. These sacred texts form the foundation of Sunni doctrine, legal principles, and spiritual life. The Quran, regarded as the direct and unaltered word of Allah, provides the ultimate guide for Muslims, while the Hadith, the recorded sayings and actions of the Prophet Muhammad (peace be upon him), serves as a complementary source that illustrates the practical implementation of Quranic teachings. Together, they form the bedrock of Sunni theology, law, and ethics.

1. The Quran – The Word of Allah

THE QURAN HOLDS A CENTRAL position in Sunni theology as the literal and final revelation from Allah. It is the unaltered and eternal word of God, revealed to the Prophet Muhammad (peace be upon him) over a period of 23 years through the angel **Jibril** (peace be upon him). Sunni Muslims believe that the Quran is a divine text that provides guidance on every aspect of life, from individual acts of worship to social justice and governance.

- **Divine Revelation**: The Quran is considered the **ultimate source of authority** in Islam, containing the final and complete message of Allah to humanity. Sunni theology emphasizes the **Tawhid** (oneness of Allah) as the central theme of the Quran, guiding all aspects of faith and practice.

- **Preservation and Integrity**: Sunni Muslims believe that the Quran has been preserved in its original form without alteration. The standardization of the Quran during the caliphate of **Uthman ibn Affan** (may Allah be pleased with him) ensured that all Muslims would recite the same text, unifying the Muslim Ummah under a single, uncorrupted scripture.

- **Source of Law and Guidance**: In Sunni Islam, the Quran is regarded as the primary source of **Sharia** (Islamic law) and is seen as the ultimate guide for ethical and moral behavior. Every aspect of life, including prayer, fasting, charity, family matters, and societal laws, is derived from the Quran. Sunni scholars interpret its verses to apply divine principles to contemporary life, ensuring that the teachings of Allah remain relevant in all contexts.

2. The Role of the Quran in Sunni Theology

THE QURAN IS MORE THAN just a book of religious instructions; it is the source of theological reflection and the basis for Sunni doctrine. Key theological concepts derived from the Quran include:

- **Tawhid (Oneness of Allah)**: The central message of the Quran is the absolute oneness of Allah. Sunni theology places Tawhid at the heart of all religious beliefs, emphasizing that Allah has no partners, equals, or intermediaries.

- **Prophethood**: The Quran confirms the role of **Prophet Muhammad (peace be upon him)** as the final messenger, sent to guide humanity to the truth. The Quran contains numerous references to the lives and messages of previous prophets, but it declares Muhammad (peace be upon him) as the **Seal of the Prophets**.

• **Day of Judgment**: Sunni theology, based on Quranic teachings, stresses the reality of the **Day of Judgment** when all humans will be held accountable for their deeds. The Quran frequently reminds believers of the importance of living a righteous life in preparation for the afterlife.

• **Divine Decree (Qadr)**: The Quran teaches that everything that happens is according to the will and decree of Allah, forming the basis for the Sunni belief in **predestination**.

---

3. The Hadith – The Sayings and Actions of the Prophet Muhammad (peace be upon him)

THE **Hadith** serves as the second most important source of theological and legal authority in Sunni Islam. The Hadith consists of reports about the words, actions, and approvals of the Prophet Muhammad (peace be upon him) as recorded by his companions (may Allah be pleased with them). These reports provide practical explanations and elaborations on the Quranic teachings, offering guidance on how to live in accordance with Islam.

• **Complement to the Quran**: While the Quran provides general principles, the Hadith offers specific examples of how the Prophet Muhammad (peace be upon him) implemented these principles in his own life. For example, the Quran commands Muslims to establish prayer, but it is through the Hadith that the details of how, when, and in what manner prayers are to be performed are explained.

● **Collections of Hadith**: Sunni Islam relies on **six major collections of Hadith** that are considered the most authentic and reliable:

○ **Sahih al-Bukhari**: Compiled by **Imam al-Bukhari** (may Allah have mercy on him), this is regarded as the most authentic Hadith collection in Sunni Islam.

○ **Sahih Muslim**: Another highly esteemed collection, compiled by **Imam Muslim** (may Allah have mercy on him).

○ **Sunan Abu Dawood, Sunan al-Tirmidhi, Sunan al-Nasa'i**, and **Sunan Ibn Majah**: These collections provide additional reports that supplement the teachings found in the Sahih collections.

Sunni scholars use these Hadith collections to interpret the Quran, develop legal rulings, and guide Muslims in their daily lives.

4. The Role of the Hadith in Sunni Theology

IN SUNNI THEOLOGY, the Hadith plays a crucial role in explaining and expanding upon the teachings of the Quran. The Prophet Muhammad (peace be upon him) is considered the best example of how to live according to Allah's guidance, and the Hadith provides insight into his behavior, character, and teachings.

- **Practical Application of Quranic Principles**: The Hadith helps Muslims understand how to implement the commandments of the Quran in daily life. For instance, the specifics of performing **Salah** (prayer), giving **Zakat** (charity), and undertaking **Hajj** (pilgrimage) are all detailed in the Hadith, providing a complete framework for worship and religious duties.

- **Moral and Ethical Guidance**: The Hadith offers guidance on moral and ethical issues, reflecting the character of the Prophet Muhammad (peace be upon him) as a role model for Muslims. His patience, kindness, humility, and justice, as recorded in the Hadith, serve as examples for how Muslims should conduct themselves in their personal and communal lives.

- **Source of Legal Authority**: Alongside the Quran, the Hadith is a primary source for deriving **Sharia** (Islamic law). Sunni scholars use the Hadith to interpret unclear Quranic verses and address issues not explicitly mentioned in the Quran. The consensus of scholars (**Ijma**) and analogical reasoning (**Qiyas**) are also informed by the Hadith when developing legal rulings.

---

5. The Interplay Between the Quran and Hadith

IN SUNNI THEOLOGY, the relationship between the Quran and Hadith is one of mutual reinforcement. The Quran provides the foundational framework of Islam, while the Hadith offers practical examples of how these teachings were lived out by the Prophet Muhammad (peace be upon him). Sunni scholars rely on both sources to ensure that religious practices are grounded in divine revelation and the Prophet's example.

- **The Quran as the Primary Source**: While the Hadith is essential in understanding the faith, the Quran remains the highest authority. Any Hadith that contradicts the teachings of the Quran is considered weak or unreliable. The **Quranic message** of Tawhid, prophethood, and moral guidance takes precedence, and the Hadith is used to support and clarify these principles.

- **The Sunnah**: The Sunnah, as derived from the Hadith, is the practical embodiment of the Quran. Together, the Quran and Sunnah form the twin pillars of Sunni theology, with the Quran providing the divine message and the Sunnah showing how that message is to be lived in the real world.

Conclusion

In Sunni theology, the Quran and Hadith are inseparable in their role of guiding Muslim belief and practice. The Quran, as the word of Allah, provides the core principles of the faith, while the Hadith, through the example of the Prophet Muhammad (peace be upon him), offers practical guidance on how to apply these principles in daily life. Together, these two sources form the foundation of Sunni thought, shaping religious doctrine, legal rulings, and personal conduct across the Muslim world.

The Four Sunni Schools of Thought (Hanafi, Maliki, Shafi'i, Hanbali)

THE DEVELOPMENT OF Islamic jurisprudence (**Fiqh**) within Sunni Islam led to the establishment of four major schools of thought, each of which provides a structured framework for interpreting Islamic law (**Sharia**) based on the Quran, Hadith, consensus (**Ijma**), and analogical reasoning (**Qiyas**). These schools—Hanafi, Maliki, Shafi'i, and Hanbali—are named after their founding scholars, and though they differ in methodology and certain rulings, all are considered valid and orthodox within Sunni Islam. These schools have historically provided guidance on legal, ethical, and ritual matters, helping to shape the practice of Islam in various regions of the world.

1. The Hanafi School

- **Founder: Imam Abu Hanifa** (may Allah have mercy on him) (699–767 CE)

- **Geographical Influence:** The Hanafi school is widely practiced in **South Asia** (Pakistan, India, Bangladesh), **Turkey**, the **Balkans**, **Central Asia**, and parts of the **Middle East**.

KEY CHARACTERISTICS:

- **Flexibility and Reasoning:** The Hanafi school is known for its emphasis on the use of **reasoning (Ra'y)** and **analogy (Qiyas)** in deriving legal rulings. Imam Abu Hanifa (may Allah have mercy on him) encouraged the application of logical reasoning to interpret the Quran and Hadith, particularly in cases where direct textual evidence was not available.

• **Ijtihad and Maslaha**: The Hanafi school allows for the practice of **Ijtihad** (independent legal reasoning) and the consideration of **Maslaha** (public welfare) in certain rulings, providing flexibility in legal matters. This has made the Hanafi school adaptable to various social and cultural contexts.

• **Role of Hadith**: While the Hanafi school respects the Hadith, it gives preference to **Ahad** (isolated) narrations only when they align with established principles from the Quran and consensus. Hanafi scholars also gave weight to the practices of the **Companions** of the Prophet Muhammad (peace be upon him) and the community of **Medina**.

Legacy:

• The Hanafi school is regarded for its intellectual openness and adaptability, which allowed it to thrive in diverse and multi-ethnic societies. Its emphasis on reasoning and jurisprudence helped it to become one of the most widespread schools of thought in the Sunni world.

---

2. The Maliki School

• **Founder: Imam Malik ibn Anas** (may Allah have mercy on him) (711–795 CE)

- **Geographical Influence**: The Maliki school is predominantly practiced in **North Africa** (Morocco, Algeria, Tunisia, Libya), parts of **West Africa**, and some regions of **Sudan** and the **Arabian Peninsula**.

KEY CHARACTERISTICS:

- **Emphasis on the Practice of Medina**: Imam Malik (may Allah have mercy on him) placed great importance on the practices and customs of the **people of Medina**, where the Prophet Muhammad (peace be upon him) lived and established the early Muslim community. Malik regarded the actions of the community in Medina as a valid source of law, viewing them as a direct continuation of the Prophet's (peace be upon him) Sunnah.

- **Strict Adherence to Hadith**: While Maliki scholars used **Qiyas** (analogy) when necessary, they prioritized **Hadith** and the established practices of Medina over personal reasoning. Imam Malik's own Hadith compilation, the **Muwatta**, is one of the earliest and most respected collections of prophetic traditions.

- **Istislah (Public Interest)**: The Maliki school allows for **Istislah**, or consideration of the **public interest**, in deriving legal rulings. This principle is used when the Quran, Hadith, and consensus are silent on a particular issue, allowing scholars to consider the welfare of the community.

Legacy:

- The Maliki school's emphasis on the preservation of the Prophet's (peace be upon him) traditions as practiced in Medina has made it a conservative school in terms of religious practices. However, its use of **Istislah** provides room for adaptability, particularly in the context of North African and West African societies, where it has had a lasting influence.

---

3. The Shafi'i School

- **Founder:** Imam Muhammad ibn Idris al-Shafi'i (may Allah have mercy on him) (767–820 CE)

- **Geographical Influence:** The Shafi'i school is practiced in **Southeast Asia** (Indonesia, Malaysia, Brunei), parts of **East Africa** (Somalia, Yemen), **Egypt**, and regions of the **Levant**.

KEY CHARACTERISTICS:

- **Systematic Approach to Fiqh:** Imam al-Shafi'i (may Allah have mercy on him) is often credited with developing a more **systematic approach** to Islamic jurisprudence. He established a clear methodology for deriving legal rulings, placing equal importance on the Quran and Hadith, while also incorporating **Qiyas** (analogy) and **Ijma** (consensus).

- **Emphasis on Hadith:** The Shafi'i school places great emphasis on the **Hadith** as a primary source of law. Imam al-Shafi'i (may Allah have mercy on him) argued that the **Sunnah** of the Prophet Muhammad (peace be upon him), as preserved in authentic Hadith, is second only to the Quran in terms of authority.

- **Use of Qiyas and Ijma:** In situations where the Quran and Hadith do not provide explicit guidance, the Shafi'i school permits the use of **Qiyas** (analogy) to derive rulings. However, Shafi'i scholars are known for their cautious approach to reasoning, always ensuring that their conclusions align with established texts and consensus.

Legacy:

- The Shafi'i school's methodical and text-based approach to Fiqh has earned it a reputation for being highly structured and scholarly. Its influence is particularly strong in **Southeast Asia**, where it has played a crucial role in shaping the religious practices and legal systems of Muslim-majority nations.

---

4. The Hanbali School

- **Founder: Imam Ahmad ibn Hanbal** (may Allah have mercy on him) (780–855 CE)

- **Geographical Influence**: The Hanbali school is the smallest of the four Sunni schools but has a significant presence in **Saudi Arabia** and parts of the **Gulf States**.

KEY CHARACTERISTICS:

- **Strict Adherence to Texts:** The Hanbali school is known for its **literalist approach** to Islamic jurisprudence, placing strong emphasis on the Quran and Hadith as the primary sources of law. Imam Ahmad ibn Hanbal (may Allah have mercy on him) rejected excessive use of **Qiyas** (analogy) and other forms of speculative reasoning, insisting that rulings should be based directly on explicit texts.

• **Reluctance Toward Ijtihad**: The Hanbali school is cautious about the use of **Ijtihad** (independent reasoning) and largely restricts its application. This reflects the school's focus on preserving the Quran and Hadith as the ultimate sources of guidance.

• **Preference for Weak Hadith**: When no strong Hadith or Quranic evidence is available, the Hanbali school is willing to accept **weak Hadith** over the use of reasoning or consensus, further emphasizing its reliance on textual evidence.

Legacy:

• The Hanbali school is known for its **conservatism** and strict adherence to the foundational texts of Islam. Its influence grew significantly through its association with **Wahhabism**, a reformist movement that emerged in the 18th century and continues to have a strong presence in Saudi Arabia. The Hanbali school's focus on **Tawhid** (oneness of Allah) and rejection of innovations (**bid'ah**) has had a profound impact on Islamic theology and practice in the Arabian Peninsula.

Conclusion

The four Sunni schools of thought—Hanafi, Maliki, Shafi'i, and Hanbali—offer distinct approaches to Islamic jurisprudence while maintaining a shared commitment to the Quran and Sunnah. Each school developed in response to different historical, social, and cultural contexts, providing Muslims with a range of interpretations to address the diverse realities of life. These schools continue to serve as pillars of Sunni orthodoxy, guiding Muslims in their legal, ethical, and spiritual lives while remaining united in their adherence to the core teachings of Islam.

Sunni Perspectives on Leadership and Governance

IN SUNNI ISLAM, THE concept of leadership and governance is deeply rooted in the events following the death of the Prophet Muhammad (peace be upon him) in 632 CE. Sunni perspectives on leadership focus on the principles of **Shura** (consultation), consensus, justice, and the adherence to Islamic law (**Sharia**). Sunni Muslims believe that the leader of the Muslim community, known as the **caliph**, should be chosen based on merit, piety, and the ability to uphold the teachings of Islam, rather than through hereditary succession. This foundational view on governance emerged during the era of the **Rashidun Caliphs** and has since shaped the Sunni approach to political authority and governance.

1. The Concept of the Caliphate

THE LEADERSHIP OF THE Muslim Ummah (community) after the death of the Prophet Muhammad (peace be upon him) was a critical issue that defined Sunni views on governance. Sunni Muslims believe that the first four caliphs, known as the **Rashidun (Rightly Guided) Caliphs**—Abu Bakr, Umar, Uthman, and Ali (may Allah be pleased with them)—established the ideal model for Islamic governance.

- **Role of the Caliph:** The caliph is regarded as the **political and spiritual leader** of the Muslim Ummah, tasked with ensuring the implementation of Sharia and the protection of the Muslim community. While the caliph is not considered infallible or divinely appointed, Sunni tradition holds that the caliph must govern according to the Quran and the Sunnah of the Prophet (peace be upon him).

● **Shura (Consultation)**: One of the key principles in Sunni governance is **Shura**, or consultation. Sunni scholars emphasize that leaders should consult with knowledgeable and pious members of the community when making important decisions. This practice is based on the Quranic injunction: *"And consult them in affairs..."* (Quran 3:159). The Shura system ensures that leadership remains accountable to the community and is guided by collective wisdom rather than arbitrary decisions.

● **Election of Leaders**: Sunni Islam traditionally supports the idea of **electing leaders** through consensus (**Ijma**) and consultation, rather than through hereditary succession. The election of Abu Bakr (may Allah be pleased with him) as the first caliph by the Prophet's companions (peace be upon them) after his death is viewed as a model for how leadership should be determined in Sunni governance.

---

2. The Rashidun Caliphs and the Ideal of Governance

THE RASHIDUN CALIPHS are considered the exemplars of Islamic leadership in Sunni Islam, as their governance reflected justice, consultation, and adherence to the teachings of the Prophet Muhammad (peace be upon him). Each of these caliphs played a significant role in shaping Sunni views on leadership.

● **Abu Bakr (may Allah be pleased with him)**: The first caliph, Abu Bakr's (may Allah be pleased with him) leadership was characterized by humility and a strong commitment to maintaining the unity of the Muslim community. His election through consensus established the Sunni precedent that leadership should not be based on familial ties but rather on the consensus of the Muslim community.

● **Umar ibn al-Khattab (may Allah be pleased with him)**: The second caliph, Umar (may Allah be pleased with him), is remembered for his administrative reforms and establishment of justice. He introduced a system of **Shura** to consult on major decisions and implemented measures to ensure fairness in governance, such as the establishment of public treasuries and social welfare systems. His reign is often cited as a model of Islamic justice in governance.

● **Uthman ibn Affan (may Allah be pleased with him)**: Uthman (may Allah be pleased with him) expanded the Islamic empire and is best known for standardizing the Quran. While his leadership faced internal dissent, his efforts to preserve the integrity of the Quran left a lasting legacy on Sunni governance.

● **Ali ibn Abi Talib (may Allah be pleased with him)**: The fourth caliph, Ali (may Allah be pleased with him), is revered for his wisdom and justice. His leadership during a time of civil conflict reinforced the Sunni belief that leadership must remain committed to justice and the principles of Islam, even in difficult circumstances.

3. Sunni Criteria for Leadership

SUNNI ISLAM OUTLINES specific criteria for those who are eligible to lead the Muslim community. These criteria are based on the teachings of the Quran, the Sunnah of the Prophet Muhammad (peace be upon him), and the example of the Rashidun Caliphs.

- **Piety and Righteousness**: A leader in Sunni Islam must be a person of deep **piety** and **righteousness**, who adheres to the teachings of the Quran and Sunnah. A leader is expected to govern with fairness, uphold justice, and prioritize the welfare of the Muslim community.

- **Knowledge of Sharia**: A leader must have a strong understanding of **Sharia** (Islamic law) and be capable of implementing it in governance. Sunni scholars emphasize that leaders should consult with qualified jurists and scholars to ensure that their rulings and policies align with Islamic principles.

- **Ability to Administer Justice**: One of the key responsibilities of a Sunni leader is to **administer justice**. This includes ensuring that the rights of all individuals—whether Muslim or non-Muslim—are protected and that any form of oppression or injustice is eliminated.

- **Consultation with Scholars and the Community**: Sunni leadership is characterized by **consultation** with scholars and the broader community. A good leader is expected to seek the advice of those who are knowledgeable in matters of religion and governance, as well as consider the needs and opinions of the people they govern.

4. Leadership and the Caliphate in Sunni History

WHILE THE RASHIDUN Caliphate is considered the ideal period of leadership in Sunni Islam, subsequent caliphates, such as the **Umayyad** and **Abbasid** dynasties, played an important role in shaping Sunni political thought.

- **Umayyad Caliphate (661–750 CE)**: The Umayyad dynasty introduced the concept of **hereditary succession**, which was a departure from the Sunni preference for electing leaders through consensus. While the Umayyads contributed to the expansion of the Islamic empire, their rule was also marked by internal dissent and challenges to their legitimacy. Nevertheless, Sunni scholars worked to maintain the religious integrity of the caliphate by emphasizing the importance of upholding Sharia.

- **Abbasid Caliphate (750–1258 CE)**: The Abbasid dynasty, which succeeded the Umayyads, is often regarded as a period of intellectual flourishing and cultural development in Sunni history. The Abbasids sought to balance political authority with religious scholarship, promoting the development of **Sunni jurisprudence** and theology through institutions of learning such as **Madrassas** and **Dar al-Hikma** (House of Wisdom) in Baghdad. While the Abbasid caliphs were often more figureheads than rulers, they provided patronage to scholars and jurists who continued to develop Sunni thought on governance.

---

5. Modern Sunni Perspectives on Leadership

IN THE MODERN ERA, the caliphate as a political institution was officially abolished in 1924 with the fall of the **Ottoman Empire**, the last Sunni empire to claim the title of caliphate. However, Sunni perspectives on leadership and governance remain relevant in contemporary discussions about Islamic politics and governance.

- **Political Movements**: Sunni movements such as the **Muslim Brotherhood** and other Islamist groups have sought to revive the idea of Islamic governance by advocating for leadership based on **Sharia** and the principles of **Shura**. These movements argue that Muslim leaders should govern according to Islamic law and principles, even within the framework of modern nation-states.

- **Consultative Governance**: Many Sunni scholars today emphasize the importance of **consultative governance** in modern Muslim-majority countries. This includes calls for greater political participation, transparency, and justice, with a focus on ensuring that leadership is accountable to the people and aligned with Islamic teachings.

- **Separation of Religious and Political Authority**: While the caliphate was historically both a political and religious institution, many modern Sunni thinkers argue for a more flexible interpretation of leadership, where religious and political authorities may be separate but mutually reinforcing. This reflects the reality of contemporary Muslim societies, where political leadership may not always be directly tied to religious authority.

Conclusion

Sunni perspectives on leadership and governance are deeply rooted in the example set by the Rashidun Caliphs and the early Muslim community. Sunni Islam emphasizes the importance of **Shura** (consultation), **justice**, and adherence to **Sharia** in leadership, with a focus on selecting leaders based on merit, piety, and the welfare of the Muslim Ummah. While the concept of the caliphate has evolved over time, the core principles of Sunni governance continue to shape discussions on leadership in both historical and modern contexts.

Chapter 2: Shia Islam and the Path of the Imamate

Shia Islam represents one of the two major branches of the Islamic faith, distinguished by its deep reverence for the family of the Prophet Muhammad (peace be upon him), especially his cousin and son-in-law **Ali ibn Abi Talib** (may Allah be pleased with him) and his descendants. Central to Shia belief is the concept of the **Imamate**, the idea that leadership of the Muslim community is divinely appointed and should remain within the Prophet's family, through the line of Ali (may Allah be pleased with him) and his progeny. This belief in the unique, spiritual authority of the Imams has shaped Shia theology, law, and identity throughout history.

The origins of Shia Islam lie in the events following the death of the Prophet Muhammad (peace be upon him), when a dispute arose over who should lead the Muslim community. While the majority chose **Abu Bakr** (may Allah be pleased with him) as the first caliph, a group of Muslims believed that the Prophet had designated Ali (may Allah be pleased with him) as his rightful successor. Over time, this division deepened, culminating in the tragic events at **Karbala** in 680 CE, where the Prophet's grandson, **Husayn ibn Ali** (peace be upon him), was martyred in his struggle against the Umayyad caliph **Yazid**.

The martyrdom of Husayn (peace be upon him) became a defining moment for Shia Islam, symbolizing the struggle for justice and the right of the Prophet's family to lead the Muslim Ummah. Shia Muslims believe that the Imams, beginning with Ali (may Allah be pleased with him), are the divinely appointed spiritual and political leaders of the Muslim community, endowed with special knowledge and authority to guide the faithful. This belief in the Imamate forms the cornerstone of Shia identity, shaping their religious practices, legal thought, and commemorations, particularly during the observance of **Ashura**, which marks the martyrdom of Husayn (peace be upon him).

This chapter explores the origins of Shia Islam, the development of the doctrine of the **Imamate**, and the central role that the family of the Prophet (peace be upon him) plays in Shia theology. By examining the key events and beliefs that have shaped Shia thought, a deeper understanding of this rich and complex tradition within Islam will emerge, illuminating its contributions to the broader Islamic world and its distinct path within the faith.

Origins of Shia Islam and the Split with Sunni Islam

THE ORIGINS OF **Shia Islam** trace back to a crucial moment in Islamic history, following the death of the Prophet Muhammad (peace be upon him) in 632 CE. The central issue that led to the split between **Sunni** and **Shia** Islam was the question of **leadership**—who would succeed the Prophet Muhammad (peace be upon him) as the rightful leader of the Muslim community. This issue of succession eventually gave rise to theological and political divisions, resulting in two distinct branches of Islam.

1. The Question of Succession After the Prophet Muhammad (peace be upon him)

THE PROPHET MUHAMMAD (peace be upon him) passed away without explicitly naming a successor, leaving the Muslim community to decide on the leadership of the Ummah (Muslim community). The companions of the Prophet (peace be upon him) debated over who should lead, and this moment of uncertainty led to differing views on the qualifications and process of selecting a new leader.

- **The Sunni Perspective**: The majority of the Prophet's companions (may Allah be pleased with them) believed that leadership should be based on **Shura** (consultation) and consensus. They elected **Abu Bakr** (may Allah be pleased with him), the Prophet's close companion and father-in-law, as the first **caliph**. This choice was seen as a pragmatic decision based on Abu Bakr's piety, leadership qualities, and close relationship with the Prophet (peace be upon him). Sunnis believe that the caliphate should be determined by consensus and that the leader should be chosen based on merit, not familial ties.

● **The Shia Perspective**: A group of Muslims, however, believed that the leadership of the Muslim Ummah should remain within the **family of the Prophet Muhammad (peace be upon him)**. They held that **Ali ibn Abi Talib** (may Allah be pleased with him), the Prophet's cousin and son-in-law, was the most qualified person to lead the community, not only because of his close familial relationship but also due to his early conversion to Islam, deep knowledge, and spiritual devotion. This group argued that the Prophet had designated Ali (may Allah be pleased with him) as his rightful successor on several occasions, including the event of **Ghadir Khumm**, where they believe the Prophet (peace be upon him) explicitly referred to Ali as his successor.

---

2. The Early Caliphate and the Development of Sunni-Shia Divisions

DESPITE THE BELIEFS of Ali's supporters, **Abu Bakr** (may Allah be pleased with him) was chosen as the first caliph, and Ali (may Allah be pleased with him) pledged his allegiance to him in the interest of unity within the Muslim community. This set a precedent for Sunni Muslims, who view the **Rashidun Caliphs**—Abu Bakr, Umar, Uthman, and Ali (may Allah be pleased with them)—as the legitimate leaders of the early Islamic state. However, tensions continued to simmer between those who supported the caliphs and those who believed that leadership rightfully belonged to Ali and his descendants.

● **Ali's Caliphate and the First Fitna**: Ali (may Allah be pleased with him) eventually became the fourth caliph in 656 CE, following the assassination of **Uthman ibn Affan** (may Allah be pleased with him). Ali's caliphate was marked by internal conflict, including the **First Fitna**, a civil war between rival factions within the Muslim community. **Muawiya**, the governor of Syria and a relative of Uthman (may Allah be pleased with him), challenged Ali's authority, leading to the **Battle of Siffin** in 657 CE. Although a temporary peace was reached, this conflict deepened the divide between those who supported Ali and those who opposed him.

● **The Assassination of Ali (may Allah be pleased with him)**: In 661 CE, Ali (may Allah be pleased with him) was assassinated by a group of extremists known as the **Khawarij**, further destabilizing the Muslim Ummah. Following Ali's death, Muawiya declared himself caliph and established the **Umayyad Dynasty**, marking a shift from the elected caliphate to a hereditary monarchy. This moment signified the end of the Rashidun period and the beginning of a deeper and more permanent divide within the Muslim community.

---

3. The Tragedy of Karbala and the Solidification of Shia Identity

THE SPLIT BETWEEN SUNNI and Shia Islam was solidified with the events surrounding the **Battle of Karbala** in 680 CE, which became a defining moment in Shia history and identity.

● **Husayn ibn Ali (peace be upon him)**: After the death of Muawiya in 680 CE, his son **Yazid** became caliph.

Husayn ibn Ali (peace be upon him), the grandson of the Prophet Muhammad (peace be upon him) and son of Ali (may Allah be pleased with him), refused to pledge allegiance to Yazid, viewing his rule as illegitimate and unjust. Husayn (peace be upon him) sought to lead the Muslim Ummah based on justice, piety, and adherence to the Prophet's teachings.

- **The Battle of Karbala**: Husayn (peace be upon him) and a small group of his followers, including family members, were surrounded by Yazid's forces at **Karbala**, in modern-day Iraq. Despite being heavily outnumbered, Husayn (peace be upon him) refused to submit to Yazid's rule, and he and his companions were killed in battle on the 10th of **Muharram**, known as **Ashura**. The martyrdom of Husayn (peace be upon him) is seen by Shia Muslims as a profound act of resistance against tyranny and injustice, and it solidified their belief in the spiritual and moral leadership of the Prophet's family, the **Ahl al-Bayt**.

- **Theological Implications**: The events of Karbala gave rise to the Shia belief in the **Imamate**, the idea that the leadership of the Muslim community must be vested in a line of **divinely appointed Imams** descended from Ali (may Allah be pleased with him) and Husayn (peace be upon him). Shia Muslims believe that the Imams, beginning with Ali (may Allah be pleased with him), are the rightful spiritual and political leaders of the Ummah, endowed with special knowledge and authority to guide the Muslim community.

4. Key Differences Between Sunni and Shia Islam

WHILE BOTH SUNNI AND Shia Muslims share fundamental beliefs in the **oneness of Allah**, the **prophethood of Muhammad (peace be upon him)**, and the divine origin of the **Quran**, there are several theological, legal, and political differences that distinguish the two branches.

- **Leadership**: The most significant difference lies in the concept of leadership. Sunni Muslims believe that leadership should be chosen through consensus and consultation, as demonstrated by the election of the Rashidun Caliphs. In contrast, Shia Muslims hold that leadership must be divinely appointed and should remain within the Prophet's family, specifically through the line of Ali (may Allah be pleased with him) and his descendants.

- **The Imamate**: Shia theology revolves around the concept of the **Imamate**, where the Imams are viewed as divinely appointed leaders with spiritual authority. Shia Muslims believe that the Imams are infallible and possess special knowledge passed down from the Prophet Muhammad (peace be upon him). Sunni Islam, on the other hand, does not recognize the concept of the Imamate and views the caliph as a political leader rather than a divinely guided figure.

- **Ashura and Karbala**: The **commemoration of Ashura** holds deep significance for Shia Muslims, who mourn the martyrdom of Husayn (peace be upon him) and his family. For Shia Muslims, Ashura is a day of reflection on the principles of justice and sacrifice. Sunni Muslims also observe Ashura but primarily commemorate it as a day of fasting, which the Prophet Muhammad (peace be upon him) practiced to commemorate the deliverance of the Prophet Moses (peace be upon him) and the Israelites from Pharaoh.

5. The Development of Shia Islam After Karbala

AFTER THE MARTYRDOM of Husayn (peace be upon him), Shia Islam continued to evolve, with the belief in the Imamate being central to their theology. Shia Muslims hold that the Imams, beginning with Ali (may Allah be pleased with him), serve as both spiritual and political leaders, guiding the Muslim community in all aspects of life.

- **The Line of Imams**: Shia Islam recognizes a line of Imams, believed to be divinely appointed, starting with **Ali** (may Allah be pleased with him) and continuing through his descendants. The most prominent branch of Shia Islam, **Twelver Shia**, believes in a succession of twelve Imams, with the twelfth Imam, **Muhammad al-Mahdi**, currently in occultation. Shia Muslims believe that al-Mahdi will return as the **Mahdi**, a messianic figure, to bring justice to the world.

- **Theological and Legal Traditions**: Shia Islam developed its own distinct theological and legal traditions, often rooted in the teachings of the Imams. Shia scholars, like their Sunni counterparts, rely on the Quran and Hadith but also give special importance to the sayings and actions of the Imams.

Conclusion

The split between Sunni and Shia Islam emerged from a disagreement over the rightful leadership of the Muslim community following the death of the Prophet Muhammad (peace be upon him). While Sunnis believed in the principle of elected leadership through consensus, Shia Muslims upheld that leadership should remain within the family of the Prophet, particularly through Ali (may Allah be pleased with him) and his descendants. The martyrdom of Husayn (peace be upon him) at the Battle of Karbala became a defining moment for Shia identity, solidifying their belief in the divinely appointed Imams. Despite these differences, both Sunni and Shia Muslims share a common faith in the core tenets of Islam and continue to coexist as two major branches of the same religious tradition.

The Concept of the Imamate and Its Theological Significance

AT THE HEART OF **Shia Islam** lies the belief in the **Imamate**, a unique doctrine that sets it apart from Sunni Islam. The Imamate refers to the divinely appointed leadership of the Muslim community, vested in the descendants of **Ali ibn Abi Talib** (may Allah be pleased with him), the cousin and son-in-law of the Prophet Muhammad (peace be upon him). Unlike the Sunni view of the caliphate, where leadership is determined by consensus and election, Shia theology holds that the Imams are divinely chosen, infallible leaders who possess special spiritual knowledge and authority.

1. The Origins of the Imamate

THE CONCEPT OF THE Imamate emerged in the aftermath of the Prophet Muhammad's (peace be upon him) death, when the Muslim community faced the critical question of succession. While the majority of Muslims accepted **Abu Bakr** (may Allah be pleased with him) as the first caliph, a group of the Prophet's followers believed that **Ali** (may Allah be pleased with him), his cousin and closest male relative, was the rightful successor. They argued that the Prophet had designated Ali (may Allah be pleased with him) as his heir at **Ghadir Khumm**, where he declared, *"For whomever I am his leader, Ali is his leader."*

For Shia Muslims, this moment was a divine endorsement of Ali's (may Allah be pleased with him) leadership, establishing the belief that leadership of the Muslim community should remain within the **Ahl al-Bayt** (the family of the Prophet), specifically through the line of Ali (may Allah be pleased with him) and **Fatimah** (peace be upon her), the Prophet's daughter. Thus, Ali (may

Allah be pleased with him) is regarded as the **first Imam** in Shia Islam, and his descendants, starting with his sons **Hasan** and **Husayn** (peace be upon them), are viewed as the rightful leaders of the Ummah.

2. The Divine Appointment of the Imams

SHIA THEOLOGY ASSERTS that the Imams are not merely political leaders but are divinely appointed by Allah to guide the Muslim community. This divine appointment sets the Imams apart from other leaders, as they are seen as the true heirs to the spiritual and temporal authority of the Prophet Muhammad (peace be upon him).

- **Infallibility (Ismah)**: One of the key theological concepts in Shia belief is the **infallibility** of the Imams. Shia Muslims believe that the Imams are free from sin and error, both in their actions and in their judgments. This infallibility (known as **Ismah**) is seen as necessary for the Imams to lead the community in matters of faith, law, and spirituality without deviation or mistake.

- **Spiritual Knowledge (Ilm al-Ladunni)**: The Imams are believed to possess a special, divine knowledge (**Ilm al-Ladunni**) that enables them to interpret the Quran and the teachings of the Prophet Muhammad (peace be upon him) with perfect understanding. This knowledge is said to have been passed down from the Prophet to Ali (may Allah be pleased with him) and from him to each subsequent Imam. It is through this divinely inspired wisdom that the Imams are able to provide guidance to the Muslim community in both religious and worldly matters.

- **Role as Intercessors**: In Shia belief, the Imams serve as **intercessors** between Allah and the Muslim community. Shia Muslims often seek the intercession of the Imams in their prayers, believing that the Imams, due to their special status and proximity to Allah, can act as intermediaries who plead on behalf of believers.

---

3. The Role of the Imams in Shia Theology

IN SHIA ISLAM, THE Imams play a crucial role not only as political leaders but also as spiritual guides and interpreters of divine law. Their leadership is believed to be continuous, stretching from **Ali** (may Allah be pleased with him) through the line of his descendants. For **Twelver Shia**, the largest branch of Shia Islam, this line of Imams culminates with the twelfth Imam, **Muhammad al-Mahdi** (peace be upon him), who is currently in occultation and is expected to return as the **Mahdi** to restore justice and bring about divine rule.

- **Guardians of the Faith**: The Imams are seen as the protectors of Islam, ensuring that the true message of the Prophet Muhammad (peace be upon him) is preserved and passed down through generations. Their role is not only to lead but also to guard the integrity of Islamic teachings, especially in the face of political corruption or misinterpretation.

- **The Model of Justice and Sacrifice**: The Imams are revered for their unwavering commitment to justice and righteousness. The most poignant example of this is the martyrdom of **Husayn ibn Ali** (peace be upon him) at the **Battle of Karbala** in 680 CE. Husayn's (peace be upon him) refusal to accept the unjust rule of **Yazid** and his sacrifice at Karbala became a defining moment for Shia identity, symbolizing the ongoing struggle against tyranny and injustice. Husayn's (peace be upon him) martyrdom is commemorated annually during the **Ashura** observance, which serves as both a religious and emotional connection to the Imams' commitment to justice.

4. Theological Significance of the Imamate

THE IMAMATE HAS PROFOUND theological implications in Shia Islam, shaping not only the political framework of leadership but also the spiritual and eschatological dimensions of the faith. The doctrine of the Imamate reflects a deep-seated belief in the continuous presence of divine guidance within the Muslim community, even after the death of the Prophet Muhammad (peace be upon him).

- **Continuity of Divine Guidance**: In Shia theology, the Imamate ensures the continuity of divine guidance. While the Prophet Muhammad (peace be upon him) is regarded as the final messenger, Shia Muslims believe that the Imams serve as **divinely appointed leaders** who continue to guide the community in spiritual and legal matters. This belief reflects a conviction that the Muslim community is never left without a source of divine direction.

- **Salvation and the Mahdi**: The twelfth Imam, **Muhammad al-Mahdi** (peace be upon him), holds a special place in Shia eschatology. Shia Muslims believe that he is in a state of occultation, hidden from the world, but will return as the **Mahdi**, a messianic figure who will bring justice to the world, defeat evil, and establish Allah's rule on earth. The return of the Mahdi is seen as a pivotal event in Shia eschatology, symbolizing the ultimate victory of justice over oppression.

- **The Imam as the Perfect Example**: In Shia Islam, the Imams are considered the **perfect examples** of how to live a righteous and pious life. Their conduct, teachings, and sacrifices are seen as a model for all believers to emulate. The Imams' lives reflect the values of patience, humility, resistance against injustice, and devotion to Allah, and these values remain central to Shia religious and spiritual practice.

5. The Imamate and Shia Identity

THE CONCEPT OF THE Imamate is central to Shia identity, shaping not only theological beliefs but also communal practices and historical consciousness. The Imams, especially Ali (may Allah be pleased with him) and Husayn (peace be upon him), are revered figures whose struggles and sacrifices are commemorated in Shia religious life.

- **Commemoration of Ashura**: One of the most significant expressions of Shia devotion to the Imams is the annual commemoration of **Ashura**, which marks the martyrdom of Husayn (peace be upon him) at Karbala. This event serves as a powerful symbol of the Imams' resistance to injustice and their dedication to truth. For Shia Muslims, Ashura is a day of mourning, reflection, and reaffirmation of their commitment to justice, inspired by the example of Husayn (peace be upon him).

- **Devotion to the Ahl al-Bayt**: Shia Muslims have a special reverence for the **Ahl al-Bayt**, the family of the Prophet Muhammad (peace be upon him). The love for and loyalty to the Ahl al-Bayt is central to Shia spirituality, with the Imams seen as the rightful heirs to the Prophet's legacy. This devotion manifests in various religious practices, such as **Ziyarat** (pilgrimages) to the shrines of the Imams and their descendants.

Conclusion

The concept of the **Imamate** is central to Shia Islam, shaping its theology, spirituality, and religious practices. The Imams, as divinely appointed leaders, serve as both spiritual guides and models of justice, carrying forward the message of the Prophet Muhammad (peace be upon him) through their wisdom, sacrifice, and leadership. The belief in the Imams' infallibility, their unique spiritual knowledge, and their role as protectors of the faith gives Shia Islam its distinct identity and provides a continuous source of divine guidance for the community. The Imamate remains a cornerstone of Shia theology, emphasizing the importance of justice, piety, and the enduring connection between the Prophet's family and the Muslim Ummah.

The Martyrdom of Husayn and Its Impact on Shia Identity

THE **martyrdom of Husayn ibn Ali** (peace be upon him), the grandson of the Prophet Muhammad (peace be upon him), at the **Battle of Karbala** in 680 CE is one of the most defining and emotionally charged events in the history of Islam, particularly for **Shia Muslims.** This event became a central symbol of **Shia identity**, representing the values of resistance against oppression, the struggle for justice, and the willingness to sacrifice for truth and righteousness. Husayn's (peace be upon him) death not only solidified the Shia community's sense of distinctness but also gave rise to enduring religious practices and annual commemorations, which continue to shape Shia spirituality and culture today.

1. The Context of the Battle of Karbala

THE EVENTS LEADING to the martyrdom of Husayn (peace be upon him) are deeply rooted in the political and moral conflicts of the early Islamic period. Following the death of **Muawiya**, the first caliph of the **Umayyad Dynasty**, his son **Yazid** was appointed as the next caliph in 680 CE. Yazid's rule was widely seen by Husayn (peace be upon him) and his supporters as illegitimate and corrupt, representing a betrayal of the principles of Islam. Yazid sought allegiance from Husayn (peace be upon him), but Husayn (peace be upon him) refused to recognize his rule, seeing it as contrary to the just and pious leadership that Islam demanded.

- **Husayn's Stand for Justice**: Husayn (peace be upon him) stood as a symbol of opposition to tyranny and oppression. He believed that Yazid's rule violated the core Islamic values of justice, morality, and righteousness.

Husayn's refusal to submit to Yazid's authority was an act of defiance rooted in his commitment to preserving the true spirit of Islam, as taught by his grandfather, the Prophet Muhammad (peace be upon him).

- **Journey to Karbala**: Despite being heavily outnumbered, Husayn (peace be upon him), along with his family and a small group of loyal followers, set out for **Kufa**, where he hoped to find support from those opposed to Yazid's rule. However, he was intercepted by Yazid's forces and forced to camp at **Karbala**, a desolate plain in present-day Iraq. On the 10th of **Muharram**, known as **Ashura**, Husayn (peace be upon him) and his companions were surrounded and cut off from access to water. Despite this dire situation, Husayn (peace be upon him) refused to pledge allegiance to Yazid.

---

2. The Martyrdom of Husayn (peace be upon him)

ON THE DAY OF **Ashura**, Yazid's forces launched a brutal assault on Husayn (peace be upon him) and his small band of followers. Despite knowing that they faced certain death, Husayn (peace be upon him) and his companions chose to fight rather than submit to an unjust ruler. One by one, Husayn's companions, including members of his family, were killed. Husayn (peace be upon him) himself fought valiantly, but he too was martyred on the battlefield. His body was desecrated, and his family taken captive.

- **The Tragedy of Karbala**: The martyrdom of Husayn (peace be upon him) was a deeply tragic event that left an indelible mark on the Muslim community. For Shia Muslims, it represented the ultimate act of sacrifice and the refusal to compromise in the face of injustice. The brutality of Yazid's forces, the suffering of Husayn's family, and the desecration of his body became powerful symbols of oppression and martyrdom that resonate throughout Shia history.

- **Symbol of Resistance**: Husayn's death came to symbolize the eternal struggle between truth and falsehood, justice and tyranny. His refusal to accept Yazid's illegitimate rule, even at the cost of his life, is seen by Shia Muslims as the highest expression of faith and commitment to Islamic principles. The martyrdom of Husayn (peace be upon him) thus became a profound act of defiance against injustice, setting a model for all Muslims to resist oppression, even under the most dire circumstances.

---

3. Ashura and the Commemoration of Husayn's Martyrdom

THE TRAGEDY OF KARBALA is commemorated annually on the **Day of Ashura**, the 10th day of the Islamic month of **Muharram**. For Shia Muslims, Ashura is a day of intense mourning, reflection, and communal solidarity, where the martyrdom of Husayn (peace be upon him) is remembered and honored. The commemoration of Ashura has become a defining feature of Shia religious life and identity.

- **Mourning Rituals**: Shia Muslims observe **mourning rituals** during Muharram, particularly on Ashura, to express their grief for the suffering and martyrdom of Husayn (peace be upon him) and his family. These rituals often include public processions, recitations of lamentations (**Marsiya** and **Noha**), reenactments of the Battle of Karbala, and expressions of sorrow and devotion to the Ahl al-Bayt (the family of the Prophet Muhammad, peace be upon them).

● **Ziyarat to Karbala**: Many Shia Muslims make **pilgrimages (Ziyarat)** to the shrine of Husayn (peace be upon him) in Karbala, which has become one of the holiest sites in Shia Islam. Visiting Karbala during Muharram, especially on Ashura or **Arbaeen** (the 40th day after Ashura), is considered a deeply spiritual act, symbolizing devotion to Husayn's cause and a reaffirmation of the principles of justice and sacrifice.

● **Ashura as a Symbol of Justice**: Beyond mourning, the commemoration of Ashura has become a powerful reminder of the importance of standing up for justice. For Shia Muslims, Husayn (peace be upon him) is not just a martyr but a symbol of the eternal struggle for truth and righteousness. His sacrifice serves as an example for all Muslims to follow, emphasizing that justice must be pursued, even in the face of overwhelming odds.

---

4. Theological and Political Impact of Karbala on Shia Identity

THE MARTYRDOM OF HUSAYN (peace be upon him) at Karbala had profound theological and political implications, solidifying the distinct identity of the Shia community and shaping its core beliefs.

● **The Centrality of the Imamate**: Husayn's martyrdom reinforced the Shia belief in the **Imamate**, the divinely appointed leadership of the Prophet's family. For Shia Muslims, Husayn's (peace be upon him) willingness to sacrifice his life for the principles of justice and truth demonstrated the moral and spiritual superiority of the **Ahl al-Bayt** and their divinely sanctioned right to lead the Muslim Ummah. Husayn's martyrdom also elevated the status of the Imams as not just political leaders but as spiritual guides who are willing to suffer for the sake of preserving Islam's true teachings.

● **Perpetual Struggle Against Oppression**: Karbala became the ultimate symbol of the Shia belief in the **struggle against oppression** and tyranny. Husayn's (peace be upon him) stand at Karbala is seen as a timeless reminder that Muslims must always fight against injustice, corruption, and oppression, regardless of the personal cost. This principle has influenced Shia political thought and action throughout history, inspiring resistance against unjust rulers and regimes.

● **Martyrdom and Redemption**: In Shia theology, **martyrdom** is seen as a path to **spiritual redemption** and closeness to Allah. Husayn's (peace be upon him) sacrifice is viewed as the ultimate act of devotion, where he gave his life not for worldly gain but for the sake of Allah and the preservation of Islam. His martyrdom is believed to hold redemptive value for the Shia community, serving as a source of inspiration and spiritual connection to the divine.

5. The Legacy of Husayn's Martyrdom in Shia History

THE MARTYRDOM OF HUSAYN (peace be upon him) has left a lasting legacy that continues to influence Shia religious practices, political movements, and identity formation.

- **Inspiration for Political Resistance**: Throughout history, the martyrdom of Husayn (peace be upon him) has inspired Shia political movements and uprisings against unjust rulers. From the **Abbasid Revolution** to modern-day resistance movements, Husayn's example of standing up against tyranny has served as a powerful symbol for Shia Muslims who fight for justice, human rights, and religious freedom.

- **Shia Identity and Solidarity**: Karbala has become a unifying event for Shia Muslims, providing a sense of **shared identity** and solidarity. The annual commemoration of Ashura and the mourning rituals associated with it reinforce the bond between Shia communities worldwide, fostering a collective memory of Husayn's (peace be upon him) sacrifice and the shared values of justice, resistance, and loyalty to the Ahl al-Bayt.

- **A Timeless Message**: The message of Karbala transcends time and place, and Husayn's (peace be upon him) legacy continues to resonate with Muslims across generations. His martyrdom is seen as a call to all believers to stand up for truth, defend the oppressed, and resist corruption, making the message of Karbala relevant in all times of moral and political crisis.

Conclusion

The martyrdom of **Husayn ibn Ali** (peace be upon him) at Karbala is a pivotal event in the history of Islam, particularly for Shia Muslims, who view it as a symbol of resistance, sacrifice, and the struggle for justice. Husayn's (peace be upon him) refusal to accept Yazid's unjust rule and his willingness to sacrifice his life for the principles of Islam established a powerful narrative that defines Shia identity. The annual commemoration of Ashura, the devotion to the Ahl al-Bayt, and the centrality of the Imamate all stem from the martyrdom at Karbala, making it a cornerstone of Shia theology, politics, and spiritual life. Husayn's legacy continues to inspire generations of Muslims to uphold justice, resist tyranny, and remain steadfast in the face of oppression.

Twelver Shia, Ismaili, and Zaydi Sects

SHIA ISLAM encompasses various sects, each of which has developed distinct theological beliefs and practices, particularly regarding the succession of Imams, or leaders, after the death of the Prophet Muhammad (peace be upon him). The three primary branches within Shia Islam are **Twelver Shia (Ithna Ashari)**, **Ismaili**, and **Zaydi**. Each of these sects traces its origins to a shared foundation—the belief in the leadership of the Prophet's family, or **Ahl al-Bayt**—but they diverge on the recognition of the rightful Imams and their respective roles in the community.

1. Twelver Shia (Ithna Ashari)

THE **Twelver Shia**, also known as **Ithna Ashari**, is the largest branch of Shia Islam, and its followers make up the majority of Shia Muslims worldwide. Twelvers believe in a line of **twelve divinely appointed Imams**, all of whom are descendants of **Ali ibn Abi Talib** (may Allah be pleased with him), the cousin and son-in-law of the Prophet Muhammad (peace be upon him).

- **The Twelve Imams:** Twelver Shia Muslims believe in a specific line of twelve Imams, beginning with **Ali** (may Allah be pleased with him), followed by his sons **Hasan** and **Husayn** (peace be upon them), and continuing through nine more Imams from Husayn's descendants. The **twelfth Imam, Muhammad al-Mahdi** (peace be upon him), is believed to have entered a state of **occultation** (hidden from the world) in 874 CE and is expected to return as the **Mahdi**, the prophesied savior who will bring justice to the world.

- **Imamate in Twelver Theology**: For Twelvers, the **Imamate** is a divinely ordained institution, with the Imams possessing both spiritual and political authority. They are regarded as **infallible** and divinely guided, serving as the true successors to the Prophet Muhammad (peace be upon him) and the rightful interpreters of Islamic law and theology. The Twelver belief in the infallibility of the Imams (known as **Ismah**) distinguishes them from other Muslim sects, who do not ascribe infallibility to their leaders.

- **The Occultation of the Twelfth Imam**: Twelvers believe that the twelfth Imam, **Muhammad al-Mahdi** (peace be upon him), is in a state of occultation and will return as the **Mahdi** at the end of time to establish a reign of justice and peace. This belief in the hidden Imam is central to Twelver eschatology and provides spiritual hope for the ultimate triumph of justice over tyranny.

- **Geographical Influence**: Twelver Shia Islam is the dominant sect in countries such as **Iran, Iraq, Azerbaijan**, and **Lebanon**, with significant communities in **Bahrain, Pakistan**, and **India**. It has had a profound influence on the political and religious landscape of these regions, particularly in Iran, where it is the official state religion.

---

2. Ismaili Shia

THE **Ismaili** branch of Shia Islam traces its origins to a split over the succession of the **seventh Imam**. While the majority of Shia Muslims (later known as Twelvers) followed **Musa al-Kadhim** (peace be upon him), a group of Shia recognized his elder brother

Isma'il ibn Jafar (peace be upon him) as the rightful successor, thus forming the **Ismaili** sect. Ismailis have a rich tradition of theological interpretation, which emphasizes the esoteric (inner) dimensions of Islam.

- **Succession of Imams**: Ismailis believe that the line of Imams continued through **Isma'il** and his descendants, in contrast to the Twelver belief in Musa al-Kadhim. The Ismaili Imams are considered to be the spiritual leaders and rightful guides for the Muslim community, with a focus on both the outer, exoteric practices of Islam and the inner, esoteric meanings of the faith.

- **Esotericism and the Role of the Imam**: Ismaili theology emphasizes the concept of **batin** (inner meaning) and **zahir** (outer meaning). The Imams are viewed as possessing special knowledge of the esoteric aspects of the Quran, which they reveal to their followers. This focus on the hidden, spiritual truths of Islam distinguishes Ismailis from other Shia groups, particularly Twelvers, who emphasize the legal and political dimensions of the Imamate.

- **Branches within Ismailism**: Over time, Ismailism developed into several branches, the most prominent of which are the **Nizari** and **Mustali** Ismailis.

  ○ **Nizari Ismailis**: The largest Ismaili branch, led by the **Aga Khan**, who is recognized as the current, living Imam. Nizari Ismailis have historically been politically active and have developed a unique form of community organization and religious practice. Today, the Nizari

Ismaili community is spread across regions such as South Asia, Central Asia, and East Africa.

○ **Mustali Ismailis**: This branch emerged after a succession dispute in the 11th century and is predominantly associated with the **Dawoodi Bohra** community, which has a significant presence in India, Pakistan, and Yemen. The Mustali Ismailis follow a line of Imams who are no longer living and are led by a spiritual leader known as the **Da'i al-Mutlaq**.

● **The Aga Khan**: The **Aga Khan**, the spiritual leader of the **Nizari Ismailis**, plays a central role in guiding the community, both religiously and socially. The Aga Khan is recognized as the living Imam who continues to provide spiritual leadership and guidance on ethical, cultural, and educational matters.

---

3. Zaydi Shia

THE **Zaydi** branch of Shia Islam differs from both Twelver and Ismaili Shia in its theological views and political orientation. Zaydi Islam, named after **Zayd ibn Ali** (peace be upon him), the great-grandson of Ali (may Allah be pleased with him), emerged in the early 8th century as a more moderate and politically oriented form of Shia Islam.

● **Zayd ibn Ali and the Revolt**: Zayd ibn Ali (peace be upon him) was a prominent figure in the early Islamic community and led an unsuccessful revolt against the Umayyad caliphate in 740 CE, seeking to restore just leadership based on the principles of Islam. His followers, who became known as **Zaydis**, viewed him as the rightful Imam and the legitimate successor to Ali (may Allah be pleased with him). Zaydis believe that leadership should belong to any qualified descendant of Ali (may Allah be pleased with him) who rises to defend Islam and justice, rather than being limited to a specific line of succession, as is the case with Twelvers and Ismailis.

- **Theological Differences**: Theologically, Zaydi Shia Islam shares more in common with Sunni Islam than Twelver or Ismaili branches. Zaydis reject the concept of **divine infallibility** for the Imams and do not believe that the Imams possess hidden, esoteric knowledge. Instead, Zaydi Imams are seen as political and religious leaders who must be chosen based on their ability to lead the Muslim community in upholding justice and Islamic law. Zaydi theology also places a strong emphasis on the **principle of justice**, which is central to their interpretation of leadership.

- **Political Leadership and the Imamate**: Zaydis do not believe in the necessity of a continuous line of Imams, and their concept of the Imamate is more political than mystical. Any descendant of Ali (may Allah be pleased with him) who is pious, learned, and capable of leading an uprising against tyranny is eligible to become the Imam. This more flexible and pragmatic approach to leadership has influenced Zaydi political movements throughout history.

- **Geographical Influence**: Zaydi Shia Islam is primarily practiced in **Yemen**, where the **Zaydi Imamate** was established in the 9th century and continued in various forms until the 20th century. Zaydis have historically played a significant role in the political and religious life of Yemen, and they continue to be a major force in the country today, particularly through the **Houthi** movement.

Conclusion

The **Twelver Shia, Ismaili,** and **Zaydi** sects each represent distinct interpretations of Shia theology, particularly regarding the **Imamate** and the rightful leadership of the Muslim community. Twelvers emphasize the divinely appointed, infallible line of twelve Imams, culminating in the occultation of the twelfth Imam, who will return as the Mahdi. Ismailis focus on the esoteric dimensions of Islam, with a line of living Imams who guide the community, while Zaydis take a more political and justice-oriented approach to the Imamate, rejecting the concept of infallibility and emphasizing the need for righteous leadership. Despite their differences, these sects share a common devotion to the **Ahl al-Bayt** and a belief in the importance of justice, righteousness, and spiritual guidance within the Muslim community.

Shia Views on Leadership, Politics, and Justice

SHIA ISLAM HAS A DISTINCT perspective on **leadership, politics, and justice**, rooted in the belief that the rightful leaders of the Muslim community are the descendants of **Ali ibn Abi Talib** (may Allah be pleased with him) and **Fatimah** (peace be upon her), the daughter of the Prophet Muhammad (peace be upon him). These views are deeply influenced by the concept of the **Imamate**, which asserts that leadership is divinely ordained and must be passed through the **Ahl al-Bayt** (the family of the Prophet). This belief has shaped Shia thought on governance, justice, and the role of the Imams in guiding the Muslim community, both in spiritual and political matters.

1. The Concept of the Imamate

THE **Imamate** is central to Shia views on leadership, and it differs fundamentally from the Sunni concept of the caliphate. Shia Muslims believe that the Imams, as descendants of Ali (may Allah be pleased with him) and the Prophet's family, are divinely appointed leaders who possess both spiritual and temporal authority.

- **Divine Appointment**: In Shia theology, the Imams are chosen by Allah to lead the Muslim community. Unlike Sunni Islam, where leaders are selected through consensus (**Shura**) or election, Shia Muslims believe that leadership must be passed down through a specific line of the Prophet's descendants, beginning with Ali (may Allah be pleased with him). The Imams are seen as infallible guides who have special knowledge and are free from sin, ensuring that they can lead the community according to the true teachings of Islam.

● **Spiritual and Political Authority**: The Imams in Shia Islam are not only political leaders but also spiritual guides. They are regarded as the legitimate successors to the Prophet Muhammad (peace be upon him) and the rightful interpreters of Islamic law. Their authority extends to both religious matters—such as interpreting the Quran and Hadith—and worldly affairs, such as governance and justice. This combination of spiritual and political leadership sets Shia views on leadership apart from the Sunni caliphate, where the caliph's role is primarily political.

---

2. Shia Views on Politics and Governance

SHIA VIEWS ON POLITICS are closely tied to their belief in the **Imamate** and the need for just, divinely guided leadership. The historical marginalization of the Shia community and the martyrdom of figures like **Husayn ibn Ali** (peace be upon him) at the Battle of Karbala have contributed to a strong emphasis on resisting injustice and tyranny in Shia political thought.

● **Resistance to Tyranny**: One of the defining aspects of Shia political ideology is the belief in resisting unjust rulers and defending the rights of the oppressed. The martyrdom of Husayn (peace be upon him) at **Karbala** in 680 CE is a powerful symbol of this resistance. Husayn's refusal to accept the corrupt rule of **Yazid** is seen as the ultimate act of defiance against tyranny and injustice. For Shia Muslims, this event represents a timeless struggle for justice, inspiring political movements that oppose oppressive regimes.

- **The Role of the Imam in Governance**: Shia Muslims believe that the **Imams** are the only rightful leaders of the Muslim community because of their divine appointment and infallibility. The Imams are tasked with establishing justice, upholding Islamic law, and protecting the rights of the people. Shia views on governance emphasize the need for a ruler who is pious, just, and divinely guided, in contrast to Sunni views, where leaders are chosen through human processes like election or consensus.

- **The Occultation and Awaited Return**: For **Twelver Shia**, the twelfth Imam, **Muhammad al-Mahdi** (peace be upon him), entered a state of occultation in 874 CE and will return as the **Mahdi** to restore justice and establish Allah's rule on earth. During the period of occultation, Shia political theory acknowledges that no leader can fully embody the divine authority of the Imam. As a result, governance in Shia communities has often been shaped by scholars and jurists who serve as interim authorities, guiding the community until the return of the Mahdi.

---

3. Justice in Shia Theology

JUSTICE (**Adl**) is a central theme in Shia theology and political thought, deeply intertwined with the concept of the **Imamate** and the events of Karbala. Shia Muslims believe that establishing justice is one of the primary responsibilities of the Imams, and the quest for justice has been a driving force behind many Shia political and religious movements throughout history.

- **Divine Justice and the Role of the Imams**: In Shia theology, Allah's justice is a fundamental attribute, and the Imams are seen as the rightful agents of divine justice on earth. The Imams are entrusted with the responsibility of ensuring that justice is upheld in society, both in terms of governance and the application of Islamic law. The infallibility of the Imams ensures that they can lead the community without error or bias, making them the perfect instruments for implementing Allah's justice.

- **Karbala as a Symbol of Justice**: The martyrdom of **Husayn ibn Ali** (peace be upon him) at the Battle of Karbala is perhaps the most significant event in Shia history, symbolizing the struggle for justice against tyranny. Husayn's (peace be upon him) refusal to pledge allegiance to Yazid, whom he viewed as an unjust and corrupt ruler, represents a rejection of illegitimate political authority. For Shia Muslims, Karbala is a reminder that justice must be pursued, even in the face of overwhelming odds, and that true leadership is defined by moral integrity and a commitment to righteousness.

- **Justice as Resistance**: Shia political thought often emphasizes the concept of **justice as resistance**. Throughout history, Shia Muslims have often been a marginalized group, facing persecution from dominant Sunni rulers. This experience has reinforced the Shia belief that true justice cannot be achieved under corrupt or oppressive rulers. As a result, Shia communities have historically aligned themselves with movements that seek to challenge tyranny and defend the rights of the oppressed, drawing inspiration from the actions of the Imams, especially Husayn (peace be upon him).

---

4. Shia Leadership in the Modern Era

IN THE ABSENCE OF THE Imam during the occultation, Shia communities have developed systems of governance and leadership to guide them, particularly in religious and political matters. These systems often involve the leadership of **scholars** and **jurists** who are regarded as the temporary representatives of the Imam.

- **The Role of the Ulama**: In the absence of the twelfth Imam, Shia scholars, or **Ulama**, play a key role in guiding the community. The most respected among them, known as **Marja' al-Taqlid** (sources of emulation), are considered authorities in matters of religious law and ethics. These scholars provide guidance on how to live according to Islamic principles in the absence of the Imam and are highly influential in both religious and political spheres.

- **Wilayat al-Faqih (Guardianship of the Jurist)**: One of the most significant developments in Shia political thought is the concept of **Wilayat al-Faqih**, or the guardianship of the jurist. This concept, developed by **Ayatollah Khomeini** and implemented in the Islamic Republic of Iran, holds that in the absence of the Imam, a qualified Islamic jurist (Faqih) can assume political authority to ensure the implementation of Islamic law and justice. This system grants jurists the power to govern on behalf of the Imam until his return. **Wilayat al-Faqih** has become the foundational principle of Iran's theocratic government, where the **Supreme Leader**, a senior Islamic jurist, holds ultimate political and religious authority.

5. Shia Movements for Justice and Reform

THROUGHOUT HISTORY, Shia Islam has been associated with movements that advocate for **justice**, **reform**, and resistance to oppression. The martyrdom of Husayn (peace be upon him) and the principles of the Imamate have inspired numerous uprisings and reform movements aimed at challenging corrupt rulers and establishing just governance.

- **The Abbasid Revolution**: Early in Islamic history, the Abbasid Revolution (750 CE) was partly motivated by support for the Ahl al-Bayt and a desire to overthrow the Umayyad dynasty, which was seen as corrupt and unjust. While the Abbasids ultimately did not establish Shia rule, the revolution was inspired by the principles of justice and opposition to tyranny that are central to Shia thought.

- **Modern Shia Resistance Movements**: In modern times, Shia political movements have continued to advocate for justice and social reform. Groups such as **Hezbollah** in Lebanon and the **Houthi** movement in Yemen have drawn on Shia ideals of resistance and justice in their political and military struggles. These movements often frame their actions in terms of the Shia tradition of standing up to oppression, following the example of the Imams.

Conclusion

Shia views on **leadership, politics, and justice** are deeply shaped by the belief in the **Imamate** and the events of **Karbala**, where Husayn (peace be upon him) sacrificed his life in the struggle against tyranny. The Imamate, as the divinely appointed leadership of the Muslim community, is seen as the true source of spiritual and political authority, entrusted with the responsibility of upholding justice and guiding the community according to Allah's will. Shia political thought emphasizes the importance of resisting unjust rulers, promoting justice, and following the moral and spiritual example set by the Imams. Even in the absence of the Imam, Shia communities look to religious scholars to provide leadership and maintain the principles of justice until the awaited return of the Mahdi, who is believed to bring about ultimate justice and restore divine rule on earth.

Chapter 3: Sufism – The Mystical Path to Divine Union

Sufism, often referred to as the mystical dimension of Islam, represents a spiritual journey aimed at deepening one's connection with the **Divine**. It is a path of inner purification, where the ultimate goal is to experience the presence of Allah in a direct and personal way. While Sufism shares the core beliefs and practices of mainstream Islam, such as the observance of prayer, fasting, and charity, it goes beyond the outward forms of worship, focusing on the cultivation of the soul, the purification of the heart, and the quest for **divine union**.

At the heart of Sufism is the belief that every human being possesses the potential to draw closer to Allah through acts of devotion, meditation, and remembrance (**dhikr**). Sufis, or practitioners of Sufism, seek to go beyond the superficial layers of faith to reach a deeper understanding of the **Truth** (al-Haq), which they believe lies at the core of all existence. This path is not simply a set of prescribed rituals but a transformative experience that encompasses all aspects of life, infusing it with a sense of divine presence and love.

Sufism is characterized by the guidance of spiritual teachers, or **sheikhs**, who lead their disciples through stages of spiritual development. These stages involve a process of inner purification, detachment from worldly distractions, and the refinement of character. The relationship between the Sufi and their spiritual guide is essential, as it mirrors the soul's journey toward Allah. Through the teachings of these masters, Sufis learn to navigate the challenges of the material world while maintaining a constant awareness of the Divine.

This chapter delves into the mystical teachings of Sufism, exploring its origins, key concepts, and practices, and the role it has played in the spiritual life of Muslims throughout history. By examining the path of the Sufi, the reader will gain insight into how this deeply spiritual tradition has inspired Muslims to transcend the boundaries of the material world and seek a more profound, intimate connection with the Divine.

Origins and Definition of Sufism

SUFISM, often described as the **mystical** or **esoteric** dimension of Islam, focuses on the inner, spiritual aspect of the faith, with the ultimate goal of attaining **direct experience** and **union with Allah**. It emphasizes the purification of the heart, self-discipline, and the cultivation of a deep personal connection with the Divine. While Sufism shares the foundational beliefs of Islam, such as the oneness of Allah and adherence to the Quran and Sunnah, it places a particular emphasis on the **inner journey** towards spiritual realization, beyond the outward rituals and formal practices.

1. Definition of Sufism

SUFISM IS OFTEN UNDERSTOOD as the quest for **spiritual perfection**, an approach that seeks to go beyond the formal aspects of religious observance. The word "Sufism" is believed to derive from the Arabic word **"suf"**, meaning "wool," referring to the simple woolen garments traditionally worn by early Muslim ascetics, or **Sufis**, as a sign of renunciation of worldly pleasures. Another interpretation links the term to **"safa"**, meaning "purity," reflecting the Sufi ideal of purifying the heart to experience divine love and presence.

Sufism involves several core concepts:

- **Ihsan**: The pursuit of spiritual excellence, as described in a Hadith of the Prophet Muhammad (peace be upon him), where Ihsan is defined as worshiping Allah as though you see Him, even though you do not.

- **Tazkiyah**: The purification of the soul from negative traits, such as pride, greed, and envy, in order to cultivate virtues like humility, patience, and love.

- **Dhikr**: The remembrance of Allah, often through the repetition of His names or phrases that glorify Him, serving as a spiritual practice to keep the heart constantly aware of the Divine.

2. Origins of Sufism

THE ORIGINS OF SUFISM can be traced back to the early centuries of Islam, when a group of Muslims began to focus intensely on the **spiritual and contemplative** dimensions of the faith. These early Sufis sought to emulate the simplicity, devotion, and piety of the Prophet Muhammad (peace be upon him) and his companions (may Allah be pleased with them), who lived lives centered around their relationship with Allah.

- **Early Ascetics and Mystics**: In the first few centuries of Islam, ascetic practices emerged as a response to the increasing material wealth and power of the Muslim empire. Many early Sufis rejected the materialism of their time, focusing on self-denial, detachment from worldly desires, and intense devotion to Allah. Figures such as **Hasan al-Basri** (642–728 CE) are considered foundational figures in the development of Sufism. Hasan al-Basri emphasized the need for constant repentance and vigilance over the heart, warning against attachment to worldly gains and urging believers to focus on the afterlife.

- **The Influence of the Quran and Hadith**: Sufism is deeply rooted in the teachings of the Quran and the

Prophet Muhammad (peace be upon him). Sufis often cite verses from the Quran that call for contemplation of Allah's signs in the universe and the need to remember Him constantly. The **Hadith**—especially those concerning the inward state of faith and the concept of **Ihsan**—also serve as key sources for Sufi teachings. For instance, the famous Hadith in which the Prophet Muhammad (peace be upon him) describes Ihsan as "worshiping Allah as if you see Him" is central to the Sufi understanding of spiritual excellence.

• **The Emergence of Sufi Orders**: Over time, as Sufism developed, **Sufi orders** (known as **Tariqas**) began to emerge, each centered around a spiritual leader or teacher, known as a **sheikh** or **pir**. These orders provided structured paths for disciples to progress through stages of spiritual development, guided by the teachings of the order's founder. Notable early Sufi figures such as **Rabi'a al-Adawiyya** (713–801 CE), known for her emphasis on **divine love**, and **Junaid al-Baghdadi** (830–910 CE), who articulated the concept of **fana** (annihilation of the self in the Divine), played key roles in shaping Sufism.

---

3. Core Concepts of Sufism

SUFISM IS NOT MERELY a set of mystical beliefs but a comprehensive approach to Islamic spirituality that integrates devotional practices, ethical self-discipline, and a profound love for Allah.

• **Tawhid (Oneness of Allah)**: At the heart of Sufism is the absolute **oneness of Allah (Tawhid)**. Sufis emphasize that all creation is a manifestation of Allah's will, and the purpose of human life is to recognize, witness, and draw near to Allah. The idea of **fana** (spiritual annihilation) reflects the desire to dissolve the ego and become fully absorbed in Allah's presence, achieving a state of divine union.

- **The Journey of the Soul**: Sufism is often described as a **spiritual journey**, where the seeker passes through various stages (called **maqamat**) and states (**ahwal**) of spiritual development. These stages involve overcoming the base desires of the **nafs** (lower self or ego) and progressing towards the ultimate goal of **ma'rifah** (gnosis or divine knowledge) and **wasl** (union with Allah).

- **Love and Devotion**: The theme of **divine love** is central to Sufi spirituality. Sufis believe that the love of Allah is the highest form of devotion and that the ultimate aim of human existence is to love and be loved by Allah. This love is often expressed in poetic terms, as seen in the works of Sufi poets like **Rumi**, who used the metaphor of love to describe the soul's longing for union with the Divine.

Conclusion

Sufism is a mystical path within Islam that emphasizes the inward journey toward Allah, focusing on self-purification, divine love, and the direct experience of the Divine. Rooted in the teachings of the Quran and the Prophet Muhammad (peace be upon him), Sufism emerged as a response to the growing materialism of the early Islamic empire, with early Sufi figures advocating for simplicity, piety, and detachment from worldly concerns. Over time, Sufi orders developed to provide structured spiritual guidance to those seeking a deeper connection with Allah. Through practices such as **dhikr** (remembrance of Allah), meditation, and love for the Divine, Sufis continue to pursue the ultimate goal of union with Allah, seeking to transcend the ego and experience His presence in every moment.

Key Beliefs and Spiritual Practices in Sufism

SUFISM, THE MYSTICAL path of Islam, revolves around a set of key beliefs and spiritual practices that aim to bring the believer closer to Allah. These practices help purify the soul, deepen one's connection with the Divine, and transcend the ego. Central to Sufism are concepts such as **Tawhid** (the oneness of Allah), the annihilation of the self in the Divine (**Fana**), and the constant remembrance of Allah through **Dhikr**. These practices reflect a commitment to living in a state of spiritual awareness, detachment from worldly distractions, and a continual quest for divine knowledge and love.

1. Key Beliefs in Sufism

- **Tawhid (Oneness of Allah)**: The concept of **Tawhid**, or the absolute oneness of Allah, is fundamental to Sufi belief. Sufis emphasize that everything in existence is a reflection of Allah's will, and that true spiritual realization involves recognizing that there is no reality other than Allah. This understanding drives the Sufi to seek **union with the Divine**, dissolving the illusion of separation between the self and Allah.

- **Divine Love and the Journey of the Soul**: Central to Sufi thought is the belief in the soul's journey toward Allah. Sufis view the human soul as being naturally inclined toward its Creator, and life is seen as a journey to return to Allah. **Divine love** is considered the most powerful force driving this journey, and many Sufis believe that the ultimate purpose of existence is to love Allah and experience His love in return. This love is often described in poetic and metaphorical terms, symbolizing the soul's longing for union with the Divine.

● **The Immanence of Allah**: While Islam traditionally teaches that Allah is transcendent and beyond human comprehension, Sufis also emphasize the **immanence** of Allah—His presence within all things. They believe that through spiritual practices, the heart can be cleansed and made aware of Allah's presence everywhere. This leads to an intimate relationship with Allah, where the seeker feels His closeness at all times.

● **The Role of the Sheikh (Spiritual Guide)**: In Sufism, the spiritual journey is often undertaken with the guidance of a **sheikh** or **pir**, a spiritual master who helps the disciple progress through the stages of self-purification and awareness of Allah. The relationship between the sheikh and disciple is one of deep trust, as the sheikh is believed to possess the wisdom and experience necessary to guide the soul toward Allah.

---

2. Key Spiritual Practices in Sufism

SUFI PRACTICES ARE designed to purify the heart, elevate the soul, and deepen the practitioner's connection with Allah. These practices include methods of devotion, contemplation, and self-discipline that enable the seeker to achieve spiritual transformation.

a. Dhikr (Remembrance of Allah)

DHIKR is one of the most fundamental and widely practiced forms of worship in Sufism. It involves the **constant remembrance of Allah**, often through the repetition of His names or phrases that glorify Him, such as **La ilaha illallah** ("There is no god but Allah") or **Subhanallah** ("Glory be to Allah").

- **Purpose of Dhikr**: The goal of Dhikr is to keep the heart and mind constantly aware of Allah's presence, cultivating a deep sense of love, devotion, and submission to His will. Through Dhikr, the Sufi seeks to transcend the distractions of the material world and focus entirely on the Divine. It is believed that regular practice of Dhikr brings spiritual purification, a sense of inner peace, and a closer relationship with Allah.

- **Types of Dhikr**: Dhikr can be performed individually or collectively, silently or aloud. In some Sufi traditions, Dhikr is accompanied by rhythmic movement, chanting, or breathing techniques to help deepen concentration and devotion. These gatherings, known as **Hadra**, can create a powerful communal experience where the participants feel united in their love for Allah.

b. Fana (Annihilation of the Self)

FANA refers to the **annihilation of the self** in Allah, a key concept in Sufi spiritual development. It involves the dissolution of the ego or the lower self (**nafs**) so that the individual's entire being is absorbed in the Divine presence. Fana is considered the ultimate goal of the Sufi path, representing the complete surrender of the self to Allah.

- **Stages of Fana**: The journey to Fana involves several stages of purification, where the Sufi gradually detaches from worldly desires, ego-driven thoughts, and personal ambitions. Through practices like Dhikr, prayer, fasting, and contemplation, the seeker learns to overcome the **nafs** (ego), which is viewed as the main barrier between the individual and Allah. Once Fana is achieved, the seeker reaches a state of complete spiritual union with Allah.

- **Baqa (Subsistence in Allah)**: After reaching Fana, the Sufi enters the state of **Baqa**, or "subsistence in Allah." This is not the loss of individuality but the transformation of the self into a purified vessel through which Allah's will can manifest. In Baqa, the Sufi is no longer focused on the self but acts with a heightened awareness of Allah's presence in every moment, living in harmony with divine guidance.

c. Sema (Listening and Devotional Music)

SEMA, meaning "listening," is a practice that involves the use of **devotional music**, poetry, and sometimes dance as a way to open the heart to divine truths. Music and poetry play a central role in the spiritual life of many Sufi orders, particularly the **Mevlevi** order, known for their **Whirling Dervishes**.

- **Purpose of Sema**: Sufi poetry, often written by figures such as **Rumi, Hafiz**, and **Attar**, is used to evoke feelings of divine love and longing. Through listening to this poetry or music, the Sufi hopes to experience a deep emotional connection with Allah. The practice of **whirling** in Sema is a form of moving meditation, symbolizing the soul's rotation around Allah, similar to how planets revolve around the sun.

• **The Role of Music**: Music in Sufi practice is seen as a way to bypass the rational mind and speak directly to the heart. Through rhythmic beats, melodies, and spiritual verses, the Sufi enters into a heightened state of awareness, which facilitates spiritual insight and closeness to Allah.

d. Murāqabah (Meditation and Contemplation)

MURĀQABAH is the Sufi practice of **meditation** or **contemplation**, where the seeker focuses inward to become fully aware of Allah's presence. It involves deep reflection and introspection, allowing the individual to quiet the mind and soul in order to connect with Allah.

• **Purpose of Murāqabah**: The goal of Murāqabah is to purify the heart, cultivate inner stillness, and reach a state of spiritual clarity where one can experience Allah's light and guidance. It is often done in seclusion or silence, creating space for the Sufi to reflect on divine mysteries and align themselves more closely with Allah's will.

---

3. The Stages of the Sufi Path (Maqamat and Ahwal)

SUFIS BELIEVE THAT the spiritual journey toward Allah is a process that involves moving through various **maqamat** (stages) and **ahwal** (states). These stages represent levels of spiritual development and transformation.

- **Maqamat (Spiritual Stations):** The **maqamat** are stages of discipline and effort that the Sufi works to achieve through devotion, self-purification, and obedience to Allah. Each stage involves the refinement of the soul and the overcoming of certain spiritual obstacles, such as pride or greed. Common maqamat include **repentance (tawbah)**, **patience (sabr)**, **gratitude (shukr)**, and **trust in Allah (tawakkul)**.

- **Ahwal (Spiritual States):** The **ahwal** are temporary spiritual states that are granted by Allah as gifts, rather than achieved through effort. These include feelings of intense love, awe, or closeness to Allah. The states are fleeting and serve to encourage the Sufi along the path, deepening their longing for Allah and affirming their spiritual progress.

Conclusion

Sufism's spiritual practices, such as **Dhikr**, **Fana**, and **Sema**, provide a structured yet deeply personal path for seekers who wish to draw closer to Allah. These practices focus on transcending the ego, purifying the soul, and experiencing the Divine in all aspects of life. Through these spiritual exercises, Sufis seek to cultivate a heart that is fully aware of Allah's presence, ultimately striving for the realization of **Tawhid** and the annihilation of the self in the Divine. The key beliefs of divine love, union with Allah, and the immanence of the Divine guide every step of the Sufi's journey toward spiritual fulfillment.

Major Sufi Orders and Their Cultural Influence

SUFISM, WITH ITS RICH spiritual tradition, is practiced through **Sufi orders**, also known as **Tariqas**. These orders are organized around a specific lineage of spiritual teachers and offer structured paths for disciples to follow in their quest for divine union. Each Sufi order has its unique practices, teachings, and cultural influence, while sharing common goals of spiritual purification and closeness to Allah. Three of the most well-known Sufi orders are the **Qadiriyya**, **Naqshbandi**, and **Chishti** orders. These orders have played a significant role in shaping the spiritual and cultural landscape of the Islamic world.

1. Qadiriyya Order

THE **Qadiriyya** is one of the oldest and most influential Sufi orders, founded by **Abdul Qadir al-Jilani** (1077–1166 CE), a renowned scholar, jurist, and mystic from **Baghdad**. The order emphasizes the importance of inner purification, humility, and adherence to Islamic law while also promoting direct personal experience of the Divine.

- **Teachings and Practices**: The Qadiriyya order emphasizes the importance of **Dhikr** (remembrance of Allah), charity, and service to others. The order encourages its followers to lead lives of piety, humility, and moral integrity, guided by a strong commitment to the **Sharia** (Islamic law). The practice of **Dhikr** in the Qadiriyya order often involves the recitation of Allah's names and attributes, as well as prayers invoking blessings on the Prophet Muhammad (peace be upon him).

- **Cultural Influence:** The Qadiriyya order has had a profound influence on Sufi thought and practice, especially in **Iraq, Turkey, India, West Africa**, and the **Maghreb** (North Africa). Through its widespread network of disciples and scholars, the Qadiriyya order has helped to shape Islamic culture, education, and spirituality in these regions. In **West Africa**, for example, the Qadiriyya order played a central role in the spread of Islam and the establishment of Sufi institutions that promoted religious education and social welfare.

- **Spread of the Qadiriyya:** Over time, the Qadiriyya spread across the Islamic world, with local variations in its teachings and practices emerging in different regions. In **West Africa**, particularly in countries like **Nigeria**, the Qadiriyya order became deeply rooted and remains one of the most influential Sufi traditions, playing a key role in the spiritual life of the region. The Qadiriyya order is also prominent in **Southeast Asia**, where it has influenced Islamic culture and education.

---

2. Naqshbandi Order

THE **Naqshbandi** order is one of the most widespread and influential Sufi orders, known for its emphasis on **silent Dhikr** and strict adherence to the **Sunnah** of the Prophet Muhammad (peace be upon him). The order traces its lineage to **Baha'uddin Naqshband** (1318–1389 CE) from **Bukhara** in Central Asia. The Naqshbandi order places a strong emphasis on the **inner purification of the heart** through contemplation, meditation, and the silent remembrance of Allah.

- **Teachings and Practices**: The Naqshbandi order is distinct in its practice of **silent Dhikr**, where followers engage in the inward, silent repetition of Allah's name or phrases of devotion. This contrasts with the more vocal and audible forms of Dhikr found in other Sufi orders. The order emphasizes the importance of **self-discipline**, living in accordance with the teachings of the Quran and Sunnah, and maintaining a state of constant awareness of Allah in daily life.

- **Emphasis on the Inner Journey**: The Naqshbandi order focuses on the **inner journey of the soul**, encouraging its disciples to engage in deep meditation and contemplation to achieve spiritual awareness and purity. It stresses the importance of balancing spiritual practice with engagement in the world, teaching that one can pursue spiritual growth without withdrawing from society.

- **Cultural Influence**: The Naqshbandi order has had a major influence on the Islamic world, particularly in **Central Asia, Turkey**, the **Indian subcontinent**, and the **Caucasus**. In **Turkey**, the Naqshbandi order has played a significant role in the religious and political life of the country, influencing Ottoman rulers and shaping the cultural identity of the region. The order also spread to the **Indian subcontinent**, where it became influential in promoting spiritual reform and revival. Naqshbandi scholars and saints have contributed significantly to Islamic scholarship, jurisprudence, and the spiritual culture of the regions in which the order is established.

3. Chishti Order

THE **Chishti** order is one of the most well-known Sufi orders in **South Asia**, especially in **India** and **Pakistan**. Founded by **Khawaja Moinuddin Chishti** (1141–1236 CE), the order is renowned for its emphasis on **love, tolerance, and openness** to people of all backgrounds, regardless of faith or social status. The Chishti order is deeply connected to Sufi music, poetry, and the practice of service to humanity.

- **Teachings and Practices**: The Chishti order focuses on **love of Allah** and the **Prophet Muhammad (peace be upon him)** as the central pillars of its spiritual practice. The order teaches the importance of **compassion, service**, and hospitality toward others. One of the core teachings of the Chishti order is the idea of **serving humanity as a form of serving Allah**, and many Chishti Sufi centers (called **khanqahs**) historically provided food, shelter, and spiritual guidance to the poor and needy.

- **Music and Poetry**: The Chishti order is known for its close connection to **Sufi music** and **poetry**, particularly **Qawwali**, a devotional form of singing that is meant to inspire spiritual ecstasy and devotion to Allah. The use of music and poetry is a hallmark of the Chishti order's approach to spirituality, emphasizing the heart's emotional connection with Allah. Chishti Sufis often engage in **Sama** (listening to music or poetry) as a way to deepen their connection to the Divine.

- **Cultural Influence**: The Chishti order has had a profound influence on the spiritual and cultural life of **India** and **Pakistan**. Sufi saints such as **Khawaja**

Moinuddin Chishti, **Nizamuddin Auliya**, and **Baba Farid** played key roles in spreading Islam in the Indian subcontinent through their teachings of love, tolerance, and spirituality. Their shrines continue to attract millions of pilgrims, both Muslim and non-Muslim, who seek spiritual blessings and guidance. The Chishti order's emphasis on inclusivity and compassion has helped bridge cultural and religious divides in South Asia, contributing to a rich spiritual and artistic heritage.

Conclusion

The **Qadiriyya**, **Naqshbandi**, and **Chishti** orders are among the most influential Sufi traditions in the Islamic world, each contributing to the rich spiritual and cultural fabric of their respective regions. The Qadiriyya order, with its emphasis on Dhikr and service, has left a deep mark on the spiritual life of West Africa, the Middle East, and beyond. The Naqshbandi order's focus on silent meditation and inner purification has inspired generations of Sufis in Central Asia, Turkey, and the Indian subcontinent. Meanwhile, the Chishti order's teachings of love, tolerance, and inclusivity have shaped the spiritual and cultural life of South Asia, with its deep connection to Sufi music and poetry. Together, these orders reflect the diversity and profound impact of Sufism on Islamic spirituality, culture, and history.

Sufism's Relationship with Sunni and Shia Islam

SUFISM, as the mystical dimension of Islam, has historically transcended the sectarian divide between **Sunni** and **Shia** Islam. While Sufism has developed distinct characteristics and practices, it shares core beliefs and spiritual values with both Sunni and Shia traditions. The relationship between Sufism and these two major branches of Islam is complex, as Sufism can be found within both Sunni and Shia communities, but it also has its own unique spiritual framework that sometimes sets it apart from more legalistic or doctrinal interpretations of Islam.

1. Sufism within Sunni Islam

SUNNI ISLAM constitutes the largest branch of Islam, and Sufism has historically been closely associated with it. Many of the major **Sufi orders** (Tariqas) that developed throughout Islamic history emerged within Sunni contexts and adhered to the fundamental beliefs of Sunni Islam, particularly regarding the **Sharia** (Islamic law) and the authority of the **Quran** and **Sunnah**.

- **Adherence to Sunni Orthodoxy**: Most Sufi orders within the Sunni tradition strictly adhere to the foundational tenets of Sunni theology, including the belief in the **Tawhid** (oneness of Allah), the **Prophethood of Muhammad (peace be upon him)**, and the centrality of the **Quran** and **Hadith** as sources of Islamic law and guidance. Sufi practices, such as **Dhikr** (remembrance of Allah), **Fana** (annihilation of the self), and spiritual mentorship under a **sheikh**, are seen as supplementary to the outward practices of Islam (such as prayer, fasting, and charity) but are not in conflict with them.

- **Relationship with Sunni Scholars**: Historically, Sufism enjoyed strong relationships with **Sunni scholars** and jurists. Prominent Sunni scholars, such as **Al-Ghazali** (1058–1111 CE), who was a key figure in integrating Sufism into mainstream Sunni Islam, wrote extensively on the importance of inner spirituality, combining Sufi mysticism with traditional Sunni jurisprudence and theology. Al-Ghazali's works, such as **"The Revival of the Religious Sciences"** (Ihya Ulum al-Din), helped bridge the gap between the legalistic aspects of Sunni Islam and the mystical quest for spiritual purity and divine presence found in Sufism.

- **Coexistence with Sunni Practices**: Sufism has flourished alongside Sunni Islam, with many practicing both the outward obligations of Sunni orthodoxy, such as following one of the **four Sunni schools of law** (Hanafi, Maliki, Shafi'i, and Hanbali), while also engaging in Sufi practices to deepen their personal relationship with Allah. Sufi **Tariqas** (orders) such as the **Qadiriyya**, **Naqshbandi**, and **Shadhili** have historically thrived in Sunni-majority regions, contributing to Islamic scholarship, culture, and spirituality.

- **Tensions with Reform Movements**: Despite its widespread acceptance in Sunni Islam, Sufism has faced opposition from certain reformist movements within the Sunni tradition, particularly from **Wahhabism** and **Salafism**, which emerged in the 18th and 19th centuries. These movements criticized Sufism for practices such as the veneration of saints, pilgrimage to Sufi shrines, and the use of **intercession** (Tawassul), viewing them as deviations from the strict monotheism of Islam. This tension has led to conflicts in certain regions where reformist groups have sought to suppress or limit Sufi practices.

---

2. Sufism within Shia Islam

SHIA ISLAM, particularly its mystical traditions, shares significant common ground with Sufism. Shia Islam already places great emphasis on the **spiritual authority** of the **Imams**, the descendants of **Ali ibn Abi Talib** (may Allah be pleased with him), and the deep mystical connection between the **Ahl al-Bayt** (the family of the Prophet Muhammad, peace be upon him) and the Divine. These shared mystical inclinations have allowed Sufism to flourish within Shia contexts, especially among certain Shia groups.

● **Common Mystical Themes:** Shia Islam's belief in the **Imamate**, where the Imams are seen as spiritual guides with esoteric knowledge (**Ilm al-Ladunni**), aligns with the Sufi quest for **divine knowledge (Ma'rifah)** and spiritual closeness to Allah. Both Sufism and Shia Islam emphasize the **inner dimensions** of faith and the importance of spiritual authority. Many Sufis regard **Ali** (may Allah be pleased with him) as the spiritual forefather of Sufism, and Shia Muslims also revere Ali (may Allah be pleased with him) as the first rightful Imam. The emphasis on **love for the Ahl al-Bayt** (the family of the Prophet, peace be upon him) is central to both Shia belief and many Sufi traditions.

- **Shia Sufi Orders**: There are specific Sufi orders that exist within Shia Islam, often sharing the spiritual goals and practices of Sunni Sufi orders while emphasizing Shia theology. The **Nimatullahi** order, for example, is one of the most prominent Shia Sufi orders. It is rooted in the teachings of **Shah Nimatullah Wali**, a revered Shia mystic. Shia Sufis, like their Sunni counterparts, engage in **Dhikr**, contemplation, and the pursuit of spiritual purification, but their practices are also intertwined with Shia theological concepts, such as the veneration of the **Imams** and a focus on the events of **Karbala** and the martyrdom of **Husayn ibn Ali** (peace be upon him).

- **The Role of the Imam**: For Shia Muslims, particularly **Twelvers**, the **Imam** is not only a political leader but also a **spiritual guide** with divine authority. This concept of spiritual leadership parallels the Sufi notion of the **sheikh** or **pir**, who acts as a mentor on the mystical path. The **12th Imam, Muhammad al-Mahdi** (peace be upon him), who is in occultation, is often viewed in a mystical light, with his return being awaited to bring ultimate justice and spiritual fulfillment. This sense of spiritual anticipation is shared by Sufis, who often speak of an **intimate connection** between the Imams and Allah.

- **Tariqas in Shia Contexts**: While Sufism is not as institutionally widespread within Shia Islam as it is in Sunni contexts, it has deep roots in certain regions, especially in **Iran**, **Iraq**, and parts of **South Asia**. The influence of Sufi thought is evident in **Shia mysticism** and **philosophy**, particularly in the writings of figures such as **Mulla Sadra** and **Ayatollah Khomeini**, both of whom integrated aspects of Sufi spirituality into their philosophical and theological works.

---

3. Common Ground Between Sufism, Sunni, and Shia Islam

SUFISM SHARES MANY core beliefs with both Sunni and Shia Islam, particularly in its devotion to Allah, the Quran, and the Prophetic tradition. Despite the doctrinal differences between Sunni and Shia Islam, Sufism's emphasis on **personal spiritual experience**, **love for Allah**, and the quest for **inner purification** transcends many of these divides.

- **Tawhid (Oneness of Allah)**: Both Sunni and Shia Sufis emphasize **Tawhid**, the oneness of Allah, as the central tenet of their faith. Sufi practices such as **Dhikr** and **meditation** are designed to cultivate an awareness of Allah's presence in every moment, transcending the outward differences between Sunni and Shia doctrines.

- **The Role of Saints and Spiritual Guides**: Both Sunni and Shia Sufism place a strong emphasis on the role of **saints** and **spiritual guides**. In Sufism, **saints** are seen as individuals who have attained spiritual proximity to Allah and can act as **intercessors** or guides for others on the mystical path. In Shia Islam, the **Imams** play a similar role, acting as spiritual leaders and models of divine guidance. The veneration of saints in Sufism and the veneration of the Imams in Shia Islam highlight the importance of spiritual authority in both traditions.

- **Mystical Love**: Sufism, whether practiced by Sunnis or Shias, revolves around the concept of **divine love**. The works of Sufi poets like **Rumi** and **Hafiz**, as well as Shia scholars and mystics, express a shared desire to experience Allah's love and unite with the Divine. This shared emphasis on love and devotion is a point of connection between Sufism and both Sunni and Shia Islam.

4. Points of Tension

DESPITE THE DEEP SPIRITUAL connections between Sufism, Sunni, and Shia Islam, there have been periods of tension and disagreement, particularly with more conservative or reformist interpretations of Islam. **Wahhabism** and **Salafism** in the Sunni world, for example, have been critical of Sufi practices such as the veneration of saints, the use of **music** and **poetry** in worship, and pilgrimage to **Sufi shrines**.

- **Shrine Veneration**: One area of contention has been the veneration of **shrines** and **Sufi saints**, which is a common practice in both Sunni and Shia Sufism. Reformist movements such as **Wahhabism** reject shrine veneration as **bid'ah** (innovation) and as a deviation from pure monotheism. Despite this opposition, Sufi shrines continue to be important centers of spirituality in both Sunni and Shia communities.

Conclusion

Sufism's relationship with both **Sunni** and **Shia** Islam is characterized by deep spiritual connections and shared beliefs, but also by differences in interpretation and practice. Sufism has historically been embedded within Sunni Islam, with many of the major **Sufi orders** adhering to Sunni orthodoxy while adding a mystical dimension to the faith. In Shia Islam, Sufism aligns with the tradition's emphasis on the **spiritual authority** of the Imams and shares many of the same mystical aspirations, such as the quest for **divine union** and **inner purification**.

Despite some tensions with more conservative or reformist movements within Sunni Islam, Sufism remains a powerful and influential force within both Sunni and Shia communities, contributing to the spiritual, cultural, and intellectual life of the broader Islamic world. Its emphasis on **personal devotion, love of Allah**, and the **inner journey** continues to resonate with Muslims from both traditions, offering a path to spiritual fulfillment that transcends sectarian boundaries.

The Role of Poetry, Music, and Art in Sufi Worship

IN **Sufism**, poetry, music, and art are powerful mediums for expressing the inner experiences of the soul's journey toward Allah. These forms of artistic expression are used to awaken spiritual longing, cultivate divine love, and bring the practitioner closer to a state of divine union. Unlike traditional forms of Islamic worship that focus primarily on the outward observance of rituals, Sufi worship emphasizes the inner, emotional, and mystical dimensions of the relationship with Allah. Poetry, music, and art are essential tools in this process, helping Sufis convey complex spiritual states and inspire others on the path toward self-purification and enlightenment.

1. Poetry in Sufi Worship

POETRY IS PERHAPS THE most iconic and celebrated form of artistic expression in Sufi worship. Throughout history, Sufi poets have used verse to express their intense love for Allah, their longing for divine union, and their spiritual insights. The themes of **divine love**, **yearning**, **self-annihilation**, and **the soul's journey** are common motifs in Sufi poetry.

- **Famous Sufi Poets:** Some of the most influential poets in the Islamic world were Sufis, including **Rumi, Hafiz, Attar**, and **Rabia al-Adawiyya**. Their works have transcended time and place, resonating with audiences far beyond the Sufi tradition. These poets expressed their profound devotion to Allah through metaphor, symbolism, and allegory, often portraying the relationship between the soul and the Divine as a lover's pursuit of the beloved.

○ **Rumi**: Perhaps the most famous Sufi poet, **Jalal al-Din Rumi** (1207–1273 CE) wrote extensively about the soul's yearning for Allah. His works, such as the **Masnavi**, are filled with allegories and metaphors that convey the struggle for divine union, the sweetness of divine love, and the joy of surrendering the self to Allah's will. Rumi's poetry is often celebrated for its universal appeal and its ability to convey the depths of spiritual experience.

○ **Rabia al-Adawiyya**: Known as one of the earliest and most prominent Sufi mystics, **Rabia al-Adawiyya** (713–801 CE) was renowned for her devotion to **divine love**. Her poetry expresses a love for Allah that transcends the fear of punishment or hope for reward, focusing entirely on love for the sake of Allah alone. Rabia's works inspired later generations of Sufis to prioritize love as the essence of their spiritual practice.

● **Poetry as a Form of Dhikr (Remembrance of Allah)**: In Sufi worship, poetry is often used as a form of **Dhikr** (remembrance of Allah). The rhythmic recitation of verses, filled with praises of Allah or expressions of longing for the Divine, serves as a way to focus the heart and mind on the presence of Allah. Poetry recitations often take place during **Sama** gatherings, where participants listen to verses that stir their hearts toward greater devotion.

● **Themes of Divine Love and Yearning**: Sufi poetry often uses the metaphor of **love** to describe the relationship between the human soul and Allah. In this context, the soul is portrayed as a lover, constantly seeking the presence of the Divine Beloved. This metaphor expresses the intense emotional and spiritual connection that Sufis feel with Allah and emphasizes the idea that the ultimate goal of the spiritual journey is to experience divine love.

---

2. Music in Sufi Worship

MUSIC plays a central role in Sufi worship, particularly in the form of **Sama** (literally meaning "listening"). Sama is a spiritual practice in which music, chanting, and sometimes dance are used to create an atmosphere of devotion and inspire spiritual states of ecstasy and closeness to Allah. For Sufis, music serves as a powerful tool for bypassing the rational mind and directly engaging the heart, allowing the practitioner to enter into a deeper, more emotional connection with the Divine.

- **Qawwali and Devotional Songs**: One of the most famous forms of Sufi music is **Qawwali**, a genre of devotional music that originated in the **Indian subcontinent**. Qawwali songs are often based on the poetry of Sufi saints and are performed in gatherings meant to invoke a state of spiritual longing and divine love. The rhythmic repetition of verses and the passionate singing of **Qawwals** (singers) help listeners become absorbed in the remembrance of Allah.

  - **Amir Khusrow** (1253–1325 CE), a notable Sufi poet and musician, is often credited with developing Qawwali and incorporating Persian, Arabic, and Indian musical traditions into Sufi music. His influence has shaped the devotional music practices of the **Chishti order** in India and Pakistan.

● **The Role of Instruments**: In some Sufi traditions, music is accompanied by musical instruments such as drums (**daf**), flutes, and stringed instruments like the **rebab**. The use of these instruments is intended to enhance the emotional impact of the Dhikr or the poetic recitations. However, different Sufi orders have varying approaches to the use of music. While some, like the **Chishti** and **Mevlevi** orders, embrace music and instruments as central to their worship, others, like the **Naqshbandi**, emphasize silent Dhikr and do not use music in their practices.

● **Sama and Spiritual Ecstasy**: The practice of **Sama** is designed to elevate the soul into a state of **spiritual ecstasy (wajd)**. Sufis believe that music, when used with pure intention, can help transcend the ego and bring the listener into a heightened awareness of Allah's presence. In some Sufi gatherings, participants may experience intense emotional or physical reactions, such as tears or ecstatic movement, as a result of their deep connection to the music and the Divine.

---

3. Dance and the Whirling Dervishes

IN ADDITION TO POETRY and music, **dance** plays an important role in certain Sufi traditions as a form of worship. The most famous example of Sufi dance is the **Whirling Dervishes** of the **Mevlevi order**, founded by followers of **Rumi** in the 13th century.

- **The Whirling Dervishes (Mevlevi)**: The **Mevlevi order** is renowned for its practice of **Sama** that includes a ritual dance known as the **whirling ceremony**. In this practice, the dervishes perform a highly symbolic dance in which they spin in circles while wearing traditional white robes. The spinning motion represents the cosmic rotation of the planets around the sun, symbolizing the soul's journey around Allah as the ultimate source of light and truth. The practice of whirling is seen as a form of moving meditation, where the dervish becomes fully absorbed in the remembrance of Allah, forgetting the self and becoming united with the Divine presence.

- **Symbolism of the Whirling Dance**: The dance of the Whirling Dervishes is full of symbolic meaning. The dervishes wear a tall conical hat called a **sikke**, representing the tombstone of the ego, and a white robe symbolizing the shroud of the ego's death. The act of spinning is intended to help the dervishes lose their sense of individual identity and become aware only of Allah's presence. As they whirl, they hold one hand up toward the heavens, receiving divine grace, and the other hand down, distributing that grace to the earth. The dance represents both the internal and external acts of devotion to Allah.

---

4. Art and Calligraphy in Sufi Worship

VISUAL ART, PARTICULARLY **calligraphy**, holds a special place in Sufi worship and is used to express spiritual truths and devotion to Allah. Islamic art generally avoids depictions of human figures in sacred contexts, focusing instead on geometric patterns, arabesque designs, and the **art of calligraphy** to convey divine beauty and order.

- **Islamic Calligraphy**: In Sufism, **calligraphy** is often used to express the names of Allah, verses from the Quran, or phrases that reflect key spiritual concepts, such as **Tawhid** (oneness of Allah) or **Bismillah** (In the name of Allah). Sufis view the writing of these sacred words as a form of worship, where the act of creating beautiful script reflects a deep reverence for the Divine. Calligraphy is not just an artistic practice but a spiritual one, where the precision and beauty of the writing are seen as reflections of Allah's perfection.

- **Symbolism in Sufi Art**: Sufi art often incorporates **symbolic imagery** that represents key mystical concepts. For example, the **rose** is a common symbol in Sufi poetry and art, representing divine beauty, while the **nightingale** symbolizes the longing of the soul for the Beloved (Allah). Geometric patterns and arabesques are also prominent in Sufi art, symbolizing the infinite nature of Allah and the interconnectedness of all creation.

Conclusion

Poetry, music, and art serve as essential elements in **Sufi worship**, providing rich avenues for expressing the mystical experiences and inner states of the soul on its journey toward Allah. **Poetry** conveys the soul's longing for divine union and the deep emotions associated with spiritual love. **Music** and **Sama** help to elevate the listener's soul into states of ecstasy and heightened awareness of Allah's presence, while practices like the **Whirling Dervishes** express the soul's movement in harmony with the Divine. **Art** and **calligraphy** reflect the beauty of Allah's creation and are used to express devotion and reverence. Together, these forms of artistic expression deepen the spiritual experience of Sufi worship, allowing practitioners to transcend the limitations of the material world and draw closer to the Divine.

Chapter 4: Wahhabism and Salafism – The Call to Purify Islam

Wahhabism and **Salafism** represent movements within Islam that call for a return to the original teachings and practices of the faith, as understood by the earliest generations of Muslims, known as the **Salaf** (the pious predecessors). These movements emerged as responses to what their proponents perceived as the decline of Islamic society due to innovations (**bid'ah**), the influence of foreign practices, and the spiritual and moral decay that had crept into the Muslim world over centuries. Their central aim is to **purify Islam** from what they see as deviations from the true path, returning to the foundational principles of **Tawhid** (the oneness of Allah) and strict adherence to the **Quran** and **Sunnah**.

Wahhabism, which emerged in the **18th century** under the leadership of **Muhammad ibn Abd al-Wahhab** (1703–1792 CE), is a reformist movement that sought to eradicate practices such as the veneration of saints, the use of intermediaries in worship, and the building of shrines, all of which were seen as forms of **shirk** (associating partners with Allah). This movement emphasized the necessity of returning to what was believed to be the pure, unadulterated form of Islam practiced during the time of the Prophet Muhammad (peace be upon him) and his companions.

Salafism, while similar to Wahhabism in its focus on purifying Islam, encompasses a broader spectrum of approaches, ranging from quietist and apolitical orientations to more activist and sometimes militant interpretations. Salafism traces its intellectual roots back to medieval scholars like **Ibn Taymiyyah** (1263–1328 CE) and promotes a literalist interpretation of the Quran and Sunnah, rejecting any form of interpretation that deviates from the practices of the early Muslim community.

Both Wahhabism and Salafism advocate for a strict, literalist approach to Islamic law and theology, emphasizing the importance of **monotheism** and rejecting practices such as Sufism, the veneration of saints, and the construction of shrines, which they view as innovations. These movements have had a significant influence on the modern Islamic world, especially in regions like **Saudi Arabia**, where Wahhabism became the dominant religious ideology, shaping the country's legal and social systems.

This chapter will explore the origins, key beliefs, and practices of **Wahhabism** and **Salafism**, as well as their impact on the broader Islamic world. It will also examine the historical and political contexts in which these movements arose and how they have shaped contemporary Islamic thought and practice. Through this analysis, a clearer understanding of their role in the ongoing debate over what it means to live an "authentic" Islamic life will emerge.

Historical Background of Wahhabism in Arabia

WAHHABISM, named after its founder **Muhammad ibn Abd al-Wahhab** (1703–1792 CE), is a religious reform movement that originated in the **18th century** in the **Najd** region of the Arabian Peninsula. It emerged in response to what Abd al-Wahhab perceived as widespread deviations from the true teachings of Islam, particularly in the form of superstitious practices, the veneration of saints, and the presence of Sufi shrines. His call for the purification of Islam focused on a strict interpretation of **Tawhid** (the oneness of Allah) and a return to the **Quran** and **Sunnah**, rejecting practices that he viewed as **shirk** (associating partners with Allah).

1. The Arabian Context: A Fragmented Society

DURING THE EARLY 18TH century, the Arabian Peninsula was a region characterized by tribal divisions, political fragmentation, and religious practices that mixed elements of Islam with pre-Islamic traditions. The Najd, where Muhammad ibn Abd al-Wahhab was born, was an especially isolated region with little centralized governance. Many people in this area practiced forms of Islam that Abd al-Wahhab considered to be corrupted by **bid'ah** (innovation) and superstition. Practices such as visiting the tombs of saints, making offerings at shrines, and seeking intercession from holy figures were common, particularly among rural communities. These practices, according to Abd al-Wahhab, diluted the pure monotheism of Islam and needed to be eradicated.

- **Religious Syncretism**: In various parts of the Arabian Peninsula, Islam had become intertwined with local traditions and practices that emphasized the veneration of saints and belief in their miraculous powers. People often visited the graves of prominent religious figures, seeking blessings and intercession, believing that these saints had special access to Allah's favor. This was seen by Abd al-Wahhab as a violation of **Tawhid** and a return to pre-Islamic polytheism (**Jahiliyyah**).

● **The Absence of Centralized Authority**: The political structure of Arabia at the time was highly fragmented, with tribal leaders wielding local authority. There was no strong, centralized Islamic government to enforce religious orthodoxy or regulate practices, which allowed diverse and sometimes unorthodox forms of Islam to flourish. In this context, Muhammad ibn Abd al-Wahhab's call for religious reform gained appeal as it promised to bring religious purity and political unity under a strict interpretation of Islam.

---

2. Muhammad ibn Abd al-Wahhab's Early Life and Influences

MUHAMMAD IBN ABD AL-Wahhab was born in the small town of **Uyayna** in the Najd region of central Arabia. His father, a religious scholar, provided him with an early education in Islamic theology and law. Ibn Abd al-Wahhab traveled widely in his youth, studying with various Islamic scholars in **Mecca**, **Medina**, and **Basra**. It was during his travels that he became deeply influenced by the works of earlier Islamic scholars, particularly **Ibn Taymiyyah** (1263–1328 CE), a medieval Sunni scholar who advocated for the purification of Islamic practice and opposed popular innovations like saint worship and shrine veneration.

- **Influence of Ibn Taymiyyah**: The teachings of **Ibn Taymiyyah** had a profound impact on Abd al-Wahhab's thinking. Ibn Taymiyyah had argued against practices that he saw as un-Islamic, such as the excessive veneration of saints and the use of intermediaries in worship. He also emphasized the importance of following the Quran and Hadith literally, without introducing speculative theology or practices that had no basis in the early Muslim community. These ideas became central to Abd al-Wahhab's own reform movement.

- **Return to Najd**: After completing his studies, Abd al-Wahhab returned to Najd, where he began preaching his message of reform. He argued that the true message of Islam had been corrupted by **innovation** and superstition, and he called for a return to the pure monotheism of the early Islamic community. His teachings quickly gained followers, but they also generated opposition from local religious and political leaders who were attached to the traditional practices that Abd al-Wahhab condemned.

---

3. Alliance with Muhammad ibn Saud and the Rise of Wahhabism

IN 1744, A PIVOTAL moment in the history of Wahhabism occurred when Muhammad ibn Abd al-Wahhab formed an alliance with **Muhammad ibn Saud**, a local tribal leader and founder of the **Al Saud** dynasty. This alliance combined the religious fervor of Wahhabism with the political ambitions of Ibn Saud, leading to the establishment of a powerful partnership that would reshape the Arabian Peninsula.

- **The Pact of Uyayna**: The alliance was formed in the town of Uyayna, where Abd al-Wahhab had been preaching. Muhammad ibn Saud agreed to support Abd al-Wahhab's religious reforms, while Abd al-Wahhab promised to legitimize Saud's rule through the enforcement of his strict interpretation of Islam. This pact gave Wahhabism a political base, and it allowed the Al Saud family to expand their influence by conquering neighboring tribes and territories under the banner of religious reform.

- **Expansion of the Saudi-Wahhabi State**: With the military support of Ibn Saud, Wahhabism spread rapidly across central Arabia. The movement grew as the Al Saud forces, motivated by both religious zeal and the desire for political dominance, waged campaigns to unite the tribes of Najd under their leadership. As they expanded their control, they implemented Wahhabi reforms, including the destruction of Sufi shrines and the enforcement of strict monotheism.

---

4. Wahhabism's Impact on Arabian Society

WAHHABISM'S RISE HAD a profound impact on Arabian society, particularly in terms of religious practice, social norms, and governance. The movement's insistence on returning to the practices of the early Muslim community led to the suppression of what were viewed as deviant practices, such as the veneration of saints, the building of tombs, and the use of intermediaries in prayer.

- **Destruction of Shrines and Tombs**: One of the key features of Wahhabi reform was the **destruction of**

tombs and **shrines** associated with saints and religious figures. Abd al-Wahhab viewed these structures as symbols of idolatry, and his followers systematically destroyed many of them, including sites revered by Sufi Muslims. This campaign to rid Islam of "un-Islamic" practices marked a dramatic shift in religious life in the Arabian Peninsula.

- **Strict Interpretation of Sharia**: Wahhabism promoted a strict interpretation of **Sharia** (Islamic law), with a focus on enforcing public morality. Music, dancing, and other forms of entertainment were discouraged, while women were expected to adhere to conservative dress codes and social roles. The Wahhabi interpretation of Sharia became the foundation of governance in areas controlled by the Al Saud-Wahhabi alliance.

---

5. The Establishment of the Saudi State

THE WAHHABI MOVEMENT reached new heights in the early 19th century when the Al Saud dynasty, with the backing of Wahhabi religious legitimacy, established a powerful state in central Arabia. By the early 1800s, the Wahhabi-Saudi forces had expanded their control to include **Mecca** and **Medina**, the two holiest cities in Islam, bringing significant portions of the Arabian Peninsula under their rule.

- **Ottoman Opposition and the Fall of the First Saudi State**: The expansion of Wahhabi influence alarmed the **Ottoman Empire**, which viewed the Wahhabi-Saudi state as a threat to its control over the Islamic holy cities. In 1818, the Ottomans, with the help of **Egyptian forces**, launched a military campaign to suppress the Wahhabis. The campaign resulted in the defeat of the first Saudi state, but the Wahhabi movement was not entirely extinguished.

● **Resurgence in the 20th Century**: In the early 20th century, Wahhabism experienced a resurgence under the leadership of **Abdulaziz ibn Saud**, who founded the **Kingdom of Saudi Arabia** in 1932. Wahhabism became the official religious ideology of the new Saudi state, and its teachings were institutionalized in the country's governance, education, and legal system. The alliance between the Al Saud family and the Wahhabi religious establishment has remained a defining feature of Saudi Arabia's political and religious identity.

Conclusion

Wahhabism emerged in the 18th century as a powerful religious reform movement aimed at **purifying Islam** from practices considered to be **innovations** and **deviations** from true monotheism. Muhammad ibn Abd al-Wahhab's strict interpretation of **Tawhid** and his rejection of practices such as saint veneration and shrine worship resonated with many in the Najd region, particularly after his alliance with **Muhammad ibn Saud**. This partnership laid the foundation for the rise of the **Saudi state**, which, under Wahhabi influence, implemented far-reaching religious reforms and expanded its control across the Arabian Peninsula. Wahhabism's impact on Arabian society and its later resurgence in the 20th century under the Al Saud family solidified its role as a dominant force in shaping the religious and political landscape of the region.

Theological Foundations: Tawhid and Rejection of Bid'ah (Innovation)

AT THE CORE OF **Wahhabism** and **Salafism** lie two key theological principles: the uncompromising emphasis on **Tawhid** (the oneness of Allah) and the rigorous rejection of **Bid'ah** (innovation). These foundational concepts shape the movements' understanding of Islam and their call to return to the original, unaltered teachings and practices of the early Muslim community, known as the **Salaf al-Salih** (the pious predecessors). By focusing on the purity of monotheism and eliminating practices they perceive as innovations, both Wahhabism and Salafism seek to **purify** Islam from what they view as deviations that have corrupted the faith over centuries.

1. Tawhid (The Oneness of Allah)

TAWHID, the belief in the **absolute oneness of Allah**, is the most fundamental concept in Islamic theology, and it serves as the cornerstone of Wahhabi and Salafi thought. For these movements, maintaining the purity of Tawhid is paramount, and they see any deviation from this principle as a form of **shirk** (associating partners with Allah), which is considered the gravest sin in Islam.

- **Tawhid al-Rububiyyah (Oneness of Lordship)**: This aspect of Tawhid refers to the belief that Allah alone is the **Creator, Sustainer,** and **Ruler** of the universe. He is the one who controls all things, gives life and death, and provides for all creatures. In Wahhabi and Salafi theology, this belief must be held without compromise, and any belief in other forces or beings having independent power or influence over the world is seen as a violation of Tawhid.

- **Tawhid al-Uluhiyyah (Oneness of Worship)**: Wahhabis and Salafis place particular emphasis on this form of Tawhid, which deals with the exclusive right of Allah to be worshipped. Worship in all its forms—whether prayer, supplication, or sacrifice—must be directed solely to Allah, without any intermediaries. Practices such as asking saints for intercession, venerating shrines, or making offerings to anyone other than Allah are considered violations of this principle and are classified as **shirk**. For Wahhabis and Salafis, Tawhid al-Uluhiyyah is the primary criterion by which the authenticity of Islamic practices is judged.

- **Tawhid al-Asma wa'l-Sifat (Oneness of Names and Attributes)**: This aspect of Tawhid refers to the belief that Allah's names and attributes, as described in the Quran and Hadith, are unique to Him and must be understood literally, without likening them to human attributes (**tashbih**) or negating their meanings (**ta'til**). Wahhabis and Salafis reject any metaphorical interpretations of Allah's attributes, insisting that they must be accepted as they are presented in the primary Islamic texts.

- **Commitment to Tawhid and Rejection of Shirk**: For Wahhabis, maintaining the purity of Tawhid requires a vigilant rejection of all forms of **shirk**. This includes practices that they believe attribute divine qualities to anyone other than Allah, such as the veneration of saints, the belief in their intercession, or the construction of shrines over graves. Wahhabis argue that these practices, common in various Islamic cultures, corrupt the essence of monotheism and must be eliminated to restore Islam to its original purity.

---

2. Rejection of Bid'ah (Innovation)

BID'AH, or **innovation**, refers to any new religious practice or belief that was not part of the original teachings of the Prophet Muhammad (peace be upon him) and his companions (may Allah be pleased with them). For Wahhabis and Salafis, eliminating bid'ah is crucial to maintaining the purity of the faith, as they believe that any addition or alteration to the practices of the early Muslim community is a corruption of Islam.

- **The Definition of Bid'ah**: In the context of Wahhabi and Salafi thought, **bid'ah** includes any religious practice or belief that was introduced after the time of the Prophet Muhammad (peace be upon him) and his companions, particularly if it has no basis in the Quran, the Sunnah, or the actions of the **Salaf al-Salih**. This definition is broad and encompasses a wide range of practices, many of which are viewed by other Muslim communities as legitimate expressions of piety.

- **The Dangers of Bid'ah**: Wahhabis and Salafis see bid'ah as a serious threat to Islam because it distorts the original message of the faith. They argue that innovations in religious practice can lead to a gradual weakening of Tawhid, eventually resulting in **shirk** or the loss of the true spirit of the religion. Muhammad ibn Abd al-Wahhab frequently warned against the dangers of bid'ah, believing that it had contributed to the spiritual decline of Muslim societies.

- **Examples of Bid'ah**: Wahhabis and Salafis classify a number of popular practices as bid'ah, including:

○ **Veneration of Saints**: Visiting the tombs of saints, making prayers or offerings at their graves, and seeking their intercession are considered forms of bid'ah. These practices are seen as violations of Tawhid because they involve seeking help from beings other than Allah.

○ **Celebrating the Prophet's Birthday (Mawlid al-Nabi)**: The celebration of the Prophet's birthday, a widespread practice in many Muslim communities, is rejected by Wahhabis and Salafis as an innovation with no basis in the Quran or Sunnah. They argue that the Prophet Muhammad (peace be upon him) did not instruct his followers to celebrate his birth, and therefore, the practice should be abandoned.

○ **Superstitious Practices**: Many folk practices, such as using charms, amulets, or talismans to ward off evil, are also classified as bid'ah. Wahhabis and Salafis see these practices as remnants of pre-Islamic traditions that have been wrongly incorporated into Islamic practice.

---

3. The Call for Purification and Reform

MUHAMMAD IBN ABD AL-Wahhab's theological focus on **Tawhid** and **rejection of bid'ah** formed the basis of his call for a **purification of Islam**. He believed that the widespread prevalence of shirk and bid'ah had led Muslims away from the true teachings of the Prophet Muhammad (peace be upon him) and that a return to the **pure monotheism** practiced by the early Muslim community was necessary to restore the strength and unity of the Ummah.

• **Reviving the Sunnah**: Central to Wahhabism's mission is the call to **revive the Sunnah**—the practices and traditions of the Prophet Muhammad (peace be upon him). Wahhabis and Salafis argue that Muslims should strictly adhere to the Sunnah as it was practiced by the **Salaf al-Salih**, without introducing new rituals or beliefs that deviate from this original model. By adhering closely to the Sunnah, they believe that Muslims can achieve a pure form of worship that is free from innovation.

• **Political Implications**: Wahhabism's emphasis on **purifying religious practices** also had political implications, as it became tied to the expansion of the Saudi state in the 18th and 19th centuries. As the Wahhabi-Saudi alliance grew, their campaign to eliminate shirk and bid'ah was enforced through military conquest, with Sufi shrines destroyed, saints' tombs leveled, and religious practices deemed un-Islamic forcibly suppressed. This approach created lasting tension between Wahhabi adherents and other Islamic groups, particularly Sufi communities and Shia Muslims, whose practices were seen as innovations.

• **Modern Salafism and Purification**: In modern times, the principles of Wahhabism have influenced the broader **Salafi** movement, which also calls for a return to the practices of the **Salaf** and the rejection of innovation. While Salafism includes a range of interpretations, from quietist to activist and sometimes militant, the emphasis on **purifying Islam** from bid'ah remains central across its different strains. Salafis often see themselves as the protectors of authentic Islamic teachings, working to rid the faith of practices that they view as foreign or un-Islamic.

Conclusion

The theological foundations of Wahhabism and Salafism are built on an uncompromising commitment to **Tawhid** and the rejection of **Bid'ah**. By emphasizing the purity of monotheism and calling for the elimination of innovations, these movements seek to return Islam to its original form, as practiced by the Prophet Muhammad (peace be upon him) and his companions. The insistence on **strict monotheism** and the **rejection of shirk**, coupled with a determination to root out any practices that deviate from the Quran and Sunnah, has been a defining feature of these movements since their inception. Their influence continues to shape the religious landscape of the Islamic world, particularly in regions where Wahhabism and Salafism have gained political and social prominence.

Salafism: Revivalism and Its Global Influence

SALAFISM is a reformist and revivalist movement within Islam that seeks to restore the faith to its original purity by emulating the practices of the **Salaf al-Salih** (the pious predecessors), the first three generations of Muslims, including the Prophet Muhammad (peace be upon him), his companions, and their immediate successors. Salafism advocates for a strict interpretation of the **Quran** and **Sunnah**, with an emphasis on literalism, avoiding innovations (**Bid'ah**), and rejecting any religious practices or beliefs that deviate from what was practiced by the early Muslim community. The movement encompasses a wide spectrum of approaches, from quietist and apolitical strains to more activist and militant interpretations.

Salafism has experienced a resurgence in modern times, and its influence has spread across the globe, impacting Islamic thought, religious education, and political movements. This revivalism, driven by a desire to **purify Islam** and **return to its roots**, has been shaped by a variety of social, political, and economic factors that have contributed to its appeal in different parts of the world.

1. Historical Origins of Salafism

THE TERM **Salaf** refers to the early generations of Muslims who are seen as models of Islamic practice and belief. The **Salafi** movement emerged as a revivalist response to what was perceived as the decline of Islamic societies due to foreign influence, internal divisions, and innovations in religious practices that were viewed as un-Islamic. While the roots of Salafism can be traced to medieval scholars such as **Ibn Taymiyyah** (1263–1328 CE), who emphasized returning to the early, uncorrupted form of Islam, the modern Salafi movement began to take shape in the **late 19th and early 20th centuries**.

- **Early Salafi Thinkers**: Key figures in the early development of Salafism included scholars like **Jamal al-Din al-Afghani** (1838–1897), **Muhammad Abduh** (1849–1905), and **Rashid Rida** (1865–1935), who were part of the **Islamic modernist** movement. They sought to reconcile Islam with modernity while advocating for a return to the practices of the Salaf as a way to revitalize the Muslim world in the face of European colonialism and intellectual decline. While their approach was more reformist than the later conservative forms of Salafism, they laid the groundwork for the broader Salafi revival.

- **Wahhabism and Salafism**: The **Wahhabi movement**, founded by **Muhammad ibn Abd al-Wahhab** in 18th century Arabia, is often considered a precursor or subset of Salafism. Both movements share a common goal of restoring pure monotheism (**Tawhid**) and eliminating innovations in religious practice. However, **Salafism** is a broader movement that includes different interpretations and approaches to reform, while **Wahhabism** is a more regionally specific movement, heavily tied to the religious and political history of **Saudi Arabia**.

---

2. Key Beliefs of Salafism

SALAFISM IS CHARACTERIZED by a strict, literal interpretation of Islam and a focus on **purity of practice**, rooted in the example of the Salaf. Some of the key beliefs and principles of Salafism include:

- **Literalism**: Salafis interpret the Quran and Sunnah literally, without relying on speculative theology or later scholarly interpretations that they view as distortions of the original message. This literalist approach leads to a focus on the direct and clear meanings of the texts, avoiding allegorical or metaphorical interpretations.

- **Tawhid and Rejection of Shirk**: Salafis emphasize the absolute oneness of Allah (**Tawhid**) and reject all forms of **shirk** (associating partners with Allah). They consider practices such as saint veneration, visiting tombs, or seeking intercession through holy figures as violations of pure monotheism. These practices are viewed as innovations that compromise the integrity of Islam.

- **Rejection of Bid'ah (Innovation)**: Like Wahhabism, Salafism places a strong emphasis on eliminating **Bid'ah**—any practice or belief that was introduced after the time of the Prophet Muhammad (peace be upon him) and his companions. Salafis argue that innovation leads to the dilution of the original message of Islam and should be avoided in all aspects of religious practice.

- **Return to the Practices of the Salaf**: Salafis seek to revive the original, authentic practices of Islam as they were observed by the first three generations of Muslims. They view the Salaf as the most trustworthy and authoritative interpreters of Islam and strive to emulate their way of life in both personal and communal aspects of worship.

3. Modern Salafism: A Diverse Movement

SALAFISM IS NOT A MONOLITHIC movement; rather, it encompasses a range of interpretations and orientations. These can broadly be classified into three categories: **quietist**, **activist**, and **jihadist** Salafism. Each of these strands reflects different approaches to the relationship between Islam and society, governance, and politics.

- **Quietist Salafism**: Quietist Salafis focus on **spiritual purification** and religious education, believing that Muslims should concentrate on perfecting their own religious practice before engaging in political activities. They avoid political activism, arguing that authority should be respected as long as rulers allow Muslims to practice their faith. Quietist Salafis are often found in religious institutions, mosques, and schools, where they emphasize the importance of teaching pure Islam as practiced by the Salaf.

- **Activist Salafism**: Activist Salafis engage in **political reform** and social activism, seeking to influence government policies and bring about a return to Sharia (Islamic law) through peaceful means. They believe in working within political systems to implement Islamic principles, often participating in elections or lobbying for legal reforms that align with Islamic teachings. This form of Salafism gained prominence in countries like **Egypt** and **Tunisia**, where Salafi political parties emerged in the wake of the **Arab Spring**.

- **Jihadist Salafism**: This strain of Salafism advocates for the use of **armed struggle (jihad)** to establish an Islamic state governed by Sharia. Jihadist Salafis are often associated with extremist groups such as **al-Qaeda** and the self-proclaimed **Islamic State (ISIS)**, which have used violence to achieve their goals of overthrowing secular governments and establishing Islamic rule. Jihadist Salafism is considered a radical interpretation of Salafi principles and has been condemned by many mainstream Islamic scholars and leaders.

---

4. Global Influence and Spread of Salafism

SALAFISM'S GLOBAL INFLUENCE has expanded significantly in the 20th and 21st centuries, largely due to the financial and ideological support it has received from countries like **Saudi Arabia** and the spread of Salafi teachings through modern media and religious institutions.

- **Saudi Arabia's Role**: Since the establishment of the **Kingdom of Saudi Arabia** in 1932, the Saudi state has promoted Wahhabism, a strict form of Salafism, as the official religious ideology of the country. Saudi Arabia has used its oil wealth to fund the spread of Salafi thought by building mosques, schools (**madrasas**), and Islamic centers around the world. This support has allowed Salafism to gain a foothold in regions such as **South Asia, Africa, Southeast Asia**, and **Western Europe**.

- **Influence in Africa and Asia**: In **Africa**, particularly in countries such as **Nigeria, Mali**, and **Somalia**, Salafism has spread through religious networks and institutions funded by Saudi Arabia and other Gulf states. The rise of Salafism has often led to tensions with local Sufi traditions, as Salafis view Sufi practices such as saint veneration as innovations that must be eliminated. In **Southeast Asia**, Salafism has gained influence in countries like **Indonesia** and **Malaysia**, where it has challenged more traditional and moderate forms of Islam.

● **Salafism in the West**: Salafism has also found followers in **Western Europe** and **North America**, often among young Muslims who are searching for a more "authentic" form of Islam. Salafi preachers use the internet, social media, and online platforms to reach global audiences, disseminating their teachings to Muslims living in the West. The rise of Salafism in Western countries has sparked debates about integration, radicalization, and the role of religion in public life, as some governments have viewed Salafism as a potential source of extremism.

● **Post-9/11 Influence**: In the wake of the **September 11, 2001** attacks, Salafism—particularly its more militant forms—came under intense scrutiny for its role in inspiring groups like al-Qaeda and ISIS. While not all Salafis endorse violence, the association of Salafi-jihadist groups with terrorism has led to efforts by governments around the world to counter the influence of extremist ideologies. At the same time, quietist and activist Salafis continue to play a role in religious education and political reform, particularly in the Middle East and North Africa.

---

5. Salafism's Impact on Global Islamic Discourse

SALAFISM HAS HAD A profound impact on **global Islamic discourse**, influencing how Muslims around the world think about religious authority, authenticity, and modernity. The movement's call to return to the practices of the Salaf has resonated with many Muslims who feel disconnected from traditional forms of Islam and are seeking a more direct, unmediated relationship with their faith.

- **Debates over Authenticity**: Salafism's insistence on a literalist interpretation of Islam and its rejection of innovations has sparked debates within the global Muslim community over what constitutes "authentic" Islam. While Salafis argue that their interpretation is the most faithful to the original teachings of the Prophet Muhammad (peace be upon him), other Muslims, including many Sunni scholars and Sufi practitioners, argue that Islamic tradition is dynamic and adaptable to changing circumstances.

- **Influence on Political Movements**: In countries like **Egypt**, **Tunisia**, and **Libya**, Salafism has become a significant force in political life, with Salafi political parties emerging as major players in the aftermath of the **Arab Spring**. These movements advocate for the implementation of Sharia and the establishment of Islamic governance, but they often face resistance from more secular or moderate Muslim groups.

- **Challenges of Radicalization**: The rise of **Salafi-jihadist** movements has led to increased global concern about radicalization and the potential for extremist ideologies to spread, particularly among disaffected youth. Efforts to combat radicalization often focus on distinguishing between mainstream Salafism and its more violent offshoots, while promoting moderate interpretations of Islam.

Conclusion

Salafism is a powerful revivalist movement within Islam that seeks to return to the practices and beliefs of the early Muslim community. Its emphasis on **Tawhid**, **literalism**, and the rejection of **Bid'ah** has made it a significant force in the global Islamic landscape. Through a combination of religious education, political activism, and, in some cases, militant jihad, Salafism has spread across the world, impacting Islamic thought, governance, and society in diverse ways. While the movement is not monolithic, its global influence continues to shape the direction of Islamic discourse and the search for authenticity in the modern Muslim world.

Differences Between Salafism and Wahhabism

WHILE **Salafism** and **Wahhabism** share many similarities, particularly in their emphasis on **Tawhid** (the oneness of Allah), rejection of **Bid'ah** (innovation), and commitment to returning to the pure teachings of the early Islamic community, they are distinct in several important ways. Wahhabism is a specific subset of Salafism with its own historical and regional context, while Salafism is a broader movement with multiple interpretations and approaches. These differences stem from the origins, development, and modern expressions of each movement.

1. Origins and Historical Context

- **Wahhabism**: Wahhabism emerged in the **18th century** in the **Najd** region of what is now Saudi Arabia, under the leadership of **Muhammad ibn Abd al-Wahhab** (1703–1792 CE). It was a response to what Ibn Abd al-Wahhab perceived as widespread deviations from the pure monotheism of Islam, particularly practices like saint veneration, shrine worship, and the use of intermediaries in worship, which he classified as **shirk** (associating partners with Allah). Wahhabism formed a close alliance with the **House of Saud**, and the movement became the dominant religious ideology of **Saudi Arabia**.

- **Salafism**: **Salafism**, on the other hand, is a broader **revivalist movement** that traces its intellectual roots to medieval scholars like **Ibn Taymiyyah** (1263–1328 CE) but developed more fully in the **19th and 20th centuries**. Salafism emerged as a response to the perceived decline of Islamic societies due to European colonialism and the influence of modernity. Early Salafi thinkers such as **Jamal al-Din al-Afghani**, **Muhammad Abduh**, and **Rashid Rida** emphasized the need to return to the practices of the early Muslim community (**Salaf al-Salih**) as a way to restore the strength of the Muslim world. While Wahhabism is closely tied to Saudi Arabia's history, Salafism developed as a more global movement, with various interpretations and strategies for reform.

---

2. Scope and Approach

- **Wahhabism's Specific Focus on Religious Reform**: Wahhabism is primarily focused on **religious purity** and **reform**, particularly in relation to **Tawhid** and the **rejection of Bid'ah**. It places heavy emphasis on the strict interpretation of **Sharia** (Islamic law) and purging practices deemed **un-Islamic**, such as shrine worship, saint veneration, and superstitions. Wahhabism is also deeply rooted in the political and historical context of Saudi Arabia, where it was used as a tool for state-building by the House of Saud.

- **Salafism's Broader Revivalist Goals**: Salafism is a more comprehensive movement that not only focuses on purifying religious practice but also seeks to **revitalize Islamic societies** as a whole. Salafism encompasses a wider range of approaches, including **educational**, **social**, and **political** reform. While Wahhabism is often concerned with religious purity in a narrow sense, Salafism can be both **reformist** and **revivalist**, engaging with modern issues like governance, social justice, and the role of Islam in public life. In its early iterations, Salafism also incorporated **Islamic modernist** thought, with some Salafis advocating for a reconciliation between Islam and modernity, while maintaining fidelity to the core tenets of the Salaf.

---

3. Relationship with Political Authority

• **Wahhabism's Ties to the Saudi State**: Wahhabism is closely associated with the rise of the **Saudi state** and has long served as the **official religious ideology** of Saudi Arabia. The alliance between **Muhammad ibn Abd al-Wahhab** and **Muhammad ibn Saud** in the 18th century laid the foundation for the political and religious partnership that continues in Saudi Arabia today. As a result, Wahhabism tends to support the **status quo** in terms of political authority, often advocating for obedience to rulers as long as they uphold Islamic law. This has made Wahhabism a stabilizing force within the Saudi state, where religious scholars legitimize the rule of the Saudi monarchy, and the state enforces Wahhabi interpretations of Islam through its institutions.

• **Salafism's Varied Approaches to Politics**: Salafism, in contrast, is more diverse in its relationship with political authority. There are **quietist** Salafis who, like Wahhabis, avoid political activism and advocate for obedience to rulers, focusing instead on personal religious reform and spiritual purity. However, **activist** and **jihadist** strains of Salafism take a more critical stance toward political rulers, especially those they perceive as un-Islamic or corrupt. Activist Salafis may engage in peaceful political reform, participating in elections and advocating for the implementation of Sharia, while jihadist Salafis seek to overthrow secular governments through violence and establish Islamic states. This diversity in political engagement distinguishes Salafism from the more state-oriented Wahhabism.

---

4. Geographic Influence and Global Reach

- **Wahhabism's Regional Focus**: While Wahhabism has had a global impact due to **Saudi Arabia's** influence, its roots and primary influence remain within the **Arabian Peninsula**. As the dominant religious ideology in Saudi Arabia, Wahhabism has been exported through **Saudi-funded** mosques, madrasas, and Islamic centers, particularly in regions like **South Asia, Africa**, and **Southeast Asia**. Despite this reach, Wahhabism's interpretation of Islam is often seen as closely tied to Saudi Arabia's political and cultural context.

- **Salafism's Global Spread**: Salafism has a much broader global reach and has been adopted by various groups and individuals across the Muslim world, from **North Africa** to **Southeast Asia, Europe**, and **North America**. The **internet, social media**, and **global networks of preachers** have played a significant role in spreading Salafi teachings. Salafism is particularly appealing to young Muslims who are searching for an "authentic" form of Islam that rejects cultural practices and innovations, offering what they perceive as a direct connection to the faith's earliest roots. As a result, Salafism has found followers in diverse contexts, from **urban centers** in

Western Europe to **rural communities** in Africa and
Asia.

---

5. Flexibility in Interpretation

- **Wahhabism's Rigidity**: Wahhabism is known for its
rigid interpretation of Islam, with a strict adherence to
the Hanbali school of law and a focus on enforcing
religious orthodoxy. In Wahhabi thought, the legal and
theological positions of Muhammad ibn Abd al-Wahhab
and his followers are seen as definitive, and there is little
room for reinterpretation or adaptation to modern
contexts. This rigidity has contributed to the perception
of Wahhabism as a particularly conservative and inflexible
movement within Islam.

- **Salafism's Diversity**: Salafism, while also committed
to a strict interpretation of Islam, is more **diverse in its
approaches**. Salafis follow no single school of law
(madhhab) and instead advocate for following the Quran
and Sunnah directly, which allows for a certain degree
of flexibility in interpreting Islamic texts. This has led to
the development of multiple strands of Salafism, from
quietist to **activist** and **jihadist** interpretations, each of
which engages with modern issues in different ways. This
diversity makes Salafism more adaptable to different
cultural and political contexts, whereas Wahhabism
remains more narrowly defined by its specific historical
and geographical origins.

6. Attitudes Toward Sufism and Shia Islam

- **Wahhabism's Strong Opposition to Sufism and Shia Islam**: One of the most well-known features of Wahhabism is its **strong opposition** to **Sufism** and **Shia Islam**. Wahhabis view the veneration of saints, visiting tombs, and other practices associated with Sufism as **Bid'ah** and **shirk** (associating partners with Allah). Similarly, Wahhabism is strongly opposed to Shia Islam, rejecting the Shia belief in the **Imamate** and criticizing many Shia rituals as innovations. In Saudi Arabia, Wahhabi teachings have been used to justify the suppression of Shia practices, particularly in regions like the **Eastern Province**, where many Shia Muslims reside.

- **Salafism's Varied Responses to Sufism and Shia Islam**: Salafism shares Wahhabism's opposition to **Sufi practices** and **Shia theology**, but its response is not always as vehement or politically motivated. While Salafis reject saint veneration and the use of intermediaries in worship, not all Salafi movements actively seek to suppress these practices in the same way Wahhabism has in Saudi Arabia. Similarly, while Salafis oppose Shia beliefs, the level of hostility varies. Some Salafis view Shia Islam as a deviant sect, while others, particularly jihadist Salafis, may view Shia Muslims as enemies. This diversity in responses reflects the broader spectrum of Salafi thought.

CONCLUSION

Although **Salafism** and **Wahhabism** share common goals of returning to the pure teachings of Islam as practiced by the **Salaf** and rejecting **Bid'ah**, they are distinct movements with different origins, scopes, and approaches. Wahhabism, with its historical roots in Saudi Arabia and its close ties to the Saudi state, is more narrowly focused on religious reform and maintaining the political status quo. In contrast, Salafism is a broader revivalist movement with diverse interpretations, ranging from quietist to activist and militant. While both movements emphasize **Tawhid** and religious purity, Salafism's global reach, political diversity, and adaptability to different contexts set it apart from the more rigid and regionally specific Wahhabi tradition.

Modern-Day Impact of Salafism and Wahhabism in the Muslim World

SALAFISM and **Wahhabism** have had significant and far-reaching impacts on the Muslim world in the modern era. These movements have shaped religious thought, politics, social norms, and international relations, particularly through their emphasis on **purity of Islamic practice, rejection of innovations** (Bid'ah), and a strict interpretation of **Sharia**. Their influence has been felt across various regions, from the Middle East and Africa to South Asia and Europe, and their roles in contemporary Islamic discourse have sparked debates, conflicts, and reform efforts.

1. Influence in Saudi Arabia and the Arabian Peninsula

WAHHABISM REMAINS DEEPLY intertwined with the **Kingdom of Saudi Arabia**, where it serves as the dominant religious ideology and continues to shape the country's governance, legal system, and social structure. The alliance between the **Al Saud** royal family and Wahhabi religious scholars has played a central role in Saudi Arabia's formation and ongoing political stability.

- **State-Sponsored Wahhabism**: Saudi Arabia has used its vast oil wealth to fund the global expansion of Wahhabi teachings by building mosques, schools (**madrasas**), and Islamic centers worldwide. Through organizations like the **Muslim World League**, Saudi Arabia has promoted Wahhabi doctrine, influencing religious education and practice in many Muslim-majority countries, particularly in **Africa**, **South Asia**, and **Southeast Asia**.

- **Social and Legal Impact**: Wahhabi principles are embedded in the **legal system** and **social norms** of Saudi Arabia, enforcing strict interpretations of Sharia, especially concerning gender roles, public morality, and religious observance. For example, women are expected to adhere to conservative dress codes, and religious police (previously known as the **Committee for the Promotion of Virtue and the Prevention of Vice**) have played a role in enforcing these laws. However, recent reforms under **Crown Prince Mohammed bin Salman** have sought to relax some of the more restrictive Wahhabi practices, particularly regarding women's rights and social freedoms.

- **Regional Influence**: Wahhabism has also influenced neighboring countries in the **Arabian Peninsula**, such as **Qatar** and **Kuwait**, where conservative religious movements have adopted similar doctrines. In **Yemen**, Wahhabi-inspired groups have played a role in the ongoing conflict, particularly through **Saudi-backed militias**.

---

2. Salafism's Global Spread and Political Influence

SALAFISM, as a broader movement, has found followers across the Muslim world, impacting religious thought, social activism, and political movements. Its appeal lies in its call for a return to the **pure practices** of early Islam, which resonates with many Muslims seeking an "authentic" form of their faith in the face of modernization, secularism, and foreign influence.

- **Political Salafism**: In the wake of the **Arab Spring** (2010–2011), Salafism gained a political foothold in several countries, particularly in **Egypt**, **Tunisia**, and **Libya**. Salafi political parties, such as **Al-Nour** in Egypt, emerged as significant players, advocating for the implementation of **Sharia** and the reform of governments to align with Islamic principles. While some Salafi movements have chosen to participate in democratic processes, others have remained more conservative, focusing on social reform without direct political engagement.

• **Salafism in North Africa**: In countries like **Morocco** and **Algeria**, Salafi movements have gained influence through grassroots activism, particularly among younger generations. These movements often challenge local religious authorities and **Sufi** traditions, which they view as deviations from true Islam. Salafism's call for a return to the teachings of the **Salaf al-Salih** has resonated with many disillusioned by the political and social stagnation in their countries.

• **Influence in Sub-Saharan Africa**: In **Sub-Saharan Africa**, Salafism has spread through **Saudi-funded** institutions and local Salafi networks. In countries like **Nigeria**, **Mali**, and **Somalia**, Salafism has influenced local Islamic movements, often in opposition to **Sufi** traditions that have historically dominated the region. In some cases, Salafi-jihadist groups, such as **Boko Haram** in Nigeria and **Al-Shabaab** in Somalia, have adopted more militant interpretations of Salafi doctrine, leading to violent insurgencies.

3. The Role of Salafism in Radicalization and Jihadist

Movements

WHILE NOT ALL SALAFIS advocate for violence, the rise of **Salafi-jihadist** movements has become one of the most significant and controversial aspects of modern-day Salafism. Groups such as **al-Qaeda** and the **Islamic State (ISIS)** have adopted militant interpretations of Salafi principles, particularly the belief in **jihad** as a means to establish an Islamic state governed by Sharia.

- **Al-Qaeda and the Islamic State (ISIS)**: Both al-Qaeda and ISIS are products of **Salafi-jihadist** ideology, which combines the theological principles of Salafism with a militant vision of global jihad. These groups view violence as a legitimate tool to overthrow **un-Islamic** governments, establish Islamic rule, and defend Muslim lands from foreign intervention. Their actions have led to devastating conflicts in regions such as **Afghanistan**, **Iraq**, **Syria**, and **Yemen**.

- **Impact on Global Security**: The rise of Salafi-jihadist groups has had a profound impact on global security, with terrorist attacks carried out by these groups in **Europe**, **North America**, the **Middle East**, and **Africa**. Governments around the world have implemented counterterrorism measures aimed at curbing the spread of Salafi-jihadist ideology, but the movement continues to attract followers, particularly through online platforms and social media.

- **Counter-Radicalization Efforts**: In response to the growing influence of Salafi-jihadist groups, many countries, including Saudi Arabia and **Egypt**, have launched **counter-radicalization** programs aimed at promoting more moderate interpretations of Islam. These efforts often focus on **education**, **religious reform**, and **community engagement** to prevent the spread of extremist ideologies.

---

4. Salafism's Influence on Religious Education and Social Movements

SALAFISM HAS HAD A major impact on **religious education** and **social movements** in the Muslim world, with many Islamic scholars, preachers, and activists adopting its teachings.

- **Educational Institutions**: Salafi teachings have been spread through **madrasas** (Islamic schools) and **universities**, particularly those funded by Saudi Arabia. Institutions like the **Islamic University of Madinah** have trained generations of scholars who disseminate Salafi doctrines across the globe. These institutions often emphasize a strict interpretation of Islamic texts, rejecting **Sufism**, **Shia Islam**, and other forms of religious expression that Salafis view as innovations.

- **Social Conservatism**: Salafism promotes a **conservative interpretation** of Islamic law and social norms, particularly regarding issues such as **gender roles**, **family life**, and **public morality**. In many Muslim-majority countries, Salafi movements have pushed for stricter dress codes for women, limitations on social interaction between men and women, and a greater emphasis on the enforcement of Sharia in public life. These movements often clash with more liberal or moderate Muslim groups who advocate for a more progressive interpretation of Islam.

● **Online Platforms and Social Media**: The internet has played a crucial role in spreading Salafi ideas, particularly among younger generations. Salafi preachers and scholars use social media platforms, YouTube channels, and online forums to reach a global audience, offering religious guidance, sermons, and fatwas (Islamic legal opinions) that align with Salafi interpretations. This has allowed Salafism to gain influence in regions where traditional religious institutions may not be as dominant.

---

5. Controversy and Criticism

DESPITE ITS GLOBAL influence, both **Salafism** and **Wahhabism** have faced significant criticism from within the Muslim world and beyond.

● **Tensions with Sufism and Shia Islam**: Salafism's rejection of **Sufism** and **Shia Islam** has led to conflicts with these communities, particularly in countries where Sufism or Shia Islam has deep historical roots. In places like **Iraq**, **Lebanon**, **Pakistan**, and **Nigeria**, tensions between Salafi groups and Shia or Sufi communities have sometimes escalated into violence. Salafi opposition to Sufi practices such as **saint veneration** and shrine visitation has also led to the destruction of religious sites in countries like **Mali** and **Somalia**.

● **Criticism from Mainstream Islamic Scholars**: Many mainstream Sunni scholars, particularly from the **Ash'ari** and **Maturidi** theological traditions, have criticized Salafism and Wahhabism for their **literalism** and **rejection of traditional Islamic scholarship**. They argue that Salafis neglect the **rich diversity** of Islamic jurisprudence and theology, particularly the **four Sunni schools of law** (Hanafi, Maliki, Shafi'i, and Hanbali) and the intellectual contributions of later Islamic scholars.

- **Impact on Muslim Unity**: Some critics argue that the strict interpretations of Salafism and Wahhabism have contributed to divisions within the global Muslim community by promoting a narrow understanding of Islam that delegitimizes other interpretations. This has led to accusations that Salafism, particularly in its more militant forms, fosters sectarianism and undermines efforts to build unity among Muslims of different backgrounds.

Conclusion

Salafism and **Wahhabism** have had a profound impact on the modern Muslim world, influencing religious thought, political movements, social norms, and global security. While these movements share a common goal of returning to the pure teachings of early Islam, they have manifested in different ways, from state-sponsored Wahhabism in Saudi Arabia to the global spread of Salafi-jihadist groups like al-Qaeda and ISIS. Their strict interpretations of **Tawhid**, rejection of **Bid'ah**, and call for religious purity have resonated with many Muslims, but they have also sparked significant controversy and conflict, both within the Muslim world and beyond. As these movements continue to shape Islamic discourse, their influence will remain a central issue in the ongoing debates over the future of Islam in a rapidly changing world.

Chapter 5: The Ahmadiyya Movement and Its Unique Beliefs

The **Ahmadiyya Movement**, founded in the late **19th century** by **Mirza Ghulam Ahmad** in **British India**, represents one of the most distinctive and controversial religious movements within Islam. The movement emerged during a period of significant political, religious, and social upheaval, as Muslims in the Indian subcontinent grappled with the challenges of colonialism, Western influence, and the internal decline of Islamic authority. Amid this backdrop, Mirza Ghulam Ahmad claimed to be the **Promised Messiah** and **Mahdi**—figures awaited by many Muslims as reformers and saviors who would restore Islam to its former glory.

The Ahmadiyya community holds a unique position within the Muslim world due to its belief in the **continuation of prophethood**—a belief that sets it apart from mainstream Sunni and Shia Islam, which hold that **Muhammad (peace be upon him)** is the **final prophet**. Ahmadis view Ghulam Ahmad as a **subordinate prophet**, whose mission was to revive Islam, restore its moral and spiritual integrity, and guide the community toward a peaceful interpretation of faith.

Despite the movement's emphasis on peaceful coexistence, intellectual reform, and interfaith dialogue, it has faced **persecution** and **rejection** from many Muslim-majority countries. This opposition largely stems from the theological disagreement over the concept of prophethood, with orthodox Sunni and Shia scholars declaring Ahmadis as **non-Muslim** due to their perceived deviation from one of Islam's core tenets. The Ahmadiyya Movement, however, continues to grow and spread globally, with millions of followers, particularly in **South Asia**, **Africa**, **Europe**, and **North America**.

This chapter will explore the **origins**, **beliefs**, and **unique practices** of the Ahmadiyya Movement, as well as the reasons for its continued **rejection** by much of the Muslim world. It will also examine the community's contributions to Islamic thought, its approach to religious reform, and its ongoing struggle for **recognition** and **religious freedom**. Through an understanding of the Ahmadiyya Movement, one gains insight into the broader challenges of sectarianism, identity, and theological diversity within the Muslim world.

The Life and Teachings of Mirza Ghulam Ahmad

MIRZA GHULAM AHMAD (1835–1908), the founder of the **Ahmadiyya Movement**, was born in **Qadian**, a small town in what is now **Punjab**, India, during a time of significant political and religious turmoil in the region. The Indian subcontinent, under British colonial rule, was experiencing shifts in its social, religious, and political fabric. This context deeply influenced Ghulam Ahmad, who became a central figure in the Islamic reformist movement. His mission, as he described it, was to **revitalize Islam**, guide Muslims back to their faith, and address the challenges posed by both Western influence and internal divisions within the Muslim community.

1. Early Life and Religious Education

MIRZA GHULAM AHMAD was born into a well-established Muslim family with a history of service to the Mughal rulers of India. His early education included the study of **Islamic jurisprudence**, **Quranic exegesis**, **Hadith**, and the **Persian** and **Arabic** languages. Though not formally trained as a scholar, Ahmad was known for his devotion to Islam and his intellectual engagement with Islamic texts. He spent much of his early life in religious contemplation, developing a deep understanding of Islamic theology and spirituality.

- **Spiritual Pursuits and Writings**: In his early adulthood, Ahmad spent much of his time in seclusion, praying and reflecting on the state of Islam and the Muslim community. His intense spiritual practices and study of religious texts led him to believe that he had been chosen by Allah for a special mission. He began writing extensively on the challenges facing Islam, producing works that addressed issues such as the decline of Muslim morality, the impact of Christian missionary efforts, and the need for Islamic revival.

---

2. Claim to Messianic and Prophetic Status

IN **1889**, Mirza Ghulam Ahmad announced that he was the **Promised Messiah** and **Mahdi**, figures prophesied to appear in the latter days to guide humanity and restore justice. Ahmad's claim was based on his belief that he had received **divine revelations** and that his mission was to revive the true teachings of Islam and promote peace. His teachings emphasized the **spiritual interpretation of jihad**, rejecting the notion of violent struggle and instead advocating for a peaceful propagation of Islam through intellectual debate and moral reform.

- **The Promised Messiah and Mahdi**: Ahmad's declaration that he was the Messiah and Mahdi was significant because it challenged traditional Islamic eschatology, which holds that Jesus (peace be upon him) will return in the flesh to restore Islam before the Day of Judgment. Ahmad taught that Jesus had died a natural death and would not return physically; instead, his own spiritual role as the Messiah fulfilled this prophecy.

- **The Continuation of Prophethood**: Perhaps the most controversial aspect of Ahmad's teachings was his claim to be a **prophet**, though not in the same sense as the **final prophethood** of Muhammad (peace be upon him). He described himself as a **non-lawbearing prophet**, whose mission was to guide Muslims back to the true path of

Islam in line with the teachings of the Prophet Muhammad (peace be upon him). Ahmadis view this as a form of **subordinate prophethood**, one that does not challenge or supersede Muhammad's role as the final law-giving prophet. This belief, however, has been the primary reason for the widespread rejection of the Ahmadiyya Movement by mainstream Sunni and Shia scholars, who view it as a deviation from the core Islamic belief that Muhammad is the final prophet.

---

3. Key Teachings and Doctrines

MIRZA GHULAM AHMAD'S teachings focus on the **revival of Islam**, **peaceful reform**, and addressing the intellectual and spiritual challenges of his time. His writings, which are extensive and cover a wide range of theological and social issues, continue to shape the doctrine of the Ahmadiyya community today.

- **Revival of True Islam**: Ahmad believed that Islam had strayed from its original teachings due to centuries of decline and the influence of foreign powers, particularly British colonial rule in India and Christian missionary efforts. He called for a return to the pure and original form of Islam, as practiced by the Prophet Muhammad (peace be upon him) and his companions. His emphasis on spiritual and moral reform was central to his message, and he called on Muslims to embody the true ethical values of Islam, such as truthfulness, justice, and compassion.

- **Rejection of Violent Jihad**: One of the most significant aspects of Ahmad's teachings was his rejection of the traditional concept of **violent jihad**. In an era when colonialism and missionary activities were perceived as threats to Islam, many Muslims called for armed resistance. Ahmad, however, preached that the true jihad was an intellectual and spiritual struggle, not a physical one. He argued that the spread of Islam should occur through peaceful means, such as dialogue, reasoning, and moral example, rather than through violence or coercion.

- **Emphasis on Interfaith Dialogue**: Ahmad placed great importance on **interfaith dialogue** and engaged in numerous debates with Christian missionaries, Hindu leaders, and other religious figures. His goal was to defend Islam from criticism while promoting mutual understanding between different faiths. His book, **"The Philosophy of the Teachings of Islam,"** is a well-known example of his efforts to explain and clarify Islamic teachings in a way that was accessible to both Muslims and non-Muslims.

- **Universal Peace and Unity**: A major theme of Ahmad's teachings was the promotion of **peace** and **global unity**. He rejected sectarianism within Islam, calling for unity among all Muslims, and emphasized the need for harmonious coexistence between different religious communities. Ahmad also advocated for loyalty to the state, teaching his followers to respect the laws of the countries they lived in, including British India.

4. The Formation of the Ahmadiyya Community

IN **1889**, Mirza Ghulam Ahmad formally established the **Ahmadiyya Movement** with a small group of dedicated followers. He invited people to take the **pledge of allegiance (Bai'at)**, symbolizing their commitment to his teachings and mission. This marked the beginning of the formal organization of the Ahmadiyya community, which grew rapidly in India and beyond.

- **Organizational Structure**: Under Ahmad's leadership, the Ahmadiyya community developed a well-structured organization with a focus on religious education, missionary work, and social welfare. The movement's emphasis on intellectual engagement and peaceful propagation of Islam helped it attract followers not only in India but also in other parts of the Muslim world and Europe.

- **Expansion and Missionary Work**: After Ahmad's death in **1908**, the Ahmadiyya Movement continued to expand under the leadership of his successors, known as **Caliphs**. The community placed a strong emphasis on **missionary work** (tabligh), sending representatives to spread its message to Africa, Europe, North America, and other regions. Today, the Ahmadiyya Movement has millions of followers worldwide and has established mosques, schools, and humanitarian projects in many countries.

5. Controversy and Persecution

FROM ITS INCEPTION, the Ahmadiyya Movement has faced significant opposition from mainstream Islamic scholars and communities. The primary source of this opposition is the Ahmadi belief in the continuation of prophethood, which many Muslims view as a direct challenge to the finality of the Prophet Muhammad (peace be upon him). As a result, Ahmadis have been declared **non-Muslim** by some Muslim-majority countries and have faced **persecution** and **discrimination**.

- **Official Declaration as Non-Muslim**: In **1974**, Pakistan's government officially declared the **Ahmadiyya community** as non-Muslim through a constitutional amendment, and in **1984**, further laws were passed restricting Ahmadis from identifying themselves as Muslims or using Islamic terminology. These laws led to widespread persecution, including mob violence, arrests, and restrictions on religious practices. Similar restrictions exist in other countries, such as **Saudi Arabia** and **Indonesia**.

- **Global Rejection**: Most Muslim-majority countries, particularly those following **Sunni** and **Shia** traditions, reject the Ahmadiyya Movement as outside the fold of Islam. Theological opposition to the belief in continued prophethood is the central reason for this rejection. Despite this, the Ahmadi community continues to grow and spread globally, with a strong presence in **Africa, Europe**, and **North America**.

Conclusion

The life and teachings of **Mirza Ghulam Ahmad** laid the foundation for one of the most unique and controversial movements within the Muslim world. His claims to **messianic** and **prophetic status**, coupled with his call for the **revival of Islam** through peaceful reform, intellectual engagement, and spiritual jihad, have left a lasting legacy. While his followers see him as a divinely guided reformer, the Ahmadiyya Movement remains a source of theological controversy and is often marginalized within the broader Muslim community. Despite facing significant opposition, the movement has continued to thrive globally, promoting its message of peace, interfaith dialogue, and unity.

The Role of the Mahdi and Messiah in Ahmadiyya Belief

IN THE **Ahmadiyya Movement**, the concepts of the **Mahdi** and the **Messiah** are central to their theology, but they are understood in a unique way that sets Ahmadis apart from mainstream Sunni and Shia Islamic beliefs. The **Mahdi** (the Guided One) and the **Messiah** are traditionally seen by Muslims as two distinct eschatological figures who are expected to appear in the latter days to restore justice, revive true Islam, and usher in an era of peace before the Day of Judgment. However, in **Ahmadiyya theology**, these two roles are combined in the person of **Mirza Ghulam Ahmad** (1835–1908), the founder of the movement.

1. The Traditional Islamic Understanding of the Mahdi and Messiah

IN MAINSTREAM **Sunni** and **Shia** Islam, the Mahdi and Messiah are viewed as separate figures:

- **The Mahdi**: In both Sunni and Shia eschatology, the Mahdi is a divinely guided leader who will appear before the Day of Judgment to restore true Islam, bring justice, and eliminate corruption and oppression in the world. For Sunnis, the Mahdi is expected to be a descendant of the Prophet Muhammad (peace be upon him), but he has not yet appeared. In **Twelver Shia Islam**, the Mahdi is believed to be the **12th Imam**, who has been in occultation and will reappear to fulfill his mission.

- **The Messiah (Isa/Jesus)**: According to Islamic teachings, Jesus (peace be upon him) was not crucified but was raised to heaven and will return in the latter days to defeat the **Dajjal** (the Antichrist) and establish a reign of peace and justice. The return of Jesus is a major part of Islamic eschatology, and Muslims believe that he will confirm the truth of Islam and follow the teachings of the Prophet Muhammad (peace be upon him).

---

2. Mirza Ghulam Ahmad's Claim to Be the Mahdi and Messiah

IN **1889**, Mirza Ghulam Ahmad declared that he was both the **Promised Messiah** and the **Mahdi** foretold in Islamic eschatology. His claim combined these two traditionally distinct roles into one, which was a significant departure from the conventional Islamic understanding. Ahmadis believe that Mirza Ghulam Ahmad's mission was to **revive Islam**, defend it against external and internal challenges, and fulfill the spiritual prophecies associated with the Mahdi and Messiah.

- **The Mahdi**: According to Ahmad, the traditional concept of the Mahdi as a militant figure who would wage war and establish a political caliphate was a misunderstanding. Instead, he taught that the Mahdi's role was **spiritual**, not military. Ahmad claimed that he was the divinely guided Mahdi who would restore Islam's true teachings through peaceful reform, intellectual engagement, and spiritual revival. His emphasis on the peaceful propagation of Islam contrasted sharply with the traditional expectation of the Mahdi as a leader who would engage in **armed jihad**.

- **The Messiah (Jesus)**: Mirza Ghulam Ahmad also claimed to be the **Messiah** whose coming was foretold in both **Islamic** and **Christian** eschatology. He rejected the idea that Jesus would return in the flesh and instead taught that the **prophecies** about the Messiah's second coming referred to a **spiritual figure** who would fulfill the mission of Jesus by restoring the moral and spiritual integrity of humanity. Ahmad argued that Jesus had already died a natural death and would not physically return to earth. Ahmadis believe that Mirza Ghulam Ahmad fulfilled the role of the Messiah by leading a peaceful revival of Islam and calling people to live according to its true principles.

---

3. The Ahmadiyya Interpretation of the Mahdi and Messiah's Mission

IN AHMADIYYA BELIEF, the roles of the Mahdi and the Messiah are deeply intertwined and focus on spiritual reformation rather than political or military leadership. The movement emphasizes that both titles represent a **spiritual mission** aimed at reviving Islam and promoting **global peace** and **justice** through non-violent means.

- **Restoration of True Islam**: Ahmadis believe that the primary mission of the Mahdi and Messiah, as embodied by Mirza Ghulam Ahmad, is to restore **Islam's original purity**. This involves returning Muslims to the core teachings of the **Quran** and **Sunnah** and eliminating the **corruptions** and **innovations** that had crept into the faith over the centuries. Ahmad's teachings focus on spiritual jihad—**striving** against one's own base desires and spreading the message of Islam through peaceful means such as preaching, dialogue, and moral example.

- **Peaceful Jihad**: One of the most significant elements of Ahmadiyya theology is the **rejection of violent jihad**. Ahmadis believe that the true jihad is an intellectual and spiritual struggle, not a physical war. Mirza Ghulam Ahmad's teachings emphasize that the **spread of Islam** should occur through peaceful **debate** and **reform**, not through military conquest or force. This message of **non-violence** is a cornerstone of Ahmadiyya belief and contrasts with the more militant interpretations of jihad associated with traditional Mahdist expectations.

- **Interfaith Dialogue and Reconciliation**: As the Messiah, Mirza Ghulam Ahmad saw his role as bridging the gap between different **religions** and promoting **interfaith harmony**. He engaged in debates with Christian missionaries and leaders of other faiths, arguing that his mission was to demonstrate the truth of Islam while also encouraging mutual understanding and respect among different religious communities. Ahmadis believe that his role as the Messiah was not just to guide Muslims but to serve as a universal figure who would bring peace and reconciliation between **Muslims**, **Christians**, **Jews**, and people of other faiths.

---

4. Significance of the Mahdi and Messiah in Ahmadiyya Practice

THE BELIEF IN MIRZA Ghulam Ahmad as the Mahdi and Messiah shapes many aspects of **Ahmadiyya practice** and religious identity. Ahmadis view their community as the fulfillment of Islamic prophecies and see their mission as one of spiritual and moral renewal, not only for Muslims but for all of humanity.

- **Khilafat (Caliphate):** After the death of Mirza Ghulam Ahmad in **1908**, the Ahmadiyya community established the **Khilafat**, a spiritual caliphate that continues to guide the movement today. The Ahmadiyya Caliphate is viewed as the continuation of Ahmad's mission as Mahdi and Messiah, and the caliphs serve as spiritual leaders who promote his teachings and provide guidance to the global Ahmadiyya community. This Caliphate is distinctly spiritual, focusing on moral leadership rather than political power, and it plays a central role in the community's unity and growth.

- **Global Outreach and Humanitarian Efforts:** Following Ahmad's emphasis on peace and moral reform, the Ahmadiyya community is heavily involved in **humanitarian work** around the world. Ahmadis believe that part of the Mahdi and Messiah's mission is to improve the material and spiritual well-being of people through education, healthcare, and social services. The community has established schools, hospitals, and charitable organizations in many countries, reflecting their commitment to **service** and **human welfare**.

- **Persecution and Identity:** The belief in Mirza Ghulam Ahmad as the Mahdi and Messiah has led to significant **persecution** of the Ahmadiyya community in many Muslim-majority countries, where Ahmadis are often declared **non-Muslim** due to their perceived deviation from the belief in the finality of the prophethood of Muhammad (peace be upon him). This has resulted in **legal restrictions**, **social ostracism**, and **violence** against Ahmadis, particularly in countries like **Pakistan** and **Indonesia**. Despite this, Ahmadis remain steadfast in their belief in Mirza Ghulam Ahmad's mission and continue to spread their message globally.

Conclusion

In **Ahmadiyya belief**, the roles of the **Mahdi** and the **Messiah** are inseparably linked in the person of **Mirza Ghulam Ahmad**, whose mission was to revive Islam, promote peace, and bring about a spiritual reformation. Ahmad's teachings emphasize the peaceful propagation of Islam, the rejection of violent jihad, and the importance of interfaith dialogue. While his claims to **messianic** and **prophetic status** have led to widespread rejection by mainstream Islamic scholars, Ahmadis believe that their community represents the fulfillment of the prophecies of the Mahdi and Messiah, with a mission to spread **truth**, **justice**, and **peace** across the world. The Mahdi and Messiah, in Ahmadiyya understanding, are not figures of war or political conquest, but of **spiritual renewal** and **moral guidance**, reflecting the movement's core values of non-violence, service, and interfaith harmony.

Key Theological Differences Between Ahmadiyya and Mainstream Sunni and Shia Islam

THE **Ahmadiyya Movement**, founded by **Mirza Ghulam Ahmad** in the late 19th century, differs significantly from mainstream **Sunni** and **Shia Islam** in several key theological areas. These differences, particularly regarding the concepts of **prophethood**, **eschatology**, and **jihad**, have led to widespread rejection of the Ahmadiyya community by both Sunni and Shia scholars. Below are the key theological differences:

1. The Concept of Prophethood

THE MOST SIGNIFICANT theological difference between **Ahmadiyya Islam** and mainstream **Sunni** and **Shia Islam** lies in the **Ahmadi belief in the continuation of prophethood** after **Muhammad (peace be upon him)**. This is the primary point of contention that has led to the Ahmadiyya community being declared **non-Muslim** in several Muslim-majority countries.

- **Ahmadiyya Belief in Subordinate Prophethood**: Ahmadis believe that **Mirza Ghulam Ahmad** was a prophet, though they distinguish this from **law-bearing** prophethood. They claim that Mirza Ghulam Ahmad was a **non-lawbearing prophet** or a **subordinate prophet**, meaning that his prophethood is not independent or superior to that of Muhammad (peace be upon him), but rather serves to **revive Islam** and guide Muslims back to the original teachings of Islam. Ahmadis affirm that Muhammad (peace be upon him) is the **Seal of the Prophets (Khatam an-Nabiyyin)**, but they interpret this to mean that no new law-bearing prophet can come after him, while **subordinate prophets** who do not bring new laws can still appear to guide the Muslim community.

• **Mainstream Islamic Belief (Finality of Prophethood)**: Both Sunni and Shia Islam uphold the belief that **Muhammad (peace be upon him)** is the **final prophet**, after whom no prophet—whether law-bearing or non-lawbearing—can come. For mainstream Muslims, the phrase **Khatam an-Nabiyyin** is interpreted to mean that Muhammad is the **last and final prophet**, closing the door to any form of prophethood after him. The belief in the finality of prophethood is a core tenet of mainstream Islamic theology, and any claim to prophethood after Muhammad is considered a **heretical deviation**. This is the principal reason why many Muslim-majority countries have legally declared Ahmadis as non-Muslim.

---

2. The Role of the Mahdi and Messiah

THE **Ahmadiyya Movement** has a unique interpretation of the eschatological figures of the **Mahdi** and the **Messiah**, which differs from traditional Sunni and Shia beliefs.

• **Ahmadiyya Belief**: Ahmadis believe that **Mirza Ghulam Ahmad** fulfilled the roles of both the **Promised Messiah** and the **Mahdi**, two figures traditionally awaited in Islamic eschatology. According to Ahmadiyya theology, the **Messiah** (identified with **Jesus**) was not to return physically but was instead to appear in the form of a **spiritual reformer**. Mirza Ghulam Ahmad claimed to be this **spiritual Messiah**, sent to **revive** Islam and

establish peace. Additionally, Ahmadis believe that the traditional understanding of the **Mahdi** as a military leader or warrior is a misinterpretation, and that Mirza Ghulam Ahmad, as the Mahdi, sought to bring about a spiritual and peaceful renewal of Islam, rather than leading a physical struggle.

● **Mainstream Sunni and Shia Belief:**

○ In **Sunni Islam**, the **Mahdi** is expected to be a descendant of the Prophet Muhammad (peace be upon him) who will come in the latter days to restore true Islam and justice, fight against the **Dajjal** (the Antichrist), and establish a global Islamic state. The **Messiah**, identified with **Jesus (Isa)**, is expected to return to earth, defeat the Dajjal, and bring about a period of peace. These figures are considered distinct in Sunni belief.

○ In **Shia Islam**, particularly in **Twelver Shia belief**, the **Mahdi** is identified as **Muhammad al-Mahdi**, the 12th Imam who is in occultation and will reappear at the end of time to restore justice. Like Sunnis, Shias also believe in the future return of **Jesus** to defeat the Dajjal.

Mainstream Muslims reject the Ahmadi claim that Mirza Ghulam Ahmad fulfilled the roles of both the Mahdi and Messiah, believing that these eschatological figures have not yet appeared and will come in the future.

3. The Concept of Jihad

THE INTERPRETATION of **jihad** is another important theological difference between Ahmadiyya Islam and mainstream Sunni and Shia Islam.

- **Ahmadiyya Belief**: The Ahmadiyya Movement promotes a **non-violent interpretation** of jihad, focusing on **spiritual** and **intellectual** struggles. Ahmadis believe that the true jihad in the modern era is a struggle for moral and spiritual reform, as well as the peaceful propagation of Islam through **dialogue**, **education**, and **reasoned arguments**. Mirza Ghulam Ahmad rejected the notion of **militant jihad**, arguing that armed struggle was no longer necessary or appropriate for spreading Islam in the modern age.

- **Mainstream Sunni and Shia Belief**: In mainstream Islam, jihad is understood in a broader context, encompassing both **spiritual** and **militant** dimensions. While the **greater jihad** is often described as the internal struggle against one's lower desires, the **lesser jihad** can include **armed struggle** in defense of Islam, particularly in cases of self-defense or when the Muslim community is under attack. Although jihad is not always understood as a call for violence, **militant jihad** remains an accepted concept in traditional Islamic jurisprudence under certain circumstances. Mainstream Islamic scholars reject the Ahmadi reinterpretation that completely discards the concept of armed jihad.

4. Mirza Ghulam Ahmad's Role in Islamic Eschatology

IN ADDITION TO THE Ahmadi interpretation of the Mahdi and Messiah, **Mirza Ghulam Ahmad's broader role in Islamic eschatology** is another key difference.

- **Ahmadiyya Belief**: Ahmadis believe that **Mirza Ghulam Ahmad** was divinely appointed to fulfill many of the **prophecies** associated with the **end times** in Islamic eschatology. He claimed to be the **reformer of the age** sent to restore Islam and establish peace, and his followers view his mission as the fulfillment of the **eschatological expectations** in Islam. Ahmadis believe that with the appearance of Mirza Ghulam Ahmad, the **promised victory** of Islam is being realized through peaceful means and spiritual guidance.

- **Mainstream Islamic View**: Mainstream Sunni and Shia Muslims reject the idea that **Mirza Ghulam Ahmad** has any role in Islamic eschatology. For Sunnis, the appearance of the **Mahdi** and the return of **Jesus (peace be upon him)** are events that are still awaited and are not believed to have been fulfilled by Mirza Ghulam Ahmad. Shias, too, reject any claim that Ahmad is connected to the reappearance of the **12th Imam** (the Mahdi) or the return of Jesus.

---

5. Relationship with the Muslim Community and Identity

THE AHMADIYYA COMMUNITY'S theological differences have had a profound impact on its relationship with the broader Muslim world, leading to significant **ostracism** and **controversy**.

- **Ahmadi Identity**: Ahmadis consider themselves **Muslim** and see their beliefs as fully aligned with the true teachings of Islam. They view the Ahmadiyya Movement as a **revivalist** movement that seeks to **reform** Islam from within and bring Muslims back to the core values of the **Quran** and **Sunnah**. Ahmadis follow the basic pillars of Islam, including prayer, fasting, and charity, and believe that their community is fulfilling the spiritual mission of Islam.

- **Mainstream Muslim Opposition**: Due to their belief in the continuation of prophethood, Ahmadis have been **rejected** by mainstream Sunni and Shia scholars, who argue that the Ahmadiyya community falls outside the fold of Islam. In countries such as **Pakistan, Indonesia**, and **Saudi Arabia**, Ahmadis have been legally declared **non-Muslim** and face **discrimination**, **violence**, and **persecution**. In Pakistan, for example, Ahmadis are forbidden from identifying themselves as Muslims or using Islamic symbols, and they are not allowed to call their places of worship **mosques**.

Conclusion

The **Ahmadiyya Movement** differs from mainstream **Sunni** and **Shia Islam** in several critical theological areas, most notably in its belief in the **continuation of prophethood**, its interpretation of the **Mahdi and Messiah**, and its approach to **jihad**. These differences, particularly the belief in **Mirza Ghulam Ahmad** as a prophet, have led to the **ostracism** and **persecution** of Ahmadis in many parts of the Muslim world. Despite these challenges, the Ahmadiyya community continues to promote its vision of **peaceful Islamic revival** and remains committed to its beliefs, while mainstream

Islamic scholars and communities continue to regard these theological differences as placing Ahmadis outside the fold of Islam.

Ahmadiyya's Approach to Jihad, Peace, and Social Justice

THE **Ahmadiyya Movement**, founded by **Mirza Ghulam Ahmad** in the late 19th century, is distinct in its interpretation of **jihad**, its commitment to **peace**, and its emphasis on **social justice**. These elements are central to Ahmadiyya theology and are rooted in the movement's overarching goal of **spiritual revival** and the peaceful propagation of Islam. Ahmadis view their approach as a return to the true teachings of Islam, focusing on moral reform, non-violence, and the betterment of humanity.

1. Ahmadiyya's Interpretation of Jihad

IN CONTRAST TO MORE traditional interpretations of jihad, which can include **militant struggle** or **armed defense** in certain contexts, the Ahmadiyya Movement offers a radically different understanding of jihad. **Mirza Ghulam Ahmad** reinterpreted jihad as primarily a **spiritual** and **moral** struggle, rather than a physical or military conflict.

- **Jihad of the Self (Jihad al-Nafs)**: According to Ahmadiyya theology, the most important form of jihad is the **internal struggle** against one's own lower desires, selfishness, and immorality. This concept, known as **Jihad al-Nafs**, emphasizes personal spiritual growth, self-discipline, and the striving to become closer to Allah through good deeds, worship, and moral behavior. Ahmadis believe that this form of jihad is central to living a righteous life and fulfilling one's responsibilities as a Muslim.

- **Jihad by the Pen (Jihad bil-Qalam)**: Ahmadis also emphasize **Jihad bil-Qalam**, or the **jihad of the pen**. This refers to intellectual and scholarly efforts to defend and propagate the message of Islam through peaceful means, such as writing, debate, dialogue, and education. Ahmadis believe that the challenges facing Islam in the modern world, particularly from **Western colonialism, secularism**, and **Christian missionary efforts**, can be best addressed through reasoned arguments, education, and the dissemination of the true teachings of Islam. Mirza Ghulam Ahmad himself wrote extensively, engaging in debates with Christian missionaries and other religious leaders, emphasizing that the spread of Islam should occur through peaceful persuasion, not violence.

- **Rejection of Violent Jihad**: The Ahmadiyya Movement firmly rejects the concept of **violent jihad** or the use of force to spread or defend Islam. Mirza Ghulam Ahmad taught that in the modern era, the need for **military jihad** had ended, as Islam should no longer be spread by the sword but through peaceful means. This rejection of violence sets Ahmadis apart from more traditional interpretations of jihad, particularly those that view armed struggle as permissible under certain conditions. Ahmadis believe that **peaceful propagation** of faith, intellectual discourse, and personal reform are the true expressions of jihad in the modern age.

---

2. Commitment to Peace

PEACE IS A FUNDAMENTAL principle of the Ahmadiyya Movement, which promotes **non-violence** and **reconciliation** as core tenets of Islamic practice. The movement's emphasis on peace is reflected in its approach to **interfaith dialogue, conflict resolution,** and **global harmony.**

- **Promotion of Non-Violence**: Ahmadis believe that Islam is a religion of peace and that its true teachings advocate for non-violence in both personal and communal matters. Mirza Ghulam Ahmad's rejection of violent jihad was rooted in the belief that Islam's message is best conveyed through **peaceful means**, and this philosophy continues to shape Ahmadiyya practices today. Ahmadis are encouraged to resolve conflicts through dialogue, patience, and understanding, rather than through aggression or force.

- **Interfaith Dialogue**: One of the ways Ahmadis promote peace is through **interfaith dialogue** and cooperation. The movement actively engages with people of other faiths, encouraging mutual understanding and respect. Ahmadis participate in **interfaith conferences**, dialogues, and humanitarian projects, emphasizing common values such as compassion, justice, and the dignity of all people. This commitment to dialogue reflects the belief that peaceful coexistence among different religious communities is not only possible but essential to achieving global peace.

- **Global Peace Initiatives**: The **Ahmadiyya community** has launched several global initiatives aimed at promoting peace and understanding between different communities. One notable example is the **"Muslims for Peace"** campaign, which seeks to build bridges between Muslims and people of other faiths by spreading the true message of Islam—one of peace, love, and respect for humanity. Ahmadis believe that it is their duty to represent Islam as a force for good in the world and to work actively toward reducing conflict and promoting peace at every level of society.

---

3. Social Justice and Service to Humanity

THE AHMADIYYA MOVEMENT places a strong emphasis on **social justice** and the **welfare of humanity**, believing that these are integral aspects of Islam. Ahmadis are encouraged to engage in acts of charity, community service, and humanitarian work as expressions of their faith. The community's commitment to **service** reflects their belief that **spirituality** must be accompanied by a dedication to improving the lives of others.

- **Service to Humanity (Khadimat-ul-Khalq):** One of the central teachings of the Ahmadiyya community is the concept of **Khadimat-ul-Khalq**, or **service to humanity**. Ahmadis believe that serving others—whether through providing education, healthcare, or humanitarian aid—is a core aspect of Islamic faith. The Ahmadiyya Movement has established a wide range of social services, including **schools**, **hospitals**, **orphanages**, and **charitable organizations**, that operate in many countries around the world. These initiatives aim to alleviate suffering, promote education, and improve living standards, particularly in underdeveloped or conflict-ridden areas.

- **Charity and Welfare:** Ahmadis are taught that **charity** is a religious obligation and an essential part of spiritual practice. The movement encourages members to give generously, both through **Zakat** (the obligatory almsgiving in Islam) and through additional voluntary contributions. The Ahmadiyya community runs a number of **humanitarian relief** programs, providing food, shelter, and medical care to those in need, regardless of their religious background. The community's **international charity organization, Humanity First**, is actively involved in disaster relief and development projects around the world, reflecting the Ahmadi belief in the importance of social justice and the dignity of every human being.

• **Educational Initiatives**: The Ahmadiyya Movement places great importance on **education** as a means of promoting social justice and empowering individuals to improve their lives. The community has established schools and educational programs in many countries, focusing on providing **quality education** to underserved communities. Ahmadis believe that education is a key driver of social change and that it is their duty to help create opportunities for learning and personal development, particularly for marginalized groups.

• **Advocacy for Human Rights**: The Ahmadiyya community is also involved in **advocacy for human rights**, particularly the rights of religious minorities. Ahmadis, who have often faced persecution themselves, are vocal in their support for **religious freedom, equality**, and the protection of vulnerable communities. Through public outreach, interfaith initiatives, and engagement with policymakers, the community works to raise awareness about issues of injustice and to promote the rights of all people to live in peace and dignity.

4. Integration of Peace, Jihad, and Social Justice

AHMADIYYA'S APPROACH to **jihad**, **peace**, and **social justice** is deeply interconnected. The movement views these concepts not as separate or conflicting ideas but as complementary aspects of a broader Islamic mission. According to Ahmadi theology, the true purpose of jihad is to **strive** for peace, justice, and the improvement of society, rather than to engage in conflict or violence.

- **Jihad for Social Justice**: Ahmadis believe that one of the most important forms of jihad is the struggle for **social justice**. This includes efforts to combat **poverty**, **injustice**, **discrimination**, and **oppression** through peaceful means. By working to create a more just and equitable society, Ahmadis see themselves as fulfilling the true spirit of jihad, which is about creating a world where everyone can live with dignity and peace.

- **Spiritual and Social Reform**: The Ahmadiyya Movement emphasizes that **spiritual reform** must go hand in hand with **social reform**. Ahmadis are taught that their religious duties include both personal moral development and active engagement in making the world a better place. This holistic approach to Islam is reflected in the community's wide-ranging efforts to promote peace, justice, education, and humanitarian aid.

Conclusion

The **Ahmadiyya Movement's approach** to jihad, peace, and **social justice** is characterized by a deep commitment to **non-violence, spiritual reform**, and the **welfare of humanity**. By reinterpreting jihad as a spiritual and intellectual struggle, rejecting violence, and emphasizing peace and service, Ahmadis present a vision of Islam that seeks to address the challenges of the modern world through peaceful means. Their work in education, humanitarian aid, and social justice reflects their belief that true Islamic practice involves not only personal piety but also the active pursuit of the common good, with a focus on creating a more just and compassionate world for all.

Global Presence and Controversies Surrounding the Ahmadiyya Community

THE **Ahmadiyya Movement**, founded by **Mirza Ghulam Ahmad** in **British India** in the late 19th century, has grown into a global religious community with millions of followers spread across **South Asia, Africa, Europe, North America**, and **the Middle East**. Despite its peaceful approach to the propagation of Islam and emphasis on social justice, the Ahmadiyya community has faced significant **controversy** and **persecution** due to its theological differences from mainstream Sunni and Shia Islam, particularly its belief in the **continuation of prophethood**. This has led to widespread rejection of Ahmadis as **non-Muslim** in many countries, resulting in **legal discrimination**, **social ostracism**, and, in some cases, **violence**.

1. Global Presence of the Ahmadiyya Community

THE AHMADIYYA COMMUNITY has expanded from its origins in **Qadian, India**, to establish a presence in over **200 countries** worldwide. It is recognized as one of the most organized and dynamic Islamic movements in the world, known for its commitment to peaceful missionary work, humanitarian efforts, and interfaith dialogue.

- **South Asia:** The largest concentration of Ahmadis is in **Pakistan**, where the movement has a complex and often difficult history due to state-imposed restrictions. **India** and **Bangladesh** also have significant Ahmadi populations. Despite facing opposition, the Ahmadi community in South Asia remains active in promoting its teachings and engaging in social welfare programs.

• **Africa:** The Ahmadiyya Movement has been particularly successful in parts of **West** and **East Africa**, including countries like **Nigeria, Ghana, Sierra Leone**, and **Kenya**. Ahmadis in Africa have established schools, hospitals, and community centers, gaining a reputation for providing critical services in underserved areas. The movement has also engaged in extensive missionary work, leading to a steady increase in conversions.

• **Europe and North America:** The Ahmadiyya community has established a strong presence in **Western Europe** and **North America**, particularly in the **United Kingdom, Germany, Canada**, and the **United States**. In these regions, Ahmadis are active in promoting interfaith dialogue, humanitarian efforts, and the peaceful image of Islam. In the UK, the **Ahmadiyya Muslim Community** organizes annual conventions that draw tens of thousands of attendees from around the world. **Canada** is home to one of the largest Ahmadi populations outside of South Asia, and the community enjoys a strong relationship with the Canadian government.

• **Southeast Asia:** The Ahmadiyya Movement has a notable presence in **Indonesia** and **Malaysia**, although it faces significant challenges due to legal restrictions and social discrimination. Ahmadis in these countries have established mosques and community organizations, but their ability to practice freely is often limited by government regulations and opposition from mainstream Islamic groups.

2. Controversies and Persecution

THE GLOBAL SPREAD OF the Ahmadiyya Movement has been accompanied by significant **controversy** and **persecution**, particularly in countries where mainstream Sunni and Shia Islam dominate. The primary source of this opposition is the **Ahmadi belief in the continuation of prophethood**, which is viewed as heretical by most Muslims, who believe in the finality of the Prophet Muhammad (peace be upon him) as the last prophet.

- **Declaration as Non-Muslim**: In **1974**, the government of **Pakistan** amended its constitution to officially declare **Ahmadis as non-Muslims**, a move that was widely supported by religious scholars and political leaders. This constitutional amendment was followed by the **Ordinance XX** in **1984**, which made it illegal for Ahmadis to identify themselves as Muslims, refer to their places of worship as mosques, or publicly practice Islamic rituals. This legal classification has led to widespread **discrimination** and **violence** against Ahmadis in Pakistan, including the destruction of Ahmadi mosques, targeted killings, and social ostracism.

- **Blasphemy Accusations**: Ahmadis in **Pakistan** and other countries with blasphemy laws have been frequently accused of **blasphemy**, which can result in severe punishment, including imprisonment or death. Blasphemy charges are often used to suppress the Ahmadi community's religious activities and to justify mob violence against them. Many Ahmadis face **social and economic discrimination**, as well as difficulties in accessing employment, education, and legal protection.

• **Persecution in Other Muslim-Majority Countries**: In **Indonesia**, **Malaysia**, **Bangladesh**, and parts of **Africa**, Ahmadis face varying levels of **persecution**. In Indonesia, for example, Ahmadis have been targets of violent attacks by extremist groups, and the government has placed restrictions on their religious activities. In Malaysia, Ahmadis are banned from practicing Islam openly, and their publications are censored. Similar challenges exist in other countries where mainstream Islamic scholars have declared Ahmadis to be outside the fold of Islam.

• **International Responses**: Human rights organizations, such as **Amnesty International** and **Human Rights Watch**, have condemned the persecution of Ahmadis and have called on governments to protect their rights to religious freedom. In countries like the **United States**, **Canada**, and **the UK**, governments have granted asylum to Ahmadi refugees fleeing persecution, and the community enjoys a greater degree of religious freedom in these regions.

---

3. Ahmadiyya Response to Persecution

DESPITE THE WIDESPREAD persecution and discrimination they face, the Ahmadiyya community has consistently adhered to its principle of **non-violence** and has sought to respond to opposition through peaceful means. Ahmadis are encouraged to remain patient in the face of adversity and to focus on **prayer**, **education**, and **service** to humanity.

• **Non-Violent Resistance**: The Ahmadiyya Movement teaches its followers to reject violence and to respond to persecution with **peace** and **dignity**. Ahmadis are encouraged to engage in **legal challenges** to defend their rights, where possible, and to work within the framework of local laws to advocate for their freedom of worship. This approach reflects the community's commitment to the peaceful propagation of Islam and the teachings of Mirza Ghulam Ahmad, who emphasized non-violence even in the face of hostility.

● **Humanitarian Work and Social Service**: One of the ways the Ahmadiyya community has responded to persecution is through its extensive involvement in **humanitarian work** and **social service**. By focusing on improving the lives of others, Ahmadis aim to demonstrate the true teachings of Islam, even in environments where they face discrimination. The Ahmadiyya community runs numerous charitable initiatives, including **healthcare programs**, **disaster relief efforts**, and **education projects** in many parts of the world.

● **Public Awareness Campaigns**: The Ahmadiyya community has launched several international campaigns to raise awareness about **religious persecution** and to promote the peaceful image of Islam. One such initiative is the **"Muslims for Peace"** campaign, which seeks to build bridges between Muslims and non-Muslims by promoting the true message of Islam as a religion of peace, love, and tolerance. Ahmadis also engage in **interfaith dialogues** and participate in **international forums** on religious freedom and human rights.

4. Controversies Within the Muslim World

THE CONTROVERSIES SURROUNDING the Ahmadiyya community are primarily theological, stemming from the belief that **Mirza Ghulam Ahmad** was a prophet. This belief challenges the core Islamic doctrine that **Muhammad (peace be upon him)** is the final prophet. Consequently, many Islamic scholars and organizations have issued **fatwas** (religious rulings) declaring Ahmadis as **non-Muslim**. This has led to a range of social, legal, and political challenges for the community.

- **Fatwas Declaring Ahmadis Non-Muslim**: Islamic scholars from across the Sunni and Shia traditions have issued fatwas declaring the Ahmadiyya community to be outside the fold of Islam. These fatwas often cite the Ahmadi belief in the continuation of prophethood as the primary reason for this declaration. In many cases, these fatwas have been used to justify the **exclusion** and **persecution** of Ahmadis, both by governments and by religious groups.

- **Sectarian Tensions**: In countries like **Pakistan** and **Indonesia**, sectarian tensions between mainstream Muslims and Ahmadis have often led to violence, including the destruction of Ahmadi mosques, attacks on Ahmadi individuals, and mob violence against Ahmadi communities. These tensions are exacerbated by the influence of extremist groups, which use anti-Ahmadi sentiment to rally support and legitimize their actions.

- **Ahmadiyya's Efforts to Gain Recognition**: Despite the widespread rejection of their beliefs, the Ahmadiyya community continues to advocate for its recognition as a legitimate Islamic movement. In countries where they face discrimination, Ahmadis have pursued legal challenges and engaged in **public diplomacy** to raise awareness about their plight and to seek protection for their religious freedoms.

---

5. Positive Global Contributions

DESPITE THE CONTROVERSIES and challenges they face, the Ahmadiyya community is widely recognized for its **positive global contributions**, particularly in the areas of **humanitarian work**, **education**, and **interfaith dialogue**. Ahmadis have earned respect for their commitment to **peace**, **service**, and **social justice**, even in the face of adversity.

- **Humanitarian Aid**: The Ahmadiyya community operates one of the largest Muslim humanitarian organizations, **Humanity First**, which provides disaster relief, healthcare, education, and food security programs in countries affected by war, natural disasters, and poverty. Humanity First operates in over 50 countries and serves people of all faiths and backgrounds.

- **Educational Initiatives**: Ahmadis have established **schools** and **universities** in many parts of the world, providing education to underserved communities. These institutions are known for their commitment to **academic excellence**, **moral education**, and **interfaith understanding**.

- **Interfaith Dialogue and Peacebuilding**: The Ahmadiyya community is actively involved in **interfaith**

dialogue and efforts to promote **peace** and **tolerance** among different religious communities. Ahmadis regularly host interfaith conferences and participate in global peace initiatives, promoting their message of harmony, mutual respect, and the peaceful coexistence of all faiths.

Conclusion

The **Ahmadiyya Movement** has grown into a global religious community known for its commitment to **peace**, **service**, and the **peaceful propagation of Islam**. However, its theological differences with mainstream Sunni and Shia Islam, particularly the belief in the **continuation of prophethood**, have led to widespread **controversy**, **rejection**, and **persecution** in many Muslim-majority countries. Despite these challenges, the Ahmadiyya community continues to make significant contributions to **humanitarian work**, **education**, and **interfaith dialogue**, demonstrating its resilience and dedication to its principles of non-violence and social justice. The movement remains a unique and influential force in the global Islamic landscape, advocating for a peaceful and inclusive vision of Islam in the modern world.

Chapter 6: Ibadi Islam – A Forgotten Tradition

Ibadi Islam, one of the most ancient and distinct branches of Islam, is a tradition that has often been overshadowed by the larger Sunni and Shia sects. Despite its rich history and unique theological perspectives, Ibadi Islam is largely unknown outside of its key stronghold in **Oman** and smaller communities in **North Africa** and **East Africa.** Unlike Sunni and Shia Islam, which emerged after significant political and theological divisions in the Muslim community, Ibadi Islam traces its roots back to the early days of the Islamic caliphate, evolving independently from the **Kharijite movement** while developing a more moderate and pragmatic identity.

Ibadis view themselves as upholding the **purest form of Islam**, adhering strictly to the values and practices of the earliest Muslim community, but without the extreme militancy that later came to characterize some Kharijite factions. This historical connection has often led to misunderstandings about the Ibadi tradition, with many incorrectly associating them with radicalism. However, Ibadi Islam emphasizes **peaceful coexistence, tolerance**, and a **just leadership** based on **piety** rather than **hereditary succession** or political power struggles, which sets them apart from both Sunni and Shia doctrines.

What is striking about Ibadi Islam is its emphasis on **quietism** in politics, a principle that encourages working within the existing political frameworks, provided they do not contradict Islamic values. This has allowed Ibadis to survive and thrive in different political contexts over centuries. In Oman, where Ibadi Islam is the dominant faith, the tradition has played a crucial role in shaping the country's **religious tolerance** and **political stability**. Oman's Ibadi rulers have maintained a unique balance between Islamic principles and pragmatic governance, fostering an environment of **religious pluralism** not commonly seen in other parts of the Muslim world.

This chapter delves into the **history, theological principles**, and **contemporary significance** of Ibadi Islam. It explores how this relatively small sect has managed to preserve its identity and influence while remaining largely insulated from the broader sectarian conflicts that have characterized Islamic history. From the Ibadi understanding of **imamate** (leadership) to their distinct **jurisprudence** and **rituals**, the chapter reveals how the Ibadis have maintained a tradition that is deeply rooted in early Islamic values while also adapting to modern challenges. By examining this often-overlooked branch of Islam, we gain a fuller understanding of the diversity within the Muslim world and the important role that the Ibadi tradition continues to play in regions where it thrives.

The Life and Teachings of Mirza Ghulam Ahmad

MIRZA GHULAM AHMAD (1835–1908), the founder of the **Ahmadiyya Movement**, was a religious reformer who emerged during a time of significant upheaval for Muslims in **British India**. Born in the small village of **Qadian** in the Punjab region, Ghulam Ahmad was deeply committed to Islamic scholarship and spirituality from an early age. His life and teachings centered on the revival of Islam, which he believed had become weakened by internal divisions, foreign colonialism, and the aggressive proselytization of Christian missionaries. His mission, he claimed, was divinely inspired—to restore the true essence of Islam and present it as a religion of peace, reason, and spiritual purity.

1. Early Life and Religious Influence

MIRZA GHULAM AHMAD was born into a well-established Muslim family with a history of service to the Mughal rulers of India. His father, Mirza Ghulam Murtaza, was a respected landowner, and young Ghulam Ahmad received a traditional education in **Islamic studies**, including **Quranic exegesis**, **Hadith**, **Islamic law**, and **Persian and Arabic languages**. Although he did not travel extensively for formal religious study, he was known for his deep personal commitment to Islam, spending much of his early life in religious reflection and writing.

- **Spiritual Inclination**: Ghulam Ahmad was known for his piety and devotion, often withdrawing from worldly affairs to focus on **spiritual contemplation**. His early writings were characterized by a strong defense of Islam against criticisms from **Christian missionaries** and

Hindu reform movements. He believed that Islam was under siege both externally and internally, and his early life was dedicated to responding to these challenges through his scholarly works and debates.

2. Claim to Messianic and Prophetic Status

IN **1889**, Mirza Ghulam Ahmad claimed to be both the **Promised Messiah** and **Mahdi**, figures expected to appear in Islamic eschatology to restore Islam and lead humanity to justice. This claim was a turning point in his life and the beginning of the **Ahmadiyya Movement**. Ahmadis believe that Ghulam Ahmad's mission was to **revive Islam**, restore its spiritual and moral teachings, and correct misunderstandings that had arisen over the centuries.

- **The Promised Messiah and Mahdi**: According to Islamic eschatology, the **Messiah** (often associated with Jesus) and the **Mahdi** are expected to arrive in the latter days to lead Muslims and bring about a just and peaceful world. Ghulam Ahmad claimed that the **second coming of Jesus** was not a physical return, but a spiritual one, and that he himself was the fulfillment of this prophecy. He argued that Jesus had died a natural death and would not physically return to earth, and that his own role as the **Messiah** was to lead the spiritual rejuvenation of Islam.

- **Subordinate Prophethood**: One of the most controversial aspects of Ghulam Ahmad's teachings was his claim to **prophethood**, although he distinguished his role from that of **Muhammad (peace be upon him)**, the final law-bearing prophet in Islam. Ghulam Ahmad asserted that his prophethood was **non-lawbearing** and

subordinate to Muhammad, and that his role was to renew the spiritual and moral teachings of Islam rather than to introduce new laws or scripture. Ahmadis believe that the **door to prophethood** remains open in the form of non-lawbearing prophets, who, like Ghulam Ahmad, serve as guides and reformers. This belief has been the main point of theological conflict with mainstream Sunni and Shia Muslims, who hold that Muhammad is the **last and final prophet**.

---

3. Key Teachings and Doctrines

MIRZA GHULAM AHMAD'S teachings were primarily focused on **spiritual revival**, **moral reform**, and presenting Islam as a **religion of peace** and **rationality**. His mission was to counter the influence of **Christian missionaries**, **Hindu reformers**, and **Western secularism**, while also addressing the internal weaknesses he saw within the Muslim world.

- **The True Essence of Islam**: Ghulam Ahmad believed that Islam, as practiced during his time, had strayed from the original teachings of the **Quran** and **Sunnah**. He emphasized the need for a return to the **true spirit** of Islam, which he saw as a religion that promoted **justice**, **compassion**, and **peace**. His teachings called for Muslims to live by the ethical and moral values of Islam, free from the **superstitions** and **innovations** (Bid'ah) that he believed had crept into Islamic practice over the centuries.

- **Jihad of the Pen**: One of Ghulam Ahmad's key contributions was his **reinterpretation of jihad**. At a time when many Muslims were calling for militant jihad in response to British colonial rule and missionary activity, Ghulam Ahmad argued that the true jihad in the modern era was not a military struggle but a **spiritual** and **intellectual** effort. He called this the **"jihad of the pen"**, meaning that Muslims should defend Islam through reasoned debate, education, and the dissemination of true Islamic teachings, rather than through violence. This peaceful understanding of jihad remains a central tenet of the Ahmadiyya Movement.

● **Interfaith Dialogue and Universal Peace**: Ghulam Ahmad was deeply committed to **interfaith dialogue** and peaceful coexistence between different religious communities. He wrote extensively to counter the arguments of Christian missionaries and Hindu reformers, but his approach was always framed in terms of **respect** and **dialogue**. Ahmadis believe that Islam teaches universal peace and that all religions contain elements of truth, advocating for mutual understanding and cooperation between faiths.

● **Miracles and Rationality**: Another notable aspect of Ghulam Ahmad's teachings was his emphasis on **rationalism** and **reason**. He sought to explain the miracles of the Quran in a way that made them compatible with **science** and **logic**, arguing that Islam was a religion of both **faith** and **intellect**. He saw his mission as aligning with the intellectual currents of the time, promoting a version of Islam that could stand up to the challenges of modernity.

4. The Establishment of the Ahmadiyya Movement

IN **1889**, Mirza Ghulam Ahmad formally established the **Ahmadiyya Movement** with the first group of followers who pledged allegiance to him. This marked the beginning of the organized spread of his teachings, which focused on **spiritual reform**, **moral education**, and the peaceful propagation of Islam.

- **Khilafat (Caliphate)**: After Ghulam Ahmad's death in **1908**, the Ahmadiyya community was led by a series of **Caliphs** (successors) who continued his mission. The **Ahmadiyya Caliphate**, which remains active today, plays a central role in guiding the community, organizing missionary efforts, and promoting the peaceful spread of Islam. The caliphs are seen as spiritual leaders who carry on the work of Ghulam Ahmad in ensuring the community's unity and adherence to its core teachings.

- **Missionary Work (Tabligh)**: The Ahmadiyya Movement places a strong emphasis on **missionary work** and the peaceful propagation of Islam through intellectual engagement and social service. The movement has established a presence in over 200 countries, with a network of **mosques, schools, hospitals**, and **charitable organizations** dedicated to spreading its message of peace, tolerance, and spiritual revival.

---

5. Controversy and Rejection by Mainstream Islam

DESPITE ITS EMPHASIS on **peace** and **reform**, the Ahmadiyya Movement has faced significant opposition from **mainstream Sunni and Shia Islam**, primarily due to its beliefs regarding the

continuation of prophethood. Ghulam Ahmad's claim to be the **Messiah** and **Mahdi**, along with his assertion of **subordinate prophethood**, has been viewed as heretical by most Islamic scholars.

- **Declaration as Non-Muslim**: In **1974**, Pakistan's government declared the Ahmadiyya community as **non-Muslim** through a constitutional amendment. This declaration was based on the mainstream belief that **Muhammad (peace be upon him)** is the final prophet, and any claim to prophethood after him is seen as a deviation from orthodox Islam. Ahmadis have since faced **persecution, violence,** and **legal restrictions** in several Muslim-majority countries, particularly in **Pakistan**, where they are prohibited from identifying themselves as Muslims.

- **Global Spread Despite Opposition**: Despite these challenges, the Ahmadiyya Movement has continued to grow and spread globally, attracting millions of followers through its message of **peace, interfaith dialogue**, and **humanitarian work**. The community remains active in promoting religious freedom and advocating for the rights of persecuted religious minorities around the world.

Conclusion

Mirza Ghulam Ahmad's life and teachings have had a profound impact on the development of the **Ahmadiyya Movement** and the broader Islamic world. His mission of **spiritual revival, peaceful reform,** and **intellectual engagement** continues to inspire millions of Ahmadis around the globe, despite the challenges and opposition they face. By reinterpreting key aspects of Islamic theology—particularly the concept of **prophethood** and

jihad—Ghulam Ahmad sought to present a version of Islam that was compatible with modernity, while remaining rooted in the **Quran** and the **Sunnah**. His legacy endures through the Ahmadiyya community's ongoing efforts to promote peace, justice, and religious understanding in the contemporary world.

The Role of the Mahdi and Messiah in Ahmadiyya Belief

IN **Ahmadiyya Islam**, the concepts of the **Mahdi** and the **Messiah** hold a central place and are interpreted differently from mainstream Sunni and Shia views. Traditionally, both figures are expected to arrive at the end of times to restore Islam, bring justice, and establish peace. However, in Ahmadiyya theology, **Mirza Ghulam Ahmad** (1835–1908), the founder of the Ahmadiyya Movement, is believed to have fulfilled both roles. This interpretation significantly distinguishes the Ahmadiyya community from mainstream Islamic sects, shaping its unique eschatological outlook and theological foundations.

1. Traditional Islamic Understanding of the Mahdi and Messiah

IN MAINSTREAM **Sunni** and **Shia Islam**, the **Mahdi** and **Messiah (Jesus)** are understood as two distinct eschatological figures:

- **The Mahdi:** The Mahdi is expected to be a **descendant of the Prophet Muhammad (peace be upon him)** who will appear before the Day of Judgment to restore the true teachings of Islam, eliminate oppression, and lead the Muslim community in the final struggle against evil forces, including the **Dajjal** (the Antichrist).

- **The Messiah (Jesus):** Islamic eschatology also teaches that **Jesus (Isa)**, who was not crucified but was raised to heaven, will return in the latter days to defeat the Dajjal and establish peace. Jesus is expected to follow and reinforce the teachings of Muhammad (peace be upon him) and play a crucial role in guiding humanity toward righteousness.

These two figures, according to mainstream beliefs, are separate individuals who will work together to bring about an era of global justice and peace before the Day of Judgment.

2. Mirza Ghulam Ahmad's Claim as the Mahdi and Messiah

IN CONTRAST TO THE traditional view, **Mirza Ghulam Ahmad** claimed that both the **Mahdi** and the **Messiah** were to be **spiritual reformers** rather than political or military leaders, and that these roles were fulfilled in his own person. He reinterpreted Islamic prophecies in a way that emphasized **spiritual renewal** over physical intervention, claiming that the purpose of these figures was to **revive Islam** rather than engage in violent conflict.

- **The Mahdi**: Ghulam Ahmad rejected the notion of the Mahdi as a **militant figure** who would engage in physical battles to restore Islam. Instead, he claimed that the Mahdi's mission was spiritual, intended to guide Muslims back to the **moral** and **spiritual principles** of the faith. Ghulam Ahmad believed that his own appearance as the Mahdi was a divine appointment meant to reform the Muslim community through peaceful means, such as **teaching, writing**, and **engaging in intellectual debates** to counter external challenges to Islam, particularly from Christian missionaries and Western secularism.

- **The Messiah (Jesus)**: Mirza Ghulam Ahmad also claimed to be the **Promised Messiah** foretold in Islamic and Christian eschatology. He argued that the traditional belief in the **physical return of Jesus** was a misinterpretation, and that the prophecies regarding Jesus' second coming referred to a **spiritual manifestation** rather than a literal descent from heaven. Ahmadis believe that Jesus had indeed died a natural death and would not return to earth. Instead, they hold that Mirza Ghulam Ahmad's mission as the Messiah was to **reform the spiritual state of the Muslim community**, bring about religious harmony, and promote global peace.

By claiming both the titles of **Mahdi** and **Messiah**, Mirza Ghulam Ahmad redefined these eschatological roles, merging them into one and emphasizing that his mission was to **revive the true spirit of Islam** through **spiritual guidance**, not through physical battles or conquest.

3. The Spiritual Mission of the Mahdi and Messiah

IN AHMADIYYA BELIEF, the roles of the Mahdi and the Messiah are primarily **spiritual**, focusing on the **moral reformation** of Muslims and humanity at large. The Ahmadi understanding of these roles reflects the movement's broader emphasis on **peace**, **intellectual engagement**, and **spiritual jihad** (the struggle against one's own desires and for the betterment of society).

- **Reviving Islam's Moral and Spiritual Integrity**: Ahmadis believe that the Mahdi and Messiah's mission is to restore Islam to its original purity by guiding Muslims back to the ethical teachings of the **Quran** and the **Sunnah** of the Prophet Muhammad (peace be upon him). The Ahmadiyya Movement teaches that **spiritual decay** and **moral decline** had taken root in the Muslim world by the time of Ghulam Ahmad, and his role as the Mahdi and Messiah was to **cleanse** these corruptions and **revive** the true essence of Islam.

- **A Peaceful Mission**: Unlike traditional interpretations that associate the Mahdi with **armed jihad** or military conquest, Ahmadis emphasize that the Mahdi's role is to promote **peace** and **tolerance**. Mirza Ghulam Ahmad taught that in the modern age, physical warfare was no longer necessary or justified for the spread of Islam, and that the true jihad was a spiritual one. His teachings promoted **non-violence** and encouraged **interfaith dialogue**, presenting Islam as a religion of reason, peace, and universal brotherhood.

- **Interfaith Harmony**: As the Messiah, Mirza Ghulam Ahmad's mission extended beyond the Muslim community. He saw his role as promoting **interfaith understanding** and **reconciliation** between different religious groups, particularly between Muslims and Christians. Ahmadis believe that the Messiah was meant to bring about **religious harmony** by emphasizing the commonalities between Islam, Christianity, and other faiths, while also correcting misunderstandings about Islam that had arisen both within and outside the Muslim world.

---

4. Significance of the Mahdi and Messiah in Ahmadiyya Practice

THE BELIEF IN MIRZA Ghulam Ahmad as the Mahdi and Messiah is central to **Ahmadi identity** and shapes many aspects of Ahmadi religious practice and community life.

- **The Caliphate (Khilafat)**: After the death of Mirza Ghulam Ahmad in **1908**, the Ahmadiyya community established the institution of **Khilafat** (Caliphate), with his successors known as **Caliphs**. The Caliphs are seen as the spiritual and administrative leaders of the community, continuing the work of Ghulam Ahmad in promoting **Islamic revival**, **peace**, and **moral reform**. The Ahmadi Caliphate plays a key role in guiding the global community and maintaining its unity.

- **Missionary Work (Tabligh)**: One of the central practices of the Ahmadiyya Movement is the peaceful **propagation of Islam** through **missionary work**. Ahmadis believe that part of the Mahdi and Messiah's mission is to spread the message of Islam to people around the world, not through force, but through **education**, **dialogue**, and **social service**. The Ahmadiyya community has a strong presence in over 200 countries, with mosques, schools, hospitals, and humanitarian projects that reflect the movement's commitment to **serving humanity**.

- **Global Humanitarian Efforts**: Reflecting the Mahdi and Messiah's mission of peace, the Ahmadiyya community is involved in numerous **humanitarian projects** around the world. From disaster relief to education and healthcare, Ahmadis believe that serving humanity is a key aspect of their religious duty. The community's charitable organization, **Humanity First**, works in various countries to provide aid to those in need, regardless of their religious background.

5. Rejection and Controversy

THE AHMADI INTERPRETATION of the Mahdi and Messiah, particularly the belief that **Mirza Ghulam Ahmad** fulfilled both roles, has led to widespread rejection of the Ahmadiyya community by mainstream Sunni and Shia Muslims. The central issue is the **belief in the continuation of prophethood** after **Muhammad (peace be upon him)**, which mainstream Islam rejects.

- **Declaration as Non-Muslim**: The claim that Mirza Ghulam Ahmad was both the Mahdi and Messiah, and his assertion of **subordinate prophethood**, led to significant opposition. In **1974**, the government of **Pakistan** officially declared Ahmadis to be **non-Muslims**, and in 1984, further restrictions were imposed that prohibited Ahmadis from identifying themselves as Muslims or practicing their faith publicly. Similar **legal and social persecution** exists in other Muslim-majority countries, including **Indonesia** and **Bangladesh**.

- **Mainstream Muslim View**: Mainstream Sunni and Shia scholars reject the Ahmadi claim that Mirza Ghulam Ahmad was the Mahdi and Messiah, holding that these figures are yet to appear. The traditional belief in the **finality of prophethood** means that any claim to prophethood, even if described as subordinate or non-lawbearing, is considered a deviation from core Islamic teachings. This theological disagreement has led to the marginalization and persecution of Ahmadis in many parts of the Muslim world.

Conclusion

In **Ahmadiyya belief**, the roles of the **Mahdi** and **Messiah** are fulfilled in the person of **Mirza Ghulam Ahmad**, whose mission was to **revive Islam** spiritually, promote **peace**, and bring about **interfaith harmony**. This reinterpretation of traditional Islamic eschatology distinguishes Ahmadis from mainstream Sunni and Shia Muslims, who await the future arrival of the Mahdi and the physical return of Jesus. Ahmadis, however, believe that these roles have already been fulfilled and that their community represents the true revival of Islam. While this belief has led to significant **controversy** and **persecution**, the Ahmadiyya community continues to promote its message of **spiritual renewal**, **peaceful jihad**, and **universal service to humanity**.

Key Theological Differences Between Ahmadiyya and Mainstream Sunni and Shia Islam

THE **Ahmadiyya Movement**, founded by **Mirza Ghulam Ahmad**, has significant theological differences with mainstream **Sunni** and **Shia Islam**. These differences primarily center around the **concept of prophethood, eschatology**, and the **interpretation of jihad**. The Ahmadiyya belief system diverges from traditional Islamic doctrines in ways that have led to widespread **rejection** of the community by both Sunni and Shia scholars, often resulting in the marginalization of Ahmadis in many Muslim-majority countries.

1. The Concept of Prophethood

ONE OF THE MOST FUNDAMENTAL theological differences between Ahmadiyya Islam and mainstream Islam is the **Ahmadi belief in the continuation of prophethood** after **Muhammad (peace be upon him).**

- **Ahmadiyya Belief in Subordinate Prophethood:** Ahmadis believe that **Mirza Ghulam Ahmad** was a **prophet**, but they distinguish his role from that of **Muhammad (peace be upon him)**, who they acknowledge as the **final law-bearing prophet**. According to Ahmadi belief, Ghulam Ahmad's prophethood is **non-lawbearing** and **subordinate** to that of Muhammad, meaning that he did not bring any new religious laws but was instead sent to revive Islam and guide the Muslim community back to its true principles. Ahmadis interpret the **"Seal of the Prophets"** (Khatam an-Nabiyyin), a title attributed to Muhammad (peace be upon him), as meaning the **seal of law-bearing prophethood**, leaving room for non-lawbearing prophets like Ghulam Ahmad.

• **Mainstream Sunni and Shia Belief (Finality of Prophethood)**: Both **Sunni** and **Shia Muslims** hold that Muhammad (peace be upon him) is the **final prophet**, after whom no prophet—whether lawbearing or non-lawbearing—can come. The majority of Islamic scholars interpret **Khatam an-Nabiyyin** as meaning that Muhammad is the last prophet in every sense, and they reject any claim of prophethood after him. This belief in the finality of prophethood is a **core tenet** of mainstream Islamic theology, and any claim to prophethood after Muhammad is considered heretical. As a result, the **Ahmadi belief** in the continuation of subordinate prophethood has been one of the main reasons for the **excommunication** and **marginalization** of the Ahmadiyya community in the Muslim world.

---

2. The Role of the Mahdi and Messiah

THE **Ahmadiyya Movement** has a distinct interpretation of the **Mahdi** and **Messiah**, which differs significantly from traditional Sunni and Shia eschatological expectations.

• **Ahmadiyya Belief**: Ahmadis believe that **Mirza Ghulam Ahmad** fulfilled the roles of both the **Mahdi** and the **Messiah (Jesus)**, two figures traditionally awaited in Islamic eschatology. According to Ahmadiyya theology, Ghulam Ahmad's role as the Mahdi and Messiah was to **spiritually reform** Islam and humanity, rather than engage in military or political struggle. Ahmadis believe that **Jesus** had already died a natural death and would not return physically to earth, as is commonly believed in mainstream Islam. Instead, they hold that the prophecies regarding Jesus' return were symbolic and were fulfilled in the spiritual mission of Mirza Ghulam Ahmad.

● **Mainstream Sunni and Shia Belief:**

○ In **Sunni Islam**, the **Mahdi** is expected to be a descendant of the Prophet Muhammad (peace be upon him) who will come in the latter days to restore true Islam and lead the Muslim community in the final struggle against the **Dajjal** (the Antichrist). **Jesus (Isa)**, who was not crucified but raised to heaven, is expected to return to earth physically to defeat the Dajjal and establish peace.

○ In **Shia Islam**, particularly **Twelver Shia belief**, the **Mahdi** is believed to be **Muhammad al-Mahdi**, the **12th Imam**, who has been in **occultation** since the 9th century. Shia Muslims await his reappearance to bring justice to the world. Like Sunnis, Shias also believe in the physical return of **Jesus** to assist the Mahdi in this eschatological role.

Mainstream Islamic scholars reject the Ahmadi claim that Mirza Ghulam Ahmad fulfilled the roles of both the Mahdi and Messiah, believing that these figures have yet to appear.

3. The Concept of Jihad

THE INTERPRETATION of **jihad** is another area where Ahmadiyya Islam differs from mainstream Sunni and Shia beliefs.

- **Ahmadiyya Belief**: The Ahmadiyya Movement promotes a **peaceful** and **spiritual** interpretation of jihad, which focuses on the **struggle for moral improvement** and the **propagation of Islam** through peaceful means. **Mirza Ghulam Ahmad** argued that in the modern era, **militant jihad** was no longer required and that the true jihad was a **jihad of the pen**—an intellectual and spiritual struggle to defend Islam against criticism and misrepresentation. Ahmadis believe that Islam should be spread through **education**, **dialogue**, and **personal reform**, rather than through warfare or violence.

- **Mainstream Sunni and Shia Belief**: In **mainstream Islam**, jihad is understood to have both **spiritual** and **military** dimensions. The **greater jihad** is considered the internal struggle against one's base desires, while the **lesser jihad** includes the possibility of **armed struggle** to defend Islam, particularly in situations where Muslims are under threat or attack. Although jihad is not always interpreted as a call to violence, traditional Islamic jurisprudence allows for **military jihad** under specific circumstances, particularly in the defense of the Muslim community. Mainstream Islamic scholars reject the Ahmadiyya reinterpretation that completely sets aside the concept of armed jihad.

4. Mirza Ghulam Ahmad's Role in Islamic Eschatology

IN ADDITION TO THE Ahmadi reinterpretation of the Mahdi and Messiah, **Mirza Ghulam Ahmad's role** in Islamic eschatology is another major point of divergence from mainstream Islam.

- **Ahmadiyya Belief**: Ahmadis believe that **Mirza Ghulam Ahmad** was divinely appointed to fulfill the **prophecies** associated with the end times in Islamic eschatology. They see his mission as the fulfillment of the eschatological expectations regarding the Mahdi and the Messiah. Ahmadis view Ghulam Ahmad's appearance as the **spiritual culmination** of Islamic prophecies, emphasizing that his role is to bring about a **spiritual revival** of Islam rather than lead a political or military campaign.

- **Mainstream Islamic View**: Mainstream Sunni and Shia Muslims reject the idea that **Mirza Ghulam Ahmad** has any role in Islamic eschatology. For them, the Mahdi and Jesus are still expected to appear in the future, and any claim that these roles have already been fulfilled is considered a **deviation** from Islamic teachings. The belief that Mirza Ghulam Ahmad is the Messiah and Mahdi is one of the reasons why Ahmadis are not accepted within the wider Muslim community.

---

5. The Position of Ahmadis Within the Muslim Community

THE THEOLOGICAL DIFFERENCES between Ahmadiyya Islam and mainstream Sunni and Shia Islam have led to significant controversy regarding the **religious identity** of Ahmadis.

- **Ahmadi Identity**: Ahmadis consider themselves to be **Muslims**, and they see the Ahmadiyya Movement as a **revivalist** movement that seeks to bring Islam back to its true teachings. They follow the basic pillars of Islam, including prayer, fasting, and charity, and believe that they are upholding the core values of the **Quran** and **Sunnah**.

- **Mainstream Muslim Opposition**: Due to their belief in the continuation of prophethood, Ahmadis have been declared **non-Muslim** in several Muslim-majority countries, most notably in **Pakistan**. In **1974**, Pakistan's government officially amended its constitution to categorize **Ahmadis as non-Muslims**, and they are prohibited from identifying themselves as Muslims. Similar **legal and social restrictions** exist in other Muslim-majority countries, including **Indonesia**, **Bangladesh**, and **Saudi Arabia**. Many mainstream Islamic scholars and organizations have issued **fatwas** (religious rulings) declaring Ahmadis to be outside the fold of Islam.

---

6. Global Presence and Controversy

DESPITE BEING MARGINALIZED in much of the Muslim world, the Ahmadiyya Movement has a significant **global presence**, with millions of followers in over **200 countries**. The community is known for its peaceful **missionary work** and commitment to **humanitarian efforts**, including building schools, hospitals, and providing disaster relief. However, the Ahmadi belief system continues to be a point of **controversy** within the broader Muslim community, leading to **persecution**, **discrimination**, and **violence** against Ahmadis in several countries.

Conclusion

The **Ahmadiyya Movement** diverges from mainstream **Sunni** and **Shia Islam** in several critical theological areas, particularly regarding the **continuation of prophethood**, the roles of the **Mahdi and Messiah**, and the interpretation of **jihad**. These differences have led to the widespread rejection of Ahmadis by mainstream Muslims, who view the Ahmadi belief system as a **deviation** from core Islamic teachings. Despite this, the Ahmadiyya community continues to grow and spread globally, promoting a vision of **peaceful Islamic revival** while facing significant challenges and opposition from the broader Muslim world.

Ahmadiyya's Approach to Jihad, Peace, and Social Justice

THE **Ahmadiyya Movement**, founded by **Mirza Ghulam Ahmad** in the late 19th century, has a distinctive approach to **jihad**, **peace**, and **social justice**, rooted in its core theological principles. Unlike traditional interpretations that often include a physical or militant aspect to jihad, the Ahmadiyya Movement emphasizes **spiritual jihad** and promotes a peaceful and non-violent understanding of Islam. These principles form the foundation of the community's mission to **spread Islam peacefully**, engage in **interfaith dialogue**, and actively contribute to **social justice** and **humanitarian work** globally.

1. Ahmadiyya's Interpretation of Jihad

IN CONTRAST TO SOME traditional Islamic interpretations of jihad, which include both spiritual and physical (militant) struggle, the Ahmadiyya Movement stresses a peaceful, **spiritual understanding of jihad**. This reinterpretation of jihad aligns with the movement's broader mission to promote peace and moral reform rather than conflict or warfare.

- **Jihad of the Pen**: For Ahmadis, the true jihad in the modern era is the **"jihad of the pen"**, a term coined by **Mirza Ghulam Ahmad**. This jihad refers to the **intellectual struggle** to defend Islam and spread its message through **education**, **reason**, and **debate**, rather than through violence or armed conflict. The Ahmadiyya Movement encourages Muslims to engage in peaceful efforts to counter misconceptions about Islam and promote its ethical and spiritual teachings. This form of jihad is seen as particularly important in the modern world, where Islam faces challenges from secularism, atheism, and other religious ideologies.

- **Rejection of Violent Jihad**: Mirza Ghulam Ahmad firmly rejected the notion of **violent jihad**, which some groups had historically interpreted as a legitimate tool for defending or spreading Islam. He argued that the **time for militant jihad** had passed and that Islam's true message should be propagated through peaceful means. Ahmadis believe that warfare in the name of religion is no longer justified and that **peaceful coexistence** and dialogue are the true expressions of jihad in the contemporary world. This interpretation stands in stark contrast to more militant interpretations of jihad that have been used by extremist groups in modern times.

- **Spiritual and Moral Struggle**: At the heart of Ahmadiyya's concept of jihad is the **struggle for self-improvement** and **moral excellence**. Ahmadis are encouraged to focus on their **personal spiritual growth**, fighting against their own inner weaknesses, desires, and sins in order to become better Muslims. This inward-focused jihad is seen as the greater jihad (jihad al-akbar) and is prioritized over any external struggle.

---

2. Commitment to Peace

THE AHMADIYYA MOVEMENT is deeply committed to **peace** as a fundamental principle of Islam. Its teachings emphasize the **non-violent** nature of Islam and the responsibility of Muslims to contribute to global peace and harmony.

• **Peaceful Propagation of Islam**: Ahmadis believe that Islam should be spread through **peaceful means**, such as **education**, **service**, and **dialogue**. The movement's missionary activities, known as **tabligh**, focus on sharing the message of Islam with others in a non-coercive manner, using reasoned arguments and moral examples to demonstrate the beauty of Islamic teachings. Ahmadis seek to engage in **interfaith dialogue** and promote mutual respect between different religious communities.

• **Interfaith Harmony**: Ahmadiyya places great importance on **interfaith harmony** and the peaceful coexistence of different religious communities. Ahmadis regularly participate in **interfaith conferences** and **peace symposiums**, where they work to build bridges between Muslims and non-Muslims. They emphasize the shared values of **compassion**, **justice**, and **love for humanity** that exist in all major world religions. By fostering an environment of mutual respect and understanding, Ahmadis seek to contribute to a more peaceful world.

• **Global Peace Initiatives**: The Ahmadiyya Movement actively promotes peace through its global campaigns, such as the **"Muslims for Peace"** initiative, which seeks to correct misconceptions about Islam and show that it is a religion of peace, love, and tolerance. The movement's leadership, particularly the Ahmadi **Caliphs**, have consistently called for peace in their sermons, advocating for **disarmament**, the **resolution of conflicts** through diplomacy, and the **elimination of extremism**.

3. Social Justice and Humanitarian Efforts

IN ADDITION TO PROMOTING peace and peaceful jihad, the Ahmadiyya Movement is deeply committed to **social justice** and the **welfare of humanity**. Ahmadis view social justice as an essential aspect of their faith and believe that Muslims are obligated to work toward creating a more just and equitable world.

- **Service to Humanity (Khadimat-ul-Khalq)**: One of the core teachings of the Ahmadiyya Movement is the concept of **Khadimat-ul-Khalq**, or **service to humanity**. Ahmadis believe that serving others—regardless of their religious, ethnic, or social background—is a fundamental part of Islamic teachings. The movement runs various humanitarian programs across the world, including providing **food**, **healthcare**, and **education** to underserved communities. This emphasis on service is based on the Quranic principle of **helping those in need** and **alleviating suffering**.

- **Humanity First**: The Ahmadiyya community operates a global humanitarian organization called **Humanity First**, which is involved in **disaster relief, development projects**, and **healthcare** in over 50 countries. Humanity First provides aid to people affected by natural disasters, conflicts, and poverty, regardless of their religious affiliation. Through its work, the organization seeks to embody the Islamic ideals of **compassion** and **justice** while fostering a spirit of global solidarity.

- **Educational and Healthcare Initiatives**: The Ahmadiyya Movement has also established **schools, universities**, and **hospitals** around the world to promote education and healthcare as essential components of social justice. In many developing countries, Ahmadi schools provide high-quality education to children from poor and marginalized communities, while Ahmadi hospitals offer medical care to those who cannot afford it. Ahmadis view education and healthcare as critical tools for empowering individuals and lifting communities out of poverty.

● **Charity and Zakat**: Like other Muslims, Ahmadis are required to give **Zakat** (the obligatory alms) as part of their religious duties. However, they also engage in additional charitable giving and volunteer work to help uplift society. The Ahmadi community organizes numerous **charity drives** to support orphans, widows, and those in need. This commitment to charity reflects their belief that **social justice** is a core principle of Islam.

---

4. Integration of Jihad, Peace, and Social Justice

IN AHMADIYYA BELIEF, the concepts of **jihad**, **peace**, and **social justice** are deeply intertwined. The movement's interpretation of jihad as a spiritual and moral struggle emphasizes the importance of **personal development** and **service to others** as the highest forms of religious practice. Ahmadis view their work for **peace** and **justice** as part of their broader jihad, striving to create a world where all people can live with **dignity**, **equality**, and **freedom**.

● **Jihad for Social Justice**: Ahmadis believe that striving for **social justice** is a form of jihad, as it involves working to end **poverty**, **oppression**, and **injustice** through peaceful means. The community's humanitarian work, advocacy for human rights, and efforts to promote equality are seen as part of their religious duty to **improve society** and uplift the disadvantaged.

- **Non-Violence and Global Responsibility**: Ahmadis are taught that they must pursue **justice** and **peace** without resorting to violence. The movement advocates for **non-violent solutions** to global conflicts and calls on its members to take personal responsibility for promoting **ethical behavior** and **humanitarian efforts** in their communities. This reflects the Ahmadi belief that true Islam requires not only personal piety but also **active engagement** in improving the world.

Conclusion

The **Ahmadiyya Movement's approach to jihad, peace, and social justice** reflects its commitment to **spiritual reform**, **non-violence**, and **humanitarianism**. By redefining jihad as a spiritual and intellectual struggle, rejecting violence, and prioritizing peace and justice, Ahmadis present a vision of Islam that aligns with modern values while remaining true to the core ethical teachings of the **Quran**. The community's global work in education, healthcare, and disaster relief embodies its belief in **service to humanity**, while its emphasis on interfaith harmony and peaceful coexistence showcases its dedication to creating a more **just** and **peaceful** world for all.

Global Presence and Controversies Surrounding the Ahmadiyya Community

THE **Ahmadiyya Movement**, founded in the late 19th century by **Mirza Ghulam Ahmad**, has grown into a global religious community with millions of followers spread across more than **200 countries**. Despite its peaceful teachings and emphasis on **interfaith harmony**, the movement has faced significant **controversy** and **persecution** due to its theological differences with mainstream **Sunni** and **Shia Islam**—particularly its belief in the continuation of prophethood after **Muhammad (peace be upon him)**. These differences have resulted in widespread **rejection** and, in some cases, **violence** against Ahmadis, especially in Muslim-majority countries.

1. Global Presence of the Ahmadiyya Community

ALTHOUGH THE AHMADIYYA community originated in **Qadian, India**, it has expanded far beyond South Asia and now has a strong presence across the world. Its ability to organize effectively and spread its message through peaceful means has contributed to its **global reach**.

- **South Asia**: The Ahmadiyya community's historical roots are in **India** and **Pakistan**, where the movement began. Despite facing intense persecution in **Pakistan**, including legal restrictions and violent attacks, Pakistan remains home to a large number of Ahmadis. **India** also has a significant Ahmadi population, where they generally enjoy more freedom, although challenges remain.

- **Africa**: The Ahmadiyya Movement has established a robust presence in **West Africa** and **East Africa**, particularly in countries like **Nigeria**, **Ghana**, **Sierra Leone**, and **Kenya**. In these regions, the Ahmadi community has played an important role in **education** and **healthcare**, often building schools and hospitals to serve underprivileged communities. Ahmadis are recognized for their contributions to social development and humanitarian work in these areas.

- **Europe**: Ahmadi Muslims have a substantial presence in **Western Europe**, especially in countries such as the **United Kingdom** and **Germany**. The UK serves as the current headquarters of the global Ahmadiyya community, particularly since the establishment of the **Ahmadiyya Caliphate** in London. Ahmadis in Europe are known for their **interfaith outreach**, **charitable work**, and efforts to promote **peace** and **religious tolerance**.

- **North America**: The Ahmadiyya community in **North America** has grown significantly in recent decades, with large populations in the **United States** and **Canada**. Ahmadis in North America are engaged in missionary work and are active in promoting their message of peace, particularly through public awareness campaigns like **"Muslims for Peace"** and **"Muslims for Life"**, which seek to counter negative stereotypes about Islam.

- **Southeast Asia**: The Ahmadiyya community is also present in **Indonesia** and **Malaysia**, though they face serious legal and social challenges in these regions. In Indonesia, Ahmadis have been targets of **sectarian violence**, and their religious activities are often restricted by law. Similarly, in **Malaysia**, Ahmadis face legal prohibitions against identifying as Muslims, and their religious practices are tightly controlled.

---

2. Controversies and Persecution

THE AHMADIYYA COMMUNITY has faced **widespread persecution** and **controversy** in many Muslim-majority countries due to its **theological differences**, particularly its belief that **Mirza Ghulam Ahmad** was a **prophet**. The rejection of Ahmadi beliefs by mainstream Sunni and Shia scholars has led to **legal discrimination**, **social ostracism**, and **violent attacks** on Ahmadis in various parts of the world.

- **Pakistan: Legal Discrimination and Persecution**: The most significant persecution of the Ahmadiyya community occurs in **Pakistan**, where Ahmadis are legally declared **non-Muslims** through a **constitutional amendment in 1974**. Under the **Blasphemy Laws** and **Ordinance XX** (1984), Ahmadis are prohibited from calling themselves Muslims, referring to their places of worship as **mosques**, or using Islamic terminology in their religious practices. Ahmadis in Pakistan face **violence, harassment**, and **murder**, with little to no legal recourse or protection from the authorities. Ahmadi mosques have been **destroyed**, their **public gatherings banned**, and **Ahmadi literature** is often censored or banned altogether.

- **Indonesia**: In **Indonesia**, the largest Muslim-majority country, Ahmadis have also faced **legal restrictions** and **mob violence**. In some areas, local governments have issued bans on Ahmadi religious activities, and Ahmadis have been attacked by hardline Islamist groups. Despite the country's official stance on religious tolerance, the Ahmadi community continues to struggle with persecution and discrimination.

• **Bangladesh**: While Ahmadis are not legally banned in **Bangladesh**, they face significant social opposition and occasional violence from extremist groups who view their beliefs as heretical. Efforts to ban Ahmadi publications and attacks on their mosques have created a hostile environment for the community.

• **Saudi Arabia and the Middle East**: In **Saudi Arabia** and other countries in the **Gulf** and **Middle East**, Ahmadiyya Islam is completely **banned**, and Ahmadis are not recognized as Muslims. They are forbidden from performing the **Hajj pilgrimage** to Mecca, and any form of public or private Ahmadi religious expression is prohibited. The Saudi government has also funded campaigns to promote anti-Ahmadi rhetoric in other Muslim countries.

• **Excommunication and Fatwas**: Islamic scholars from both the **Sunni** and **Shia** traditions have issued **fatwas** (religious rulings) declaring Ahmadis to be **outside the fold of Islam**. These fatwas have played a significant role in justifying the **marginalization** and **persecution** of Ahmadis in countries where these rulings hold considerable influence.

3. Ahmadiyya's Response to Persecution

DESPITE FACING PERSECUTION and legal restrictions in many countries, the Ahmadiyya community remains committed to its principles of **non-violence** and **peaceful resistance**. The movement advocates for **religious freedom, interfaith dialogue,** and **humanitarian service**, regardless of the challenges it faces.

- **Non-Violent Resistance:** The Ahmadiyya Movement teaches its members to respond to persecution with **patience, prayer**, and **non-violent protest**. Ahmadis are encouraged to use legal channels and international forums to advocate for their religious freedom while maintaining a peaceful stance. The movement's commitment to **non-violence** reflects the teachings of **Mirza Ghulam Ahmad**, who emphasized the need for peaceful solutions to conflict and religious disputes.

- **Humanitarian Work:** Ahmadis have responded to persecution by increasing their efforts in **humanitarian work** and **community service**. Through their international charity organization, **Humanity First**, Ahmadis provide **disaster relief, medical care, education**, and **food security** in underdeveloped and conflict-ridden regions. These efforts are seen as part of their religious duty to **serve humanity** and promote **social justice**, regardless of the difficulties they face in practicing their faith.

- **Advocacy for Religious Freedom:** The Ahmadiyya community actively advocates for **religious freedom** at the international level, often working with **human rights organizations** such as **Amnesty International** and

Human Rights Watch to highlight the persecution of religious minorities. Ahmadis have been vocal at forums like the **United Nations** and in **Western countries** to call attention to their plight and to press for greater protections for religious freedom globally.

- **Migration and Asylum**: Due to persecution in countries like **Pakistan**, many Ahmadis have sought asylum in countries such as **Canada**, the **United States**, and several **European nations**. These countries have often granted asylum to Ahmadis fleeing religious persecution, allowing them to practice their faith freely in a supportive environment.

---

4. Positive Contributions and Global Influence

DESPITE THE CHALLENGES it faces, the Ahmadiyya community has made significant positive contributions to global society through its **charitable work**, **interfaith outreach**, and **educational initiatives**.

- **Humanitarian Efforts**: The Ahmadiyya community's **Humanity First** organization is involved in various humanitarian projects, including providing **clean water**, **medical aid**, **education**, and **disaster relief** in countries affected by poverty, conflict, and natural disasters. Humanity First operates in over 50 countries and serves all people, regardless of their religious background.

- **Interfaith Dialogue**: Ahmadis are known for their active participation in **interfaith dialogue** and **peacebuilding initiatives**. They regularly organize interfaith **conferences** and **peace symposiums** to promote understanding and respect among different religious groups. Ahmadis believe that dialogue is essential for building a more peaceful world and reducing the misunderstandings and conflicts that arise from religious differences.

• **Educational Contributions**: The Ahmadiyya community has established numerous **schools** and **universities**, particularly in **Africa** and **South Asia**, to provide high-quality education to underprivileged communities. Many of these institutions are open to students of all faiths and have gained a reputation for academic excellence. In addition, the movement places great emphasis on the **moral education** of its students, instilling values of **peace**, **service**, and **integrity**.

Conclusion

The **Ahmadiyya Movement** has a strong **global presence** and continues to grow despite the **controversies** and **persecution** it faces, particularly in Muslim-majority countries. Its belief in the **continuation of prophethood** and its distinct interpretation of **Islamic teachings** have led to **rejection** and **marginalization** by mainstream Sunni and Shia scholars. Despite these challenges, the community has made significant contributions to **humanitarian efforts**, **education**, and **interfaith harmony**, demonstrating resilience and a deep commitment to **peace** and **social justice**. Through its peaceful approach and dedication to serving humanity, the Ahmadiyya Movement continues to play an influential role in the global Islamic landscape.

Chapter 7: Modern Islamic Movements and Contemporary Thought

In the rapidly changing world of the **20th** and **21st centuries**, Islam has experienced a remarkable evolution, shaped by both global dynamics and internal theological developments. As Muslim societies confronted **colonialism**, **modernization**, **globalization**, and **political upheaval**, a diverse array of **modern Islamic movements** emerged to address the challenges of these new realities. These movements have sought to reinterpret Islam in light of contemporary issues, grappling with questions about **identity**, **political authority**, **social justice**, and **spiritual renewal**.

From **revivalist movements** that advocate a return to what they perceive as the pure teachings of the Prophet **Muhammad (peace be upon him)** and his companions, to **progressive reformists** who emphasize the need for Islam to adapt to modern values such as **human rights** and **democratic governance**, the landscape of Islamic thought has become highly diverse. Some of these movements have sought to assert Islam as a solution to political and social issues, while others have focused on personal spiritual reform or the reconciliation of Islam with **modern science** and **philosophy**.

At the heart of these discussions are debates over how to interpret **sharia** (Islamic law), the role of **jihad** in the modern world, the place of **women** in Muslim societies, and the relationship between Islam and the **West**. Movements like **Salafism**, **Islamism**, **modernist Islam**, and **Sufism** each offer different answers to these questions, reflecting the complexity and adaptability of Islamic thought in the face of contemporary global challenges.

This chapter will explore the major **modern Islamic movements** and their responses to the issues of the contemporary world. By examining the ideologies and objectives of these movements, as well as their impact on Muslim societies and global politics, it becomes clear that Islam is not a monolithic tradition but one that is dynamic and continually evolving. Through understanding these movements, we gain insight into how Muslims are navigating the complexities of modernity, striving to balance the demands of faith with the realities of the modern world.

Liberal Islam: Reinterpreting Traditional Doctrines in the Modern Era

LIBERAL ISLAM is a modern movement within the Islamic world that seeks to reinterpret traditional Islamic doctrines in ways that align with contemporary values, such as **democracy**, **human rights**, **gender equality**, and **freedom of expression**. Advocates of liberal Islam emphasize the need for a more **flexible** and **contextual interpretation** of the **Quran** and **Hadith**, arguing that Islam's core principles are compatible with modern ideals when understood within their historical and social context.

Liberal Islamic thinkers challenge the rigid interpretations of **sharia** that have dominated much of Islamic legal tradition, advocating instead for a **progressive approach** that accounts for changes in society, science, and human knowledge. They argue that Islamic teachings on **justice**, **compassion**, and **reason** provide a foundation for modern social reforms, including the advancement of **women's rights**, the **abolition of harsh punishments**, and the **promotion of individual freedoms**.

Key aspects of liberal Islam include:

- **Reinterpretation of Sharia**: Liberal Muslims call for a **reinterpretation of sharia** to fit the realities of contemporary society, focusing on its ethical principles rather than rigid legal rulings. They argue that many Islamic laws were developed in a specific historical context and are not necessarily applicable to modern governance and justice systems.

- **Human Rights and Social Justice**: Liberal Islam promotes the idea that **human rights**, including **freedom of religion**, **freedom of speech**, and **gender equality**, are compatible with Islamic values. By emphasizing the **Quran's teachings on justice** and the inherent dignity of all people, liberal Muslims advocate for an inclusive approach that respects the rights of minorities and marginalized groups within Muslim societies.

- **Gender Equality**: One of the central concerns of liberal Islam is **gender equality**. Many liberal Muslim scholars and activists challenge traditional interpretations of Islamic law that restrict the rights of women, particularly in areas such as **inheritance**, **marriage**, and **public leadership**. They argue that early Islamic principles promoted women's empowerment and that contemporary Muslim societies should reflect these values by advancing **women's rights** in all spheres of life.

- **Democracy and Pluralism**: Liberal Islam supports the idea of **democratic governance** and **political pluralism**. Proponents argue that Islam's principles of **consultation (shura)** and **justice** can support democratic practices, such as **representative government**, **rule of law**, and **freedom of political expression**. Liberal Muslims reject the notion of **theocracy** and advocate for a separation between religious authority and the state, emphasizing that political power should be derived from the people.

- **Engagement with Modernity**: Liberal Islam encourages engagement with modern intellectual currents, including **science**, **philosophy**, and **global ethics**. Liberal Muslim thinkers promote the idea that Islam is not incompatible with modern scientific knowledge and that Muslims can embrace technological and intellectual advancements while remaining faithful to their religious principles.

Although liberal Islam has gained support in various parts of the world, it faces significant opposition from **conservative** and **traditionalist Islamic scholars** who argue that such reinterpretations undermine the foundations of Islamic law and tradition. Nonetheless, liberal Islam continues to influence discussions about **religious reform** and **social justice** within Muslim communities, offering a vision of Islam that is adaptable, inclusive, and responsive to the needs of the modern era.

Political Islam: The Muslim Brotherhood and Its Influence

POLITICAL ISLAM, also known as **Islamism**, refers to movements and ideologies that seek to integrate Islamic principles into political governance. Among the most influential and well-known groups within Political Islam is the **Muslim Brotherhood** (Ikhwan al-Muslimin), founded in **1928** in Egypt by **Hassan al-Banna**. The movement aimed to reform society through the application of Islamic values in both personal and political life, eventually expanding into a global movement with chapters and affiliates in many countries across the **Middle East, North Africa,** and beyond.

The **Muslim Brotherhood** advocates for an Islamic state governed by **sharia law**, but its approach to achieving this goal has varied between **gradualist, democratic participation** and at times, support for **revolutionary tactics**. Unlike extremist groups that favor violent methods, the Muslim Brotherhood has generally promoted a **moderate and pragmatic approach**, working within political systems to gain power through **elections, social welfare programs**, and **grassroots activism**.

1. The Founding and Ideals of the Muslim Brotherhood

THE MUSLIM BROTHERHOOD was established during a period of **colonialism** and **Western domination** in the Muslim world, particularly in **Egypt**. Its founder, Hassan al-Banna, sought to revive Islamic values in response to the perceived decline of Muslim societies under Western influence. Al-Banna's vision for the Brotherhood was twofold:

- To bring about a **spiritual and moral revival** of the individual and society based on Islamic principles.

- To establish an **Islamic government** where Islamic law (sharia) would be implemented to guide both personal and public life.

The Brotherhood's core message emphasized the **comprehensive nature of Islam**, viewing it not just as a religion but as a complete way of life, including politics, economics, and social organization. Al-Banna famously stated, "**Islam is the solution**," arguing that Islamic governance would lead to justice, equality, and the elimination of corruption and oppression.

2. The Muslim Brotherhood's Political and Social Influence

THROUGHOUT ITS HISTORY, the Muslim Brotherhood has employed a mix of **political activism** and **social welfare** to gain influence. It established schools, hospitals, and charitable organizations, providing services to communities neglected by the government. This focus on **grassroots support** allowed the Brotherhood to build a strong base among the lower and middle classes, especially in countries where governments were seen as corrupt or authoritarian.

- **Political Engagement:** The Brotherhood's strategy has often involved working within the existing political framework to gain power through **elections** and **parliamentary participation**. In Egypt, the Brotherhood remained a banned organization for much of its history, but it operated through proxy political parties and ran candidates as independents. In 2011, after the Egyptian Revolution, the Brotherhood's political wing, the

Freedom and Justice Party, won a significant number of seats in parliamentary elections. This success culminated in the election of **Mohamed Morsi** as Egypt's first democratically elected president in 2012.

● **Social Welfare and Charitable Work**: The Brotherhood has always placed a strong emphasis on **social services** and charity, establishing networks of hospitals, schools, and community centers that provide much-needed services to the poor. This focus on social welfare has endeared the Brotherhood to many Muslims, particularly in countries where government services are lacking. By addressing **education**, **healthcare**, and **poverty**, the Brotherhood built a broad base of popular support, which helped it expand its influence across the Arab world and beyond.

---

3. The Ideology and Goals of Political Islam within the Brotherhood

THE MUSLIM BROTHERHOOD'S ideology is based on the belief that **Islamic governance** is the only way to ensure justice and well-being in Muslim societies. The movement emphasizes the need for a **gradual Islamization** of society, starting with the individual, then the family, and finally the state. The ultimate goal is to establish an Islamic state where **sharia** law governs all aspects of life.

● **Sharia as a Comprehensive System**: The Brotherhood believes that **sharia** is not merely a set of legal rulings, but a comprehensive system that encompasses **morality**, **economics**, **social justice**, and **politics**. They argue that by implementing sharia, Muslims can create a just and prosperous society that adheres to the will of God. However, their approach is generally **gradualist**, aiming to work through existing political and legal systems rather than through violent revolution (though some offshoots and factions have taken more militant stances).

• **Democracy and Islam**: The Brotherhood's relationship with **democracy** is complex. While it advocates for **free elections** and **pluralism** as a means to gain political power, its vision of democracy is filtered through an **Islamic lens**. The movement does not advocate for secular liberal democracy but rather for a form of governance where **Islamic principles** underpin the state and guide the legislative process. This has led to criticism from secularists who view the Brotherhood's long-term goal as theocratic.

---

4. The Brotherhood's Influence and Expansion Beyond Egypt

THE MUSLIM BROTHERHOOD'S ideology and organizational structure have inspired **Islamist movements** in many countries. Through both direct chapters and indirect ideological influence, the Brotherhood has established a global network that spans the Middle East, North Africa, and even parts of Europe and Asia.

• **Middle East and North Africa**: The Brotherhood's influence has been particularly strong in countries like **Jordan**, **Syria**, and **Tunisia**. In **Jordan**, the Brotherhood has played a significant role in opposition politics, while in **Syria**, it led a major resistance movement against the Assad regime in the 1980s. The Tunisian political party **Ennahda**, founded by **Rached Ghannouchi**, is ideologically aligned with the Brotherhood and gained significant power after the Arab Spring.

• **Global Reach**: Beyond the Arab world, the Brotherhood has influenced Islamist movements in countries like **Turkey**, where the **Justice and Development Party (AKP)**, led by **Recep Tayyip Erdoğan**, has incorporated elements of the Brotherhood's ideology. In **Palestine**, the Brotherhood's ideology directly inspired the founding of **Hamas**, the militant group and political party that governs the **Gaza Strip**.

---

5. Controversy and Opposition

DESPITE ITS BROAD APPEAL, the Muslim Brotherhood has faced significant opposition, both from secular regimes and conservative Islamic scholars. Governments in many Muslim-majority countries have viewed the Brotherhood as a threat to their power, especially given its focus on political Islam and grassroots activism.

• **Suppression by Governments**: The Brotherhood has been banned in several countries, including **Egypt** (under **Gamal Abdel Nasser**, **Anwar Sadat**, and **Hosni Mubarak**) and **Saudi Arabia**. In 2013, after a popular uprising and military coup in Egypt, the Brotherhood was declared a **terrorist organization**, and its members were subjected to mass arrests and trials. Similar measures have been taken against Brotherhood affiliates in countries like **the UAE** and **Saudi Arabia**, where the group's influence is seen as a challenge to monarchical and authoritarian rule.

- **Tensions with Salafism**: While both the Muslim Brotherhood and **Salafi movements** advocate for an Islamic state, there are tensions between them. Salafis often criticize the Brotherhood for its **political pragmatism** and willingness to engage with non-Islamic political systems, accusing it of compromising Islamic principles. Conversely, the Brotherhood criticizes Salafis for their **narrow interpretations of Islam** and their reluctance to engage with modern political realities.

---

6. The Muslim Brotherhood's Legacy and Contemporary Impact

DESPITE FACING REPRESSION and challenges, the Muslim Brotherhood remains a key player in the landscape of **Political Islam**. Its influence on **Islamist parties** and movements across the Muslim world is undeniable, and its ideology continues to resonate with many Muslims who seek to reconcile Islamic principles with political and social life.

- **Impact on Islamist Movements**: The Brotherhood's intellectual and organizational framework has laid the foundation for many contemporary Islamist movements, including those that have come to power through democratic means. Islamist political parties across the Arab world continue to draw on the Brotherhood's model of **grassroots mobilization**, **political engagement**, and **social welfare** as strategies for gaining influence.

- **Post-Arab Spring Politics**: In the wake of the **Arab Spring**, the Muslim Brotherhood saw both significant gains and devastating losses. In Egypt, while the Brotherhood initially won significant political power following the ousting of **Hosni Mubarak**, it was swiftly removed from power by a military coup in **2013** and has since faced severe repression. Despite these setbacks, Islamist parties inspired by the Brotherhood, like **Ennahda** in Tunisia, remain key players in the political systems of several countries.

Conclusion

The **Muslim Brotherhood** has had a profound influence on the development of **Political Islam** in the modern era. Its ability to mobilize popular support through **social welfare**, **education**, and **political participation** has made it one of the most influential Islamist movements in the world. However, its blending of **Islamic values** with **political ambitions** has also made it a target of repression by both secular and authoritarian regimes. Despite these challenges, the Brotherhood's legacy continues to shape the political and social landscape of the Muslim world, influencing a wide range of Islamist movements that seek to integrate Islam into governance and public life.

Secularism and Islam: The Debate Over Religion's Role in Public Life

THE RELATIONSHIP BETWEEN **secularism** and **Islam** has long been a subject of intense debate within Muslim societies. Secularism, often defined as the separation of religion from the affairs of the state and public life, is seen by many as a **Western concept** that emerged from European struggles to limit the political power of the church. In contrast, Islam traditionally views religion as encompassing all aspects of life, including politics, governance, and law. This fundamental difference has sparked ongoing discussions about whether Islam can coexist with secularism and what role **Islamic principles** should play in shaping public policies, laws, and governance in Muslim-majority countries.

At the heart of the debate is a tension between two opposing views: those who advocate for a **secular state** that limits religion to the private sphere and those who believe that **Islamic governance**—rooted in sharia (Islamic law)—should be integral to the functioning of society. This chapter examines the key arguments on both sides, exploring the historical roots of secularism in the Muslim world, its challenges, and the various ways in which Muslim societies have navigated this complex relationship between faith and public life.

1. Historical Roots of Secularism in the Muslim World

SECULARISM IN THE MUSLIM world has often been a byproduct of **colonialism** and the influence of Western political ideologies. European colonial powers introduced secular ideas of governance, legal systems, and education into Muslim societies, often as part of their broader mission to modernize and "civilize" the regions they ruled. As a result, many post-colonial Muslim-majority countries adopted elements of **secular governance** when they gained independence.

- **Ataturk's Secular Reforms in Turkey**: Perhaps the most well-known example of secularism in the Muslim world is the case of **Turkey** under **Mustafa Kemal Ataturk**. In the early 20th century, Ataturk sought to modernize and Westernize Turkey by implementing a series of radical **secular reforms**. These included abolishing the **Ottoman Caliphate**, disbanding Islamic courts, replacing Islamic law with a secular legal code, and banning religious clothing in public institutions. Turkey remains one of the most secular Muslim-majority countries today, though debates over the role of Islam in public life continue.

- **Secularism in Egypt**: Egypt also experienced secularization, especially during the rule of **Gamal Abdel Nasser** in the 1950s and 60s. Nasser's vision of **Arab nationalism** and **socialism** involved reducing the influence of **Islamist movements** like the Muslim Brotherhood and promoting a **secular state** that prioritized modernization and economic development. However, the resurgence of Islamist movements in Egypt, especially in the post-Arab Spring period, has kept the debate over secularism alive.

- **Colonial Legacy in North Africa**: In countries like **Algeria**, **Tunisia**, and **Morocco**, the experience of **French colonialism** introduced secularism as a model of governance. While these countries maintained strong ties to Islamic traditions after independence, secular legal codes and educational systems remained in place, creating a complex relationship between Islam and public life that continues to this day.

---

2. Arguments for Secularism in Muslim Societies

PROPONENTS OF SECULARISM in Muslim societies argue that a **secular state** is essential for ensuring **pluralism, individual freedoms**, and **democratic governance**. They maintain that by separating religion from public life, the state can guarantee **equal rights** and **freedoms** for all citizens, regardless of their religious beliefs. Secularism, in this view, is seen as a way to protect religious diversity and prevent the state from favoring one religious group over others.

- **Pluralism and Religious Freedom**: Advocates of secularism argue that in a diverse society, where multiple religions or interpretations of Islam may exist, secularism allows for **equal treatment** of all citizens. They claim that a **secular government** can better protect the rights of minorities, including non-Muslims, by ensuring that no religious group dominates the public sphere or imposes its beliefs on others.

- **Protecting Individual Freedoms**: Secularism is often associated with the protection of **freedom of expression, freedom of religion**, and **personal autonomy**. By separating religious authority from the state, secularism ensures that individuals are free to practice—or not practice—religion as they see fit. In secular systems, personal freedoms, such as **women's rights, freedom of speech**, and **gender equality**, are often prioritized over religious doctrines that might impose restrictions on these liberties.

- **Avoiding Religious Conflict**: Secularism is also seen as a safeguard against **sectarianism** and **religious conflict**. In many Muslim-majority countries, different sects of Islam (such as Sunni and Shia) coexist, and secular governance can prevent one sect from imposing its version of Islam on others. Secularism, in this sense, promotes **social harmony** by ensuring that no single religious authority has control over public life.

---

3. Opposition to Secularism: The Islamic Perspective

ON THE OTHER SIDE OF the debate, many Muslims argue that Islam, unlike Christianity, does not support the separation of religion from politics or public life. They contend that **Islam is a complete way of life**, encompassing not just personal beliefs but also social, legal, and political structures. As such, secularism, which confines religion to the private sphere, is seen as incompatible with the teachings of Islam.

- **Islam as a Comprehensive System**: For many Muslims, Islam provides a **holistic framework** for life, including governance. They argue that the Quran and the teachings of the Prophet **Muhammad (peace be upon him)** offer guidance on how to structure a just society, including laws on **family matters, business ethics**, and **criminal justice**. In this view, the separation of religion from public life is not only unnecessary but also a deviation from the true nature of Islam.

- **Sharia and Justice**: Opponents of secularism often argue that **sharia law** provides a more just and equitable system than secular laws, particularly in terms of **social welfare**, **justice**, and **morality**. They believe that sharia is divinely ordained and provides a set of **moral principles** that guide personal and public conduct. For many, the application of sharia in governance is essential to creating a society that reflects **Islamic values** and ensures **social justice**.

- **Western Secularism and Colonialism**: Secularism is frequently viewed with suspicion in the Muslim world due to its association with **Western colonialism** and **imperialism**. Many Islamic thinkers argue that secularism was imposed on Muslim societies by colonial powers as a means of **cultural domination**, aiming to weaken the influence of Islam. As a result, secularism is often seen as a foreign ideology that undermines **Islamic identity** and values.

---

4. Varied Approaches to Secularism and Islam

DIFFERENT MUSLIM-MAJORITY countries have taken varied approaches to balancing **Islam** and **secularism**. Some have adopted **strict secularism**, while others maintain a more **blended approach** where Islam plays a significant role in public life.

- **Turkey**: As a **secular republic**, Turkey has long sought to limit the role of Islam in politics and governance, particularly under the leadership of **Mustafa Kemal Ataturk**. However, the rise of the **Justice and Development Party (AKP)** under **Recep Tayyip**

Erdoğan has seen a resurgence of **political Islam** in Turkey, with increasing emphasis on Islamic values in public life, education, and governance.

- **Tunisia**: Tunisia presents a unique case, where **secularism** and **Islamism** have been in constant negotiation, especially following the **Arab Spring**. The **Ennahda Party**, an Islamist political party, has sought to balance Islamic values with democratic principles, advocating for **moderate Islamism** while respecting **secular traditions**.

- **Saudi Arabia**: In contrast, countries like **Saudi Arabia** have embedded **Islamic governance** into the state structure, with **Wahhabi Islam** serving as the official interpretation of Islam. In such systems, Islamic law and religious authorities play a dominant role in shaping public policies, laws, and social norms.

---

5. Contemporary Debates and the Future of Secularism in Muslim Societies

THE DEBATE OVER SECULARISM and Islam remains ongoing and reflects broader questions about **identity, modernity**, and **globalization**. As Muslim societies grapple with the pressures of **modernization, globalization**, and **Western influence**, the role of Islam in public life continues to evolve. Movements advocating for greater **Islamization of public life** coexist alongside those calling for a more **secular, pluralistic** approach.

- **Reformist and Progressive Movements**: Some Islamic thinkers and movements advocate for a **reformist** approach, seeking to reconcile Islamic principles with modern concepts of **democracy**, **human rights**, and **gender equality**. These groups argue that Islam is fully compatible with modernity and that it can play a role in public life without infringing on individual freedoms or minority rights.

- **Resurgence of Political Islam**: At the same time, the rise of **Political Islam**, particularly through movements like the **Muslim Brotherhood**, highlights the ongoing desire for a system that integrates Islamic values into governance. These movements argue that secularism has failed to address the moral and social crises of the modern world, and that a return to Islamic governance is necessary to restore justice and prosperity.

Conclusion

The debate over **secularism and Islam** touches on fundamental questions about the role of religion in society, governance, and personal freedom. While some argue that **secularism** is essential for protecting **individual rights**, **pluralism**, and **modern democratic values**, others believe that **Islam** provides a comprehensive framework for all aspects of life, including politics. As Muslim-majority societies continue to navigate these competing visions, the relationship between **faith** and **public life** will remain a central issue in the ongoing evolution of **Islamic thought** and **governance**.

How Modern Movements Navigate Islamic Tradition and Reform

MODERN ISLAMIC MOVEMENTS have emerged in response to the complex challenges faced by Muslim societies in a rapidly globalizing world. These movements, while diverse in their ideologies and goals, all grapple with the central question of how to balance **Islamic tradition** with the need for **reform** in the face of political, social, and economic change. This balancing act involves interpreting sacred texts in light of contemporary realities while staying true to core Islamic values. The result is a wide spectrum of approaches, from **conservative** revivalism to **progressive** reinterpretation.

At the heart of these modern movements is the desire to maintain Islam's relevance in a world shaped by **colonialism**, **modernity**, and **globalization**, all of which have had a profound impact on Muslim societies. From efforts to revive Islamic governance and law to attempts at reforming social practices and embracing **democratic ideals**, modern Islamic movements represent a dynamic and ongoing engagement with tradition and the forces of modernity.

1. Conservative Movements: Revivalism and the Return to Tradition

ONE MAJOR TREND WITHIN modern Islamic movements is the call for a return to **authentic Islamic practices** through **revivalism**. Conservative movements argue that the challenges facing the Muslim world are a result of straying from the original teachings of **Islam** and the Prophet **Muhammad (peace be upon him)**. They advocate for a **literal interpretation** of the Quran and

Hadith, often seeking to reestablish **sharia law** as the foundation for personal and public life.

- **Salafism**: The **Salafi movement** is one of the most prominent examples of Islamic revivalism. It promotes a strict adherence to the practices of the first three generations of Muslims, known as the **Salaf**, and seeks to **purify** Islam from what it considers to be innovations (bid'ah) and cultural influences that have crept into Islamic practice over the centuries. Salafis emphasize the **literal interpretation** of Islamic texts and advocate for a return to early Islamic governance models, often rejecting democratic principles as incompatible with Islamic law.

- **Wahhabism**: In **Saudi Arabia**, the **Wahhabi movement**, a branch of Salafism, has had a profound influence on the state's governance and religious policy. Founded in the 18th century by **Muhammad ibn Abd al-Wahhab**, Wahhabism calls for a strict application of sharia and opposes practices it views as un-Islamic, such as **Sufi rituals** and the veneration of saints. Wahhabism's influence extends beyond Saudi Arabia through its promotion of **conservative Islamic values** across the Muslim world via funding for mosques, schools, and religious publications.

- **Islamism and the Muslim Brotherhood**: Another key conservative movement is **Islamism**, particularly as represented by the **Muslim Brotherhood**. Founded in **Egypt** by **Hassan al-Banna** in 1928, the Brotherhood advocates for the **gradual establishment of an Islamic state** through political participation, social activism, and education. While the Brotherhood supports democratic processes, it ultimately seeks to implement sharia as the foundation of the state. The Brotherhood's influence has spread globally, inspiring Islamist movements in **Jordan**, **Syria**, **Sudan**, and beyond.

These conservative movements navigate Islamic tradition by arguing for a **return to the fundamentals** of Islam. They resist modern innovations they see as incompatible with Islam and prioritize the **implementation of sharia** as a solution to the moral and social challenges faced by Muslim societies.

2. Reformist Movements: Engaging with Modernity

IN CONTRAST TO CONSERVATIVE revivalism, **reformist movements** seek to reinterpret Islamic tradition in ways that align with modern values such as **human rights**, **democracy**, and **gender equality**. These movements argue that Islam is a dynamic religion capable of adapting to changing circumstances and that **ijtihad** (independent reasoning) should be used to address contemporary issues.

- **Modernist Islam: Modernist** Islamic thinkers and movements emerged in the late 19th and early 20th centuries in response to the decline of the Muslim world in the face of **Western colonialism** and the rise of **scientific rationalism**. Figures like **Jamal al-Din al-Afghani**, **Muhammad Abduh**, and **Rashid Rida** advocated for a **reform** of Islamic thought, arguing that the Muslim world needed to embrace modern science, education, and rational inquiry while remaining true to Islamic principles. They called for the **reinterpretation of Islamic law** to reflect modern realities, particularly in areas like social justice, governance, and education.

● **Liberal Islam**: Building on modernist ideas, **liberal Islamic movements** take a more progressive approach to the interpretation of Islam. Liberal Muslims advocate for a reexamination of the Quran and Hadith in light of contemporary values, such as **gender equality**, **freedom of speech**, and **human rights**. They argue that Islamic law should evolve to meet the needs of modern societies and that Muslims should engage with democratic processes, pluralism, and global ethics. **Feminist Islamic movements** are part of this broader liberal trend, advocating for the **reform of gender roles** in Muslim societies by highlighting the egalitarian aspects of early Islamic teachings.

● **Muslim Reformists and Democratic Islam**: In countries like **Tunisia**, where secularism and Islamism intersect, reformist movements have sought to **balance Islamic values with democratic governance**. The **Ennahda Party**, led by **Rached Ghannouchi**, is an example of this approach. Ennahda advocates for a moderate interpretation of Islam that supports democratic principles while grounding governance in **Islamic ethics**. This pragmatic approach allows for **compromise** between secular and religious factions in Tunisia, making it a model for how Islamic movements can engage with modern political systems.

Reformist movements navigate Islamic tradition by advocating for **ijtihad** (independent reasoning) and reinterpretation of Islamic texts to fit the modern world. They view Islam as compatible with **democracy, human rights**, and **scientific progress**, and argue that Islam can evolve without losing its core values.

3. Sufi Movements: Balancing Tradition and Spiritual Renewal

SUFI ISLAM, with its emphasis on **mysticism**, **spiritual practice**, and inner transformation, presents another approach to navigating Islamic tradition in the modern era. Sufism focuses on the **esoteric** aspects of Islam, seeking a deeper connection with God through practices like **dhikr** (remembrance of God), **meditation**, and **poetry**. While Sufism is often viewed as apolitical, it has played a significant role in the social and political life of many Muslim societies.

- **Sufi Orders and Social Reform**: Sufi orders, such as the **Qadiriyya**, **Naqshbandi**, and **Chishti**, have historically been involved in **social welfare** and **education**, providing moral and spiritual leadership in their communities. In countries like **Turkey** and **Indonesia**, Sufi movements have promoted a **moderate interpretation of Islam**, emphasizing **tolerance** and **coexistence** with other religious traditions. Sufi leaders have also engaged in **peacebuilding** and **conflict resolution** in regions plagued by violence and extremism.

- **Sufi Response to Modernity**: While Sufi movements tend to emphasize **spiritual renewal** over political activism, they have adapted to modernity by focusing on **inner reform** as a way to address the moral and spiritual crises of the contemporary world. Some Sufi leaders argue that the **moral decay** and **materialism** of modern societies can only be countered through a return to the spiritual values of **compassion, love,** and **service to humanity**, which are central to Sufi teachings.

Sufi movements navigate tradition by focusing on **personal spiritual reform** and **inner transformation** as a means of addressing modern challenges. They offer a mystical interpretation of Islam that emphasizes the universal values of **love**, **peace**, and **unity**, making them adaptable to diverse cultural contexts.

4. Progressive Movements: Embracing Social Change

PROGRESSIVE ISLAMIC movements represent some of the most forward-thinking attempts to navigate Islamic tradition in the modern era. These movements seek to integrate Islam with modern social and political ideals, including **human rights**, **feminism**, and **environmentalism**. They argue that Islam is a **progressive religion** at its core and that its ethical teachings align with contemporary struggles for **justice** and **equality**.

- **Feminist Islam**: One of the most prominent progressive movements within Islam is **Islamic feminism**. Islamic feminists advocate for **gender equality** and **women's empowerment** within the framework of Islamic teachings. They reinterpret Quranic verses related to gender roles, arguing that early Islam was progressive in its treatment of women and that modern Muslim societies have misinterpreted or distorted these teachings. Figures like **Amina Wadud** and **Asma Barlas** are leading voices in this movement, calling for equal participation of women in religious leadership and challenging patriarchal interpretations of Islam.

- **Environmentalism and Islam**: Another area of progressive Islamic thought is the integration of **environmental ethics** into Islamic practice. Progressive Muslim thinkers argue that Islam teaches **stewardship** of the earth and that Muslims have a responsibility to address **climate change** and **environmental degradation**. They highlight Quranic teachings that emphasize the **balance of nature**, the **protection of animals**, and the importance of **sustainability**.

Progressive movements navigate tradition by drawing on the **ethical teachings of Islam** to address contemporary social issues. They view Islam as inherently aligned with **social justice** and **human rights**, and advocate for a reformist interpretation that promotes **equality, peace**, and **environmental responsibility**.

Conclusion

Modern Islamic movements, whether **conservative, reformist, Sufi**, or **progressive**, all face the challenge of navigating the rich traditions of Islam while addressing the complexities of the modern world. Each movement offers a different vision for how Islam can remain relevant in a globalized society, from strict adherence to **sharia** to more flexible interpretations that engage with **democracy, human rights**, and **social justice**. These diverse movements reflect the dynamic nature of Islam and its ability to adapt, reform, and respond to the needs of contemporary Muslim societies. Through their engagement with both **tradition** and **reform**, modern Islamic movements continue to shape the future of Islam in an ever-changing world.

Gender Equality, Human Rights, and Islam in the 21st Century

IN THE 21ST CENTURY, the discourse surrounding **gender equality** and **human rights** within the context of **Islam** has gained increasing prominence. As Muslim societies confront modern values and evolving social norms, the relationship between **Islamic teachings** and the promotion of **human rights**, particularly the **rights of women**, has sparked vibrant debates. This discourse is shaped by varying interpretations of Islamic texts and the ways in which they are reconciled with contemporary issues such as **women's empowerment**, **freedom of speech**, **political participation**, and **individual rights**.

At the heart of these discussions is the question of whether Islam, as traditionally understood, supports **gender equality** and **universal human rights**, or whether a **reinterpretation** of its teachings is necessary to address the challenges of the modern world. While **conservative interpretations** of Islam often emphasize traditional gender roles and the application of **sharia law**, **progressive Islamic movements** argue that Islam is inherently compatible with **gender justice** and **human rights**, and they call for a **reexamination** of certain religious interpretations.

1. Gender Equality in Islam: Traditional Perspectives

TRADITIONAL ISLAMIC perspectives on gender roles are rooted in the **Quran**, the **Hadith** (sayings of the Prophet Muhammad, peace be upon him), and **sharia law**. Many conservative scholars argue that these sources prescribe distinct but complementary roles for men and women, often emphasizing women's roles as **mothers**, **wives**, and **caretakers of the household**, while assigning men the primary responsibility of being the **providers** and **leaders** of the family.

- **Complementary Roles**: Traditionalists argue that Islam upholds **gender justice** by assigning men and women different roles that complement one another. According to this view, men and women are inherently different in nature, and Islamic law acknowledges these differences in the ways it prescribes responsibilities. For example, the Quran provides guidelines on **inheritance**, with men generally receiving a larger share than women because they are considered financially responsible for the family. Similarly, sharia outlines **guardianship** laws that emphasize men's roles in protecting and providing for their families.

- **Modesty and Public Life**: Another area where gender roles are emphasized in traditional Islamic thought is the concept of **modesty** and **segregation in public life**. Many conservative Islamic communities enforce strict codes of dress and behavior, such as the wearing of the **hijab** or **niqab** by women, and limitations on **interactions between men and women** in public spaces. These practices are seen as upholding moral values and protecting women's honor, while critics argue that they restrict women's freedoms.

While these traditional perspectives are still prevalent in many parts of the Muslim world, they have come under increasing scrutiny as Muslim women and progressive scholars call for a more egalitarian interpretation of Islamic teachings.

2. Progressive Interpretations: Gender Equality in Islam

IN CONTRAST TO TRADITIONAL perspectives, **progressive Muslim scholars** and activists argue that Islam, at its core, promotes **gender equality** and that the teachings of the Quran have been **misinterpreted** or **distorted** over time to justify **patriarchal structures**. They advocate for a **reexamination** of Islamic texts in light of modern values of **gender justice** and **human rights**, contending that early Islam was **progressive** in its treatment of women compared to other societies of the time.

- **The Quran and Women's Rights**: Progressive scholars point to the Quran as a source of **empowerment** for women, highlighting verses that emphasize women's rights to **education**, **property**, and **independence**. They argue that many restrictive interpretations stem from cultural practices rather than Islamic principles. For example, the Quran grants women the right to **inheritance**, **consent in marriage**, and **divorce**, rights that were groundbreaking in 7th-century Arabia but have been undermined by later interpretations that favor male authority.

- **Ijtihad and Reinterpretation**: A key concept for progressive Islamic movements is **ijtihad**, or independent reasoning, which they believe should be applied to reexamine Islamic teachings on gender roles. They argue that certain interpretations of the Quran and Hadith that restrict women's rights are the result of **historical and cultural contexts** and are not immutable. By engaging in **ijtihad**, progressive scholars seek to reinterpret these teachings in ways that align with modern values of **equality** and **justice**.

- **Women in Religious Leadership**: One of the most debated issues within progressive Islamic thought is the question of **women's leadership** in religious and public life. While many traditional scholars argue that women are not permitted to hold leadership roles, especially in the mosque or judiciary, progressive movements challenge this view by pointing to examples of **female leaders** in early Islamic history. Figures like **Aisha** (the wife of the Prophet Muhammad, peace be upon him) and **Khadijah** (the Prophet's first wife) are often cited as examples of empowered women who played influential roles in the early Muslim community.

---

3. Human Rights and Islam: Debates and Challenges

THE RELATIONSHIP BETWEEN **human rights** and **Islam** is a complex and often contentious issue. While many Islamic scholars assert that Islam promotes universal human rights, others argue that certain rights, particularly those related to **freedom of expression**, **religious freedom**, and **gender equality**, must be understood through the lens of **sharia**. The question of whether **Islamic law** can be fully reconciled with **international human rights standards**, as defined by documents like the **Universal Declaration of Human Rights**, remains an area of significant debate.

- **Human Rights in Islamic Law**: Many Muslim scholars argue that the **maqasid al-sharia** (the higher objectives of Islamic law) include the protection of **life**, **property**, **dignity**, **religion**, and **family**, all of which align with core human rights principles. They emphasize that Islam seeks to ensure **justice**, **compassion**, and **equality** for all people, and that sharia provides mechanisms for protecting these rights within the framework of an Islamic society.

- **Challenges with International Human Rights Norms**: However, tensions arise when Islamic teachings are perceived to conflict with certain **Western conceptions of human rights**, particularly in areas such as **freedom of religion** (including the right to convert from Islam), **freedom of expression**, **women's rights**, and **LGBTQ+ rights**. For example, many Muslim-majority countries have laws that restrict **apostasy** (leaving Islam) and **blasphemy**, which are seen as contrary to international human rights standards that protect freedom of belief and expression.

- **Muslim Human Rights Activists**: Despite these challenges, there is a growing movement of **Muslim human rights activists** who argue that Islam can be harmonized with global human rights standards. These activists advocate for legal and social reforms that uphold **democratic principles**, **individual freedoms**, and **gender equality** while remaining faithful to Islamic teachings. They call for a reinterpretation of sharia to reflect contemporary understandings of **justice** and **equality**, arguing that Islam is inherently compatible with the protection of human dignity and rights.

---

4. Women's Rights in Muslim Societies

WOMEN'S RIGHTS in Muslim-majority countries vary widely, with some countries implementing progressive reforms to advance **gender equality** and others maintaining more restrictive laws based on traditional interpretations of **sharia**. In recent years, there has been a growing movement for the empowerment of Muslim women, with women's rights activists working to address issues such as **education, marriage, inheritance, political participation**, and **workplace rights**.

- **Education and Employment**: In many Muslim-majority countries, women's access to **education** and **employment** has increased significantly over the past few decades. Countries like **Indonesia, Malaysia**, and **Tunisia** have made strides in promoting women's education and ensuring equal opportunities in the workplace. However, in other countries, such as **Saudi Arabia** (prior to recent reforms) and **Afghanistan**, women face significant barriers to education and professional advancement due to **cultural restrictions** and **conservative interpretations of Islamic law**.

- **Marriage and Family Law**: One of the key areas of contention regarding women's rights in Islam is **family law**, particularly the issues of **marriage, divorce**, and **inheritance**. In many Muslim-majority countries, family law is governed by sharia, which can result in unequal treatment of women, especially in areas such as divorce rights and child custody. However, progressive movements in countries like **Morocco** and **Tunisia** have reformed family law to ensure greater equality for women in matters of marriage and divorce.

- **Political Participation**: Women's political participation in Muslim-majority countries has been another area of progress. In countries like **Pakistan, Bangladesh**, and **Senegal**, women have held high political offices, including **prime minister** and **president**. Women's representation in **parliaments** and **local governments** has also increased in many Muslim-majority countries, although challenges remain in countries where political and religious conservatism limit women's involvement in public life.

---

5. The Future of Gender Equality and Human Rights in Islam

AS THE 21ST CENTURY progresses, the conversation around **gender equality** and **human rights** in Islam continues to evolve. The rise of **social media** and **global activism** has empowered Muslim women and human rights advocates to challenge traditional structures and call for reform. While **conservative** and **progressive** interpretations of Islam often clash, the diversity of thought within the Muslim world reflects a dynamic and evolving engagement with these critical issues.

- **Ongoing Reforms**: Many Muslim-majority countries are witnessing significant legal and social reforms aimed at advancing women's rights and aligning with global human rights standards. For instance, **Saudi Arabia** has recently introduced reforms allowing women to drive and participate more fully in the workforce, while **Tunisia** continues to lead the way in promoting **gender equality** through legal reforms.

- **Challenges to Progress**: Despite these advancements, challenges remain, particularly in regions where **extremist groups** or **conservative governments** resist efforts to reform gender roles or expand individual freedoms. The struggle for **gender equality** and **human rights** in the

Muslim world is far from over, and ongoing debates about the role of **Islamic tradition** in shaping these rights will continue to shape the future.

Conclusion

The 21st century has brought significant developments in the conversation surrounding **gender equality** and **human rights** in Islam. While traditional interpretations of Islamic law continue to shape gender roles in many Muslim-majority countries, progressive movements are advocating for reforms that align with modern values of **equality** and **justice**. Through ongoing engagement with **ijtihad**, **reform**, and **activism**, the future of gender equality and human rights in Islam remains a central issue, with the potential for significant progress as more voices call for a balanced and just interpretation of Islamic teachings.

Chapter 8: Comparative Theological and Jurisprudential Views

Throughout Islamic history, a rich diversity of theological and jurisprudential interpretations has shaped the practice of Islam across the world. From the early days following the death of the Prophet **Muhammad (peace be upon him)**, different groups of scholars, leaders, and thinkers sought to interpret Islamic texts in ways that addressed the evolving social, political, and spiritual needs of their communities. These differences gave rise to distinct **theological schools of thought** and **jurisprudential traditions** that have continued to influence how Islam is understood and practiced today.

At the heart of this diversity are the questions of how to interpret the **Quran**, the **Hadith**, and the **principles of sharia law**. While all Muslims share core beliefs—such as the oneness of God, the finality of the prophethood of Muhammad (peace be upon him), and the Day of Judgment—there are varying perspectives on the nature of **faith, divine justice**, and the role of **human reasoning** in interpreting the divine will. These perspectives are reflected in the differences between **Sunni** and **Shia Islam**, as well as within the **four Sunni madhabs (schools of jurisprudence): Hanafi, Maliki, Shafi'i**, and **Hanbali**.

This chapter explores these **comparative theological** and **jurisprudential views**, highlighting the distinctive features of the major schools and sects within Islam. By examining how each school approaches key issues such as **leadership, divine justice,**

interpretation of Islamic law, and the role of human reasoning, we can better understand the rich diversity within Islam and how these differences have shaped the religion's development over time. This comparative study underscores how Muslim scholars have navigated complex theological questions and legal challenges while remaining committed to the core principles of their faith.

Theological Differences on God, Prophethood, and the Afterlife Across Sects

ISLAM'S CORE BELIEFS in **the oneness of God**, **prophethood**, and the **afterlife** are shared by all Muslims, yet different Islamic sects have developed varying interpretations of these concepts. These theological differences have emerged over centuries and continue to influence the way different Muslim communities understand the relationship between God and humanity, the role of prophets, and what awaits in the afterlife. The most significant distinctions arise between **Sunni** and **Shia Islam**, but there are also nuanced differences within these broader categories, as well as among other sects like **Ibadi Islam**.

1. The Concept of God (Tawhid) Across Sects

THE BELIEF IN THE **oneness of God (Tawhid)** is the foundational principle of Islam and is accepted universally by all Muslims. However, theological schools differ in their interpretations of certain attributes of God, particularly when it comes to understanding His **nature** and **interaction with creation**.

- **Sunni Theology**: Sunnis traditionally adhere to one of two main theological schools, the **Ash'ari** and **Maturidi** schools, which focus on the balance between God's **sovereignty** and human **free will**. Both emphasize that **God's attributes**—such as His knowledge, power, and will—are eternal and beyond human comprehension. While **Ash'arism** stresses that humans cannot fully understand God's nature, it maintains that all of God's actions are inherently just, even if they seem beyond human logic. **Maturidism**, on the other hand, gives a greater role to **human reasoning**, arguing that certain aspects of God's justice and wisdom can be understood by humans.

● **Shia Theology**: In **Shia Islam**, particularly in the **Twelver Shia** tradition, there is a strong emphasis on **God's justice (Adl)**, which is one of the core theological tenets of their belief system. Shia scholars argue that God's justice must be understandable to human beings, and therefore, His actions are always just and good. The **Imamate** is also seen as a manifestation of God's guidance on Earth, with **Imams** considered divinely appointed leaders who are infallible and have a unique connection to God's wisdom.

● **Ibadi Theology**: **Ibadi Islam**, an often-overlooked sect, holds a moderate and unique position on God's attributes. The Ibadis emphasize that God's actions are always just and fair, and they lean toward **rationalism** in interpreting divine justice. Ibadis reject both extreme determinism (where humans have no free will) and the idea that God's actions are beyond human understanding, advocating for a balance between divine sovereignty and human responsibility.

---

2. Prophethood (Nubuwwah)

ALL ISLAMIC SECTS BELIEVE that **Muhammad (peace be upon him)** is the **final prophet** and **seal of the prophets (Khatam an-Nabiyyin)**. However, theological differences emerge in how different sects view the role of **other prophets** and the **concept of guidance** after the death of Muhammad.

● **Sunni View**: Sunnis uphold that **prophethood** ended with Muhammad (peace be upon him) and that the **Quran** and **Sunnah** (traditions of the Prophet) provide complete guidance for the Muslim community. Sunnis believe that no new **divinely appointed leaders** are necessary after the Prophet's death, and the role of guiding the community falls to the **ulema (scholars)**, who derive their authority from the Quran and Sunnah.

● **Shia View**: Shia Islam places a significant emphasis on the role of the **Imams**, who are seen as **infallible** and divinely guided successors to the Prophet Muhammad (peace be upon him). In **Twelver Shia Islam**, the belief is that the line of Imams, starting from **Ali ibn Abi Talib**, was divinely appointed to provide spiritual and political leadership. The **12th Imam**, known as **Al-Mahdi**, is believed to be in **occultation** and will return to restore justice before the Day of Judgment. This concept of **Imamate** is central to Shia theology, marking a key difference with Sunni Islam, which denies the necessity of infallible successors.

● **Ibadi View**: Ibadis reject the concept of divinely appointed **Imams** and the Shia understanding of **infallibility**. They emphasize that **prophethood** ended with Muhammad (peace be upon him), and after his death, leadership should be determined by the Muslim community based on **merit, piety,** and **competence**. Ibadis believe that the role of guiding the community belongs to a just and righteous leader (Imam) chosen by consensus, who must always prioritize justice and adherence to Islamic principles.

- **Ahmadiyya Belief**: The **Ahmadiyya** community presents a unique view on prophethood. Ahmadis believe that **Mirza Ghulam Ahmad** was a non-lawbearing prophet sent to revive Islam, but that his prophethood is subordinate to that of Muhammad (peace be upon him). This belief has led to widespread rejection of Ahmadis by mainstream Sunni and Shia scholars, who regard the **finality of Muhammad's prophethood** as absolute and non-negotiable.

---

3. The Afterlife (Akhirah) and Eschatology

BELIEF IN THE **afterlife** and **Day of Judgment** is a core tenet of Islamic theology across all sects. However, differences exist in how various sects interpret certain aspects of **eschatology**, including the events leading up to the Day of Judgment and the nature of **divine justice** in the hereafter.

- **Sunni Views on the Afterlife**: Sunni Muslims believe that after death, souls enter a state of **barzakh** (intermediary realm) until the **Day of Resurrection**. On the Day of Judgment, individuals will be judged based on their deeds, and they will either be rewarded with **Paradise (Jannah)** or punished in **Hell (Jahannam)**. Sunni eschatology emphasizes the role of **individual accountability** and **God's mercy**, with the Prophet Muhammad (peace be upon him) interceding on behalf of the righteous.

- **Shia Views on the Afterlife**: Shia eschatology shares many similarities with Sunni views, but with additional emphasis on the **intercession of the Imams**. In **Twelver**

Shia Islam, it is believed that the Imams will intercede on behalf of their followers on the Day of Judgment, and that the **12th Imam (Al-Mahdi)** will return to bring justice to the world before the final judgment. This concept of **Mahdism** plays a central role in Shia theology, as the **occulted Imam** is expected to lead the final battle between good and evil, establish a reign of justice, and prepare the world for the Day of Judgment.

• **Ibadi Views on the Afterlife**: Like other Islamic sects, Ibadis believe in the **resurrection** and **judgment** after death. However, they emphasize **God's justice** and the idea that **divine punishment** or **reward** is based strictly on one's deeds. Ibadis maintain that no one can intercede on behalf of another, rejecting the Shia and Sunni ideas of intercession by the Prophet or the Imams. For Ibadis, the emphasis is placed on **individual accountability** and the importance of living a righteous life in accordance with Islamic principles.

4. The Role of Human Reason and Divine Justice

ANOTHER KEY THEOLOGICAL difference across sects concerns the role of **human reason** in understanding **divine justice** and making ethical decisions.

• **Sunni Views on Divine Justice and Human Reason:** Sunni theologians, particularly in the **Ash'ari** school, tend to limit the role of human reasoning in interpreting divine justice. They argue that while humans have free will, God's justice is **beyond human comprehension**, and believers must trust in God's wisdom, even if certain events or actions appear unjust from a human perspective. The **Maturidi** school, however, gives more weight to human reasoning and maintains that **ethical truths** can be discerned through reason, though ultimately, God's justice prevails.

● **Shia Emphasis on Divine Justice**: Shia Islam, especially in **Twelver Shia theology**, places a strong emphasis on **divine justice** and believes that **human reason** plays a significant role in understanding good and evil. Shia scholars argue that God's actions are always just and that humans are capable of understanding this justice through reason. The concept of **Adl (divine justice)** is one of the five pillars of Shia theology, and it underpins their belief in the **Imamate** as divinely guided leadership meant to ensure justice on earth.

● **Ibadi Views on Human Responsibility**: Ibadi Islam also emphasizes **divine justice** and human responsibility. Ibadis believe that individuals are fully accountable for their actions and that **God's justice** ensures that each person will be rewarded or punished according to their deeds. Like Shia scholars, Ibadis believe that **reason** can help humans understand the moral principles laid out in the Quran, but they stress the importance of adhering strictly to God's commandments.

Conclusion

Theological differences between **Sunni**, **Shia**, **Ibadi**, and **Ahmadi** interpretations of Islam reveal the diversity of thought within the Muslim world regarding core beliefs about **God, prophethood,** and the **afterlife**. While all Muslims share a belief in the oneness of God, the finality of Muhammad's prophethood, and the reality of the afterlife, each sect offers unique perspectives on how to understand these concepts. These differences have shaped the evolution of Islamic thought, jurisprudence, and religious practice, reflecting the rich and dynamic nature of Islamic theology across time and regions.

Comparative Approaches to Sharia Law and Ijtihad (Independent Reasoning)

SHARIA LAW, or **Islamic law**, is a comprehensive system that governs not only religious rituals but also personal conduct, social justice, and legal matters within Islamic societies. It is derived from two primary sources: the **Quran** and the **Hadith** (sayings and actions of the Prophet Muhammad, peace be upon him), along with secondary sources such as **consensus (ijma)** and **analogy (qiyas)**. However, the interpretation and application of sharia have varied across different Islamic sects and schools of thought, particularly regarding the role of **ijtihad** (independent reasoning).

Ijtihad refers to the process of applying independent reasoning to derive legal rulings or resolve new issues not explicitly addressed in the Quran or Hadith. Throughout Islamic history, different schools of thought have debated the extent to which **ijtihad** should be employed and the level of flexibility allowed in interpreting sharia law. This chapter examines how **Sunni, Shia**, and **Ibadi** traditions, as well as **modern reformist movements**, approach sharia law and ijtihad, highlighting the diversity of thought within Islamic jurisprudence.

1. Sunni Approaches to Sharia Law and Ijtihad

IN **Sunni Islam**, the four major schools of jurisprudence (madhabs)—**Hanafi, Maliki, Shafi'i**, and **Hanbali**—each offer distinct interpretations of sharia law, particularly in relation to ijtihad.

- **Hanafi School:** The **Hanafi** school, the largest of the four, is known for its flexibility and willingness to incorporate **ijtihad**. It places a strong emphasis on the use of **qiyas** (analogy) and **istihsan** (juristic preference) to address issues not explicitly covered in the Quran or Hadith. The Hanafi school's openness to ijtihad allowed it to adapt to diverse legal and cultural environments, especially in regions like the **Ottoman Empire** and **South Asia**.

● **Maliki School**: The **Maliki** school emphasizes the **practice of the people of Medina** (Amal Ahl al-Madina) as a source of law, in addition to the Quran and Hadith. Although it uses ijtihad, it places greater weight on historical practice and consensus, seeing the early Muslim community in Medina as a model for Islamic law. **Istislah** (public interest) is also an important concept in Maliki jurisprudence, allowing for legal decisions that promote the common good.

● **Shafi'i School**: The **Shafi'i** school is more conservative in its use of ijtihad compared to the Hanafi school. **Imam al-Shafi'i** is credited with formalizing the principles of Islamic jurisprudence (usul al-fiqh), and his school relies heavily on the **Quran**, **Hadith**, and **ijma (consensus)**. While the Shafi'i school acknowledges the role of qiyas (analogy) for deriving legal rulings, it limits the use of ijtihad to prevent excessive innovation.

● **Hanbali School**: The **Hanbali** school, the most conservative of the four, places the greatest emphasis on strict adherence to the Quran and Hadith and is often skeptical of ijtihad. **Imam Ahmad ibn Hanbal** preferred to rely on the **literal texts** of the Quran and Hadith, using ijtihad only sparingly. The Hanbali school has influenced modern movements like **Wahhabism** and **Salafism**, which advocate for a literal interpretation of sharia and generally oppose extensive use of independent reasoning.

2. Shia Approaches to Sharia Law and Ijtihad

IN **Shia Islam**, particularly in the **Twelver Shia** tradition, the concept of **ijtihad** plays a significant role in jurisprudence. Shia scholars emphasize the continued need for independent reasoning to interpret Islamic law, especially in the absence of the **12th Imam (Al-Mahdi)**, who is believed to be in **occultation**.

- **Role of the Ulama**: In Twelver Shia Islam, the **ulama** (scholars) hold a special status as **mujtahids**—those qualified to engage in ijtihad. They are responsible for interpreting sharia law and guiding the community in the absence of the Imam. Shia Muslims are often required to follow the rulings of a **marja' al-taqlid** (source of emulation), a senior jurist who is regarded as highly knowledgeable in Islamic law and capable of issuing legal rulings (fatwas) based on ijtihad.

- **Ijtihad in Shia Tradition**: Unlike some Sunni schools that view ijtihad as a practice that was closed after the early centuries of Islam, **Twelver Shia scholars** maintain that ijtihad remains open and necessary. They argue that new circumstances and challenges require fresh interpretations of Islamic law, and therefore, jurists must continuously apply reasoning to address contemporary issues. This approach has allowed Shia scholars to develop legal rulings on modern matters such as **bioethics**, **politics**, and **technology**.

- **Divine Justice and Reason**: Shia jurisprudence is closely tied to the theological principle of **Adl (divine justice)**, which asserts that humans can discern right and wrong through **reason**. This belief supports the idea that **ijtihad** is a legitimate and necessary process for understanding God's will, as human reasoning can help interpret the principles of justice enshrined in the Quran and Hadith.

---

3. Ibadi Approaches to Sharia Law and Ijtihad

IBADI ISLAM, which is primarily practiced in **Oman** and parts of **North Africa**, takes a more moderate and pragmatic approach to sharia and ijtihad. While Ibadis share many similarities with Sunni Islam, they have their own jurisprudential traditions and place a strong emphasis on **justice, moderation**, and **reason** in legal matters.

- **Ijtihad in Ibadi Tradition**: The Ibadi approach to ijtihad is rooted in their belief in the importance of **human reasoning** to address legal and ethical challenges. Ibadis argue that Islamic law must be adaptable to changing circumstances and that scholars should engage in ijtihad to ensure that sharia remains relevant to modern life. Unlike the **Hanbali** school, which restricts the use of ijtihad, Ibadi scholars advocate for **pragmatism** in interpreting sharia law, particularly in matters of governance, social justice, and ethics.

- **Focus on Public Interest**: Ibadi jurisprudence emphasizes the **public interest (maslaha)** in legal rulings, similar to the **Maliki school**. This allows for flexibility in applying sharia law to ensure that decisions benefit the broader community. Ibadis view justice and fairness as central to Islamic law, and they are willing to adapt legal rulings to serve the common good, provided they remain consistent with Islamic principles.

---

4. Modern Approaches: Reform and Ijtihad in the 21st Century

IN THE 21ST CENTURY, there has been renewed interest in **reopening the doors of ijtihad** to address contemporary issues faced by Muslim communities worldwide. **Reformist Islamic movements** argue that sharia law must be adapted to the realities of modern life, including issues like **democracy, human rights, women's rights,** and **technology.**

- **Liberal and Progressive Movements: Liberal Muslim thinkers** advocate for a broad use of ijtihad to reinterpret Islamic texts in ways that align with modern values such as **gender equality, freedom of expression,** and **human rights.** They argue that many traditional interpretations of sharia are the result of historical contexts and that new interpretations are necessary to ensure that Islamic law is consistent with contemporary ethical standards.

- **Islamic Modernism: Islamic modernists,** such as **Muhammad Abduh** and **Rashid Rida,** have called for a revival of ijtihad to reform Islamic law and align it with modern science, education, and rationalism. Modernists seek to balance Islamic tradition with the demands of modernity by promoting an interpretation of sharia that is flexible and forward-thinking.

- **Contemporary Fatwas and Legal Opinions**: In many Muslim-majority countries, contemporary scholars issue **fatwas** (legal rulings) based on ijtihad to address new challenges such as **bioethics, financial regulation**, and **international relations**. These fatwas often reflect an effort to reconcile Islamic principles with modern legal and social norms, ensuring that Islamic law remains relevant in a rapidly changing world.

Conclusion

The comparative approaches to **sharia law** and **ijtihad** across Islamic sects and schools of thought illustrate the diversity and flexibility within Islamic jurisprudence. While some schools prioritize strict adherence to traditional legal rulings, others emphasize the importance of **independent reasoning** to adapt sharia to contemporary challenges. Whether through the cautious use of ijtihad in **Sunni Islam**, the central role of ijtihad in **Shia jurisprudence**, or the pragmatic approach of **Ibadi Islam**, the ongoing process of interpreting Islamic law demonstrates the dynamism of the **sharia** in addressing the evolving needs of Muslim societies. As modern reform movements continue to call for greater engagement with ijtihad, the debate over how to reconcile tradition with modernity will remain central to the future of Islamic jurisprudence.

Views on Social Justice, Human Rights, and Governance Across Islamic Traditions

ISLAMIC TEACHINGS ON **social justice**, **human rights**, and **governance** have been central to Muslim thought and practice since the early days of the faith. These concepts are deeply rooted in the **Quran**, the **Hadith**, and the **Sharia** (Islamic law), which emphasize the importance of **justice**, **compassion**, and **equality** in all aspects of life. However, different Islamic sects and schools of thought have interpreted and applied these principles in diverse ways, reflecting the rich variety of approaches within the Muslim world to questions of governance, law, and social order.

This chapter explores how **Sunni**, **Shia**, **Ibadi**, and **modern reformist movements** conceptualize social justice, human rights, and governance. Each tradition offers distinct perspectives on issues such as **economic justice**, **political authority**, **individual rights**, and the role of the state in ensuring the welfare of its citizens.

1. Sunni Views on Social Justice, Human Rights, and Governance

IN **Sunni Islam**, the principles of social justice and governance are rooted in the example of the **Prophet Muhammad (peace be upon him)** and the early **Caliphate**. Sunni thought emphasizes the role of **Sharia** in guiding society toward justice, but there is a range of views on how to balance Islamic law with modern concepts of **human rights** and **democratic governance**.

- **Social Justice in Sunni Islam**: Social justice is a central theme in Sunni thought, with the Quran and Hadith emphasizing the importance of caring for the **poor**, the **orphan**, and the **marginalized**. Key Islamic practices, such as the **obligatory charity (zakat)**, are designed to redistribute wealth and ensure that the most vulnerable members of society are protected. Sunni scholars argue that Islam's principles of **economic justice** align with modern concepts of **social welfare**, and many advocate for a system where the state plays a role in regulating wealth and ensuring fairness.

- **Governance and Political Authority**: The Sunni tradition places great importance on the idea of the **Caliphate** as the ideal form of Islamic governance, where a leader (caliph) ensures that the Sharia is implemented for the benefit of the entire community. However, modern Sunni thought has adapted to various forms of governance, from monarchies to republics, with scholars debating the extent to which **Sharia** should be applied in these systems. While some Sunni scholars advocate for **Islamic governance** with Sharia as the legal foundation, others promote the idea of **secular governance** where Islamic values guide personal ethics but not state law.

- **Human Rights in Sunni Thought**: Sunni scholars generally agree that Islam promotes **human rights**, including the right to **life**, **property**, **dignity**, and **justice**. However, debates arise around issues such as **freedom of religion**, **gender equality**, and **political freedoms**. While many Sunni scholars argue that Islamic law is compatible with international human rights norms, more conservative voices assert that **Sharia** must take precedence over human rights frameworks when the two are in conflict, particularly in areas like **apostasy** or **blasphemy** laws.

2. Shia Views on Social Justice, Human Rights, and Governance

IN **Shia Islam**, the concepts of social justice, human rights, and governance are closely tied to the theological belief in **Imamate**, the divinely guided leadership of the community by the **Imams**. Shia thought emphasizes the role of **justice (Adl)** as a core principle, not only in personal and social relationships but also in governance.

- **Social Justice in Shia Thought**: Twelver Shia Islam places a strong emphasis on social justice, rooted in the belief that the **Imams** serve as models of justice and righteousness. The martyrdom of **Imam Hussein** at **Karbala** is viewed as a powerful symbol of the fight against oppression and injustice, and Shia thought often frames social justice in terms of resistance to tyranny. **Zakat** and **khums** (an additional obligatory charity) are important tools in redistributing wealth to the needy and ensuring that the economic structure benefits the marginalized.

- **Governance and the Role of the Imam**: Shia governance is traditionally tied to the **Imamate**, with the belief that the **Imams**, as divinely appointed leaders, are responsible for guiding the community toward justice. In **Twelver Shia theology**, the **12th Imam (Al-Mahdi)** is in **occultation** and will return to establish a just and righteous Islamic state. In his absence, Shia scholars developed the concept of **Wilayat al-Faqih** (guardianship of the jurist), where senior religious scholars assume the role of guiding the community. This principle has been implemented in **Iran**, where the Supreme Leader, a jurist, oversees the Islamic Republic.

Other Shia communities, however, advocate for secular or democratic forms of governance guided by Islamic values.

● **Human Rights in Shia Islam**: Shia scholars argue that **divine justice** underpins human rights and that Islamic teachings promote dignity, equality, and freedom for all people. However, like in Sunni Islam, there are debates around the scope of these rights, particularly regarding **freedom of speech** and **religious freedom**. Shia scholars are more open to **ijtihad (independent reasoning)** in interpreting Islamic law, which has allowed for more flexibility in adapting to modern human rights frameworks in areas such as **women's rights** and **legal reforms**.

---

3. Ibadi Views on Social Justice, Human Rights, and Governance

IBADI ISLAM, practiced primarily in **Oman** and parts of **North Africa**, offers a distinctive approach to social justice, human rights, and governance, shaped by its emphasis on **moderation**, **justice**, and **rationalism**.

● **Social Justice in Ibadi Thought**: Ibadis place a strong emphasis on **egalitarianism** and **social justice**, viewing economic and social fairness as essential components of Islamic governance. The Ibadi tradition encourages community-oriented solutions to address poverty and inequality, with a focus on **charity** and **fair treatment** for all individuals. **Zakat** is viewed as a social obligation that ensures the just distribution of wealth, and Ibadis stress the importance of **ethics** and **righteous behavior** in both personal and public life.

• **Governance in Ibadi Islam**: Ibadis emphasize **consensus** and **meritocracy** in governance. They reject the concept of dynastic rule or inherited leadership, advocating instead for the selection of a **just and righteous leader (Imam)** based on merit, piety, and competence. In Oman, where Ibadi Islam is the dominant sect, the governance model reflects this principle, with a focus on **stability, consultation**, and **moderation**. Ibadi political thought advocates for **justice** and **accountability**, with leaders expected to rule in accordance with Islamic principles while serving the public good.

• **Human Rights and Moderation**: Ibadis are known for their **moderate** approach to human rights and their emphasis on **rationalism** in interpreting Islamic teachings. Ibadi scholars advocate for **human dignity**, **social justice**, and **individual responsibility**, and they are generally more flexible in adapting to modern human rights frameworks. The Ibadi tradition's emphasis on **justice** ensures that rights are protected, though like other Islamic schools, there are areas of tension regarding **freedom of belief** and **freedom of expression**.

---

4. Modern Reformist Movements and Their Approaches

IN THE 21ST CENTURY, **reformist Islamic movements** have emerged, advocating for a reinterpretation of Islamic principles to better align with modern concepts of **democracy, human rights**, and **social justice**. These movements seek to address the challenges posed by **globalization, secularism,** and **political authoritarianism** while remaining faithful to the core teachings of Islam.

- **Social Justice in Reformist Islam**: Reformist movements emphasize the Quranic principles of **justice, compassion**, and **equity** as a foundation for modern social justice. They advocate for the expansion of **women's rights, labor rights**, and **economic justice**, arguing that Islam's ethical teachings provide a framework for addressing contemporary issues such as **poverty, inequality**, and **environmental justice**. Many reformist scholars argue that Islamic law must be reinterpreted to promote social welfare and protect the most vulnerable in society.

- **Governance and Democracy**: Many reformist movements support the idea of **democratic governance** within an Islamic framework. They argue that Islamic principles of **consultation (shura)** and **justice** are compatible with democratic ideals such as **elections, political pluralism**, and **freedom of expression**. These movements often advocate for **constitutionalism**, where **Sharia** provides ethical guidance but does not dominate the political or legal system. In countries like **Tunisia** and **Turkey**, reformist Islamist parties have sought to balance Islamic values with democratic governance, promoting political participation and social justice.

- **Human Rights in Reformist Thought**: Reformist Islamic scholars place a strong emphasis on **human rights**, arguing that Islam is inherently aligned with the protection of individual freedoms, **gender equality**, and

social justice. They call for the **reopening of ijtihad (independent reasoning)** to address issues such as **freedom of belief, gender equality**, and **human rights**, advocating for a reinterpretation of Islamic teachings that reflects the ethical demands of the modern world. Reformist movements often challenge conservative interpretations of Islamic law that restrict human rights, calling for a more inclusive and compassionate approach to governance and legal systems.

Conclusion

The diverse approaches to **social justice**, **human rights**, and **governance** across Islamic traditions reflect the rich complexity of Islamic thought. While **Sunni**, **Shia**, and **Ibadi** scholars share common concerns about justice and the welfare of society, their interpretations of how to achieve these goals differ, particularly in their views on governance, the application of **Sharia**, and the role of the state. **Modern reformist movements** add another layer to these discussions, advocating for **democratic** and **human rights-based approaches** that engage with Islamic ethics while addressing the challenges of the contemporary world. Together, these perspectives demonstrate how Islamic thought continues to evolve in response to changing social, political, and economic conditions.

How Different Sects Interpret and Practice Islamic Rituals (Prayer, Fasting, Pilgrimage)

ISLAMIC RITUALS, PARTICULARLY the **Five Pillars of Islam**—prayer (Salah), fasting (Sawm), pilgrimage (Hajj), almsgiving (Zakat), and the testimony of faith (Shahada)—are central to the practice of Islam across all sects. However, the way these rituals are interpreted and performed can vary significantly between different Islamic sects, especially between **Sunni, Shia**, and **Ibadi** traditions. While the **core elements** of these rituals remain the same, differences in **timing, methodology**, and **theological emphasis** have shaped the distinct practices of these communities.

This chapter will explore how **Sunni, Shia, Ibadi**, and other Islamic sects interpret and perform key rituals like **prayer, fasting**, and **pilgrimage**, highlighting both shared beliefs and unique traditions.

1. Prayer (Salah) Across Islamic Sects

SALAH, or the ritual prayer, is a fundamental act of worship performed five times a day by most Muslims. It is considered the direct link between a believer and God. While all Islamic sects observe the obligation of prayer, differences in **timing, posture**, and certain ritual details distinguish how these prayers are conducted across various sects.

- **Sunni Islam**: In **Sunni Islam**, prayers are performed five times a day at specific times: **Fajr** (dawn), **Dhuhr** (midday), **Asr** (afternoon), **Maghrib** (sunset), and **Isha** (night). Sunni prayers involve a set of **movements (rak'ahs)**, including standing, bowing, and prostrating, all of which follow a structured sequence. Sunni Muslims place their hands on their chest or below the navel during the standing position, depending on the school of thought they follow (for example, the **Hanafi**, **Shafi'i**, or **Maliki** traditions). The **Friday congregational prayer (Jumu'ah)** is particularly important and takes place in place of the midday prayer on Fridays.

● **Shia Islam**: Shia Muslims also pray five times a day but often combine the **Dhuhr** and **Asr** prayers, as well as the **Maghrib** and **Isha** prayers, reducing the number of daily prayer sessions to three distinct times. In **Twelver Shia Islam**, believers typically place their hands at their sides during prayer, rather than folding them across the chest or below the navel. Another distinguishing feature is the use of a **small clay tablet (Turbah)**, often made from the soil of **Karbala**, where they rest their forehead during prostration. The Shia emphasis on the events of **Karbala** and the martyrdom of **Imam Hussein** also influences their communal prayers, especially during the month of **Muharram**.

● **Ibadi Islam**: Ibadis, primarily found in **Oman** and parts of North Africa, perform five daily prayers similarly to Sunnis. However, Ibadis have their own distinctive **rituals** in the way they perform Salah. For instance, in Ibadi prayer, the **qunut** (a special supplication) is recited during the **Fajr** prayer, which differs from some Sunni practices. Additionally, Ibadis place a strong emphasis on **purity** and **intent**, ensuring that their prayers are free from distractions.

● **Ismaili Islam**: Among **Ismaili Muslims**, a sect within Shia Islam, prayers are distinct in that many Ismailis perform **du'a** (invocations) rather than the traditional Salah. These prayers are recited privately, and while Ismailis may attend Friday prayers, their approach to prayer tends to emphasize **spiritual contemplation** and **individual connection with God**.

---

2. Fasting (Sawm) in Ramadan

FASTING DURING THE month of **Ramadan** is a shared practice across all Islamic sects, requiring Muslims to abstain from food, drink, and other physical needs from dawn until sunset. While the overall practice of fasting is similar, there are slight variations in how different sects observe the fast and the surrounding rituals.

- **Sunni Islam**: In **Sunni Islam**, fasting begins at **dawn (Fajr)** and ends at **sunset (Maghrib)** each day during the month of Ramadan. The fast is broken with a meal called **Iftar**, which traditionally starts with dates and water, followed by a larger meal. **Suhoor**, the pre-dawn meal, is also recommended before the fast begins each day. Sunni Muslims also engage in **extra prayers (Tarawih)** at night during Ramadan, which are performed in congregation after the Isha prayer.

- **Shia Islam**: **Shia Muslims** observe the same fast but often differ slightly in their timing for **breaking the fast**. Shia scholars often recommend waiting a little longer after sunset to ensure that the sun has fully set before breaking the fast. Shia Muslims also place a strong emphasis on the **spiritual significance** of Ramadan, often reflecting on the events of **Karbala** during this month. Shia communities recite special supplications and attend **Majlis** (religious gatherings) where they reflect on the martyrdom of **Imam Hussein** and the importance of patience and sacrifice. Additionally, Shia Muslims do not perform **Tarawih** prayers, as they believe that extra prayers should not be performed in congregation after the **Isha** prayer.

- **Ibadi Islam**: **Ibadis** follow a similar fasting routine to Sunnis, but with a particular emphasis on **purity** and **spiritual reflection**. Ibadis focus on ensuring that the fast is not just a physical exercise but also a time to purify the soul through ethical behavior and self-restraint. The breaking of the fast in Ibadi communities is often marked by simplicity, reflecting their emphasis on modesty and spirituality.

---

3. Pilgrimage (Hajj) and Differences in Rituals

THE **Hajj**, the pilgrimage to **Mecca**, is an obligation for all Muslims who are physically and financially able to undertake the journey at least once in their lifetime. While the core rituals of Hajj are the same across all Islamic sects, such as the **Tawaf** (circumambulation of the Kaaba) and **Sa'i** (walking between the hills of Safa and Marwah), some sects emphasize different aspects of the pilgrimage or have unique practices associated with it.

- **Sunni Islam**: For Sunni Muslims, the Hajj follows the traditional structure laid out in the Quran and Hadith, including the **Day of Arafah**, the **stoning of the pillars** in Mina, and the sacrifice on **Eid al-Adha**. Sunnis also perform a **lesser pilgrimage (Umrah)**, which can be undertaken at any time of the year and involves some of the same rituals as Hajj, though it is not a substitute for the obligatory Hajj.

- **Shia Islam**: **Shia Muslims** perform the same core rituals of Hajj, but they emphasize additional supplications and reflect deeply on the **spiritual and historical significance** of the pilgrimage. For instance, Shia pilgrims often include visits to the graves of **Imam Ali** and **Imam Hussein** in **Najaf** and **Karbala** before or after the Hajj, seeing this as an extension of the pilgrimage experience. Shia scholars also emphasize the **Imam's guidance** during the Hajj and use the pilgrimage as an opportunity to reflect on the leadership of the **Imams** in the broader spiritual journey of life.

- **Ibadi Islam**: **Ibadis** undertake Hajj in a similar manner to Sunnis, adhering closely to the rituals laid out in Islamic tradition. However, Ibadis place particular emphasis on the **ethical dimensions** of the pilgrimage, ensuring that their actions during Hajj reflect the values of **justice**, **modesty**, and **piety**. Like other sects, Ibadis also see the pilgrimage as an opportunity for personal **spiritual renewal** and transformation.

- **Ismaili Islam**: **Ismailis** have a unique approach to the Hajj and may prioritize spiritual pilgrimage in different forms. While some Ismailis undertake the Hajj to Mecca, they often place greater emphasis on the inner, spiritual journey of **self-purification** and closeness to God, which can be achieved through other forms of worship and devotion. The Ismaili understanding of pilgrimage is thus more symbolic and reflects their focus on **spirituality** over ritual.

Conclusion

The **interpretation** and **practice** of key Islamic rituals such as **prayer**, **fasting**, and **pilgrimage** demonstrate the rich diversity within the Muslim world. While all Islamic sects agree on the importance of these rituals as fundamental acts of worship, their unique approaches reflect varying theological perspectives, historical influences, and cultural practices. From the use of the **turbah** in Shia prayer to the emphasis on **spiritual purity** in Ibadi fasting and the symbolic meanings behind **Ismaili pilgrimage**, these differences highlight the dynamic nature of Islamic practice across different communities while maintaining a shared commitment to the core principles of the faith.

Chapter 9: Sacred Texts and Interpretations Across Islamic Sects

The Quran, the final revelation of **God (Allah)** to the Prophet **Muhammad (peace be upon him)**, serves as the foundational scripture for all Muslims. However, beyond the Quran, different Islamic sects follow various collections of **Hadith** (the sayings and actions of the Prophet), as well as theological and jurisprudential texts, that shape their understanding of Islamic law and practice. The way these texts are interpreted and the **emphasis placed on certain sources** over others differ across **Sunni, Shia, Ibadi,** and other sects within Islam. These differences are often linked to the sect's historical development, theological priorities, and jurisprudential methods.

This chapter will explore the **core texts** and the specific books followed by different Muslim sects, detailing the primary sources of authority and interpretation for **Sunni, Shia, Ibadi,** and **Ahmadi** traditions, as well as the schools of thought that have developed around these texts.

1. The Quran: The Universal Sacred Text

ACROSS ALL SECTS OF Islam, the **Quran** is the primary sacred text. It is viewed as the literal word of God, revealed to the Prophet **Muhammad (peace be upon him)** over 23 years, and it forms the basis of Islamic beliefs, rituals, and laws. While the **Quran** itself is universally accepted, its **interpretation (tafsir)** differs between sects. The Quran is often interpreted in light of the Hadith and the jurisprudential traditions each sect adheres to.

2. Sunni Islam: The Quran, Hadith, and the Four Madhabs

IN **Sunni Islam**, the **Quran** is supplemented by the **Hadith**, which are collections of the sayings, actions, and approvals of the Prophet Muhammad (peace be upon him). Sunni scholars compiled several authoritative Hadith collections that serve as key sources for **jurisprudence (fiqh)** and theology.

- **Primary Books in Sunni Islam:**

  ○ **Sahih al-Bukhari**: One of the most authoritative Hadith collections in Sunni Islam, compiled by **Imam al-Bukhari**. It is considered highly reliable (Sahih) and widely referenced in Sunni legal and theological discourse.

  ○ **Sahih Muslim**: Another core Hadith collection, compiled by **Imam Muslim**, also considered highly authentic and often paired with Bukhari in importance.

  ○ **Sunan Abu Dawood, Jami' at-Tirmidhi, Sunan an-Nasa'i**, and **Sunan Ibn Majah**: These collections, known as the **Kutub al-Sittah (Six Books)**, also hold significant weight in Sunni jurisprudence.

  ○ **Tafsir al-Tabari**: An early and respected Quranic exegesis (tafsir) by **Imam al-Tabari**, offering explanations and commentary on the verses of the Quran.

- **The Four Sunni Schools of Thought**: Sunni jurisprudence is based on four main schools, each with its own books and texts that guide legal interpretations:

  - **Hanafi**: Founded by **Imam Abu Hanifa**, the Hanafi school relies on texts like **Al-Hidayah** and **Fath al-Qadir**.

  - **Maliki**: The **Muwatta** of **Imam Malik** is one of the earliest works of Hadith and jurisprudence used by the Maliki school.

  - **Shafi'i**: **Al-Risala** by **Imam al-Shafi'i** is a foundational text for Shafi'i legal methodology.

  - **Hanbali**: **Musnad Ahmad ibn Hanbal** is a significant text in the Hanbali tradition, in addition to the reliance on direct Quranic and Hadith sources.

---

3. Shia Islam: The Quran, Hadith, and the Books of the Imams

IN **Shia Islam**, while the Quran remains central, the Hadith collections they rely on are distinct from those of the Sunnis. Shia Muslims prioritize the sayings and actions of the **Imams**, who are considered the rightful successors to the Prophet **Muhammad (peace be upon him)**, as divinely appointed leaders.

- **Primary Books in Shia Islam**:

  - **Al-Kafi**: Compiled by **Al-Kulayni**, this is one of the most important Hadith collections for **Twelver Shia Islam**. It covers a range of theological, legal, and ethical teachings attributed to the Prophet and the Imams.

○ **Man La Yahduruhu al-Faqih**: Written by **Al-Saduq**, this book is another key source of Hadith and Shia legal opinions.

○ **Tahdhib al-Ahkam** and **Al-Istibsar**: Both compiled by **Shaykh Tusi**, these books serve as primary texts in Twelver Shia jurisprudence.

• **The Role of the Imams**: In Shia Islam, particularly among **Twelvers**, the teachings of the twelve **Imams** (starting from **Imam Ali**) are considered a central source of religious authority. Their sayings are collected in Hadith books that are highly regarded. Shia scholars also produce **tafsir** (exegesis) that includes the interpretations of the Imams.

• **Key Tafsir Texts**: Shia tafsir often incorporates the insights of the Imams. Important works include **Tafsir al-Qummi** and **Tafsir al-Mizan** by **Allama Tabatabai**, which are highly regarded in Shia intellectual circles.

---

4. Ibadi Islam: Unique Texts and Early Islamic Sources

IBADI ISLAM, a smaller but significant sect primarily based in **Oman**, follows the Quran and Hadith like other Islamic sects but has its own Hadith collections and jurisprudential sources that differentiate it from both Sunni and Shia traditions.

• **Primary Books in Ibadi Islam:**

○ **Jami Sahih**: A Hadith collection compiled by **Al-Rabi bin Habib**, which is considered one of the earliest collections of prophetic traditions in Islam. Unlike Sunni or Shia Hadith collections, this work reflects the unique theological and legal priorities of the Ibadi sect.

○ **Al-Mudawwana**: A significant Ibadi legal text that outlines the core principles of Ibadi jurisprudence and law.

○ **Kitab al-Mabsut**: Another foundational text in Ibadi jurisprudence, which focuses on legal rulings and ethical practices in line with Ibadi thought.

● **Focus on Early Islamic Sources**: Ibadis emphasize **early Islamic sources** and seek to return to what they consider the pure practices of the early Muslim community. Their scholars have produced extensive theological works that discuss governance, law, and ethics in ways that are distinct from both Sunni and Shia perspectives.

---

5. Ahmadiyya Islam: Unique Interpretations and Texts

THE **Ahmadiyya** movement, founded by **Mirza Ghulam Ahmad** in the late 19th century, claims to follow the Quran and the Hadith but with significant theological differences that set them apart from mainstream Sunni and Shia Islam.

● **Primary Books in Ahmadiyya Islam**:

○ **The Writings of Mirza Ghulam Ahmad**: As the founder of the Ahmadiyya movement and believed to be the **Mahdi** and **Messiah**, Ghulam Ahmad's extensive writings, including books like **Barahin-e-Ahmadiyya** and **The Philosophy of the Teachings of Islam**, are central to Ahmadi belief.

○ **Tafsir al-Kabir**: A Quranic exegesis written by **Mirza Bashir-ud-Din Mahmud Ahmad**, the second caliph of the Ahmadiyya community, offering unique interpretations of Quranic verses in line with Ahmadi theology.

● **Ahmadiyya Hadith Interpretation**: Ahmadis accept many of the same Hadith collections as mainstream Sunni Islam but interpret them through the lens of Ghulam Ahmad's teachings, which are seen as fulfilling certain prophecies mentioned in the Hadith.

Conclusion

ACROSS THE VARIOUS Islamic sects, while the **Quran** remains the central sacred text, the **interpretation** of its verses and the **Hadith collections** followed by different communities create distinct religious traditions and practices. **Sunni Muslims** follow widely recognized Hadith collections and legal texts from the **four madhabs,** while **Shia Muslims** prioritize the teachings of the **Imams** and have their own Hadith sources. **Ibadi Muslims** maintain a unique body of literature distinct from both Sunni and Shia traditions, while **Ahmadi Muslims** incorporate the writings of their founder as an essential source of religious knowledge.

These variations in textual authority and interpretation reflect the rich diversity within Islam, as different sects seek to understand and practice their faith in ways that align with their theological and jurisprudential principles.

Key Texts in Sunni Islam: Foundations of Jurisprudence and Theology

THE SUNNI ISLAMIC TRADITION is built upon a rich collection of **Hadith** and **Tafsir** texts that complement the **Quran** in shaping religious, legal, and theological understanding. These books provide critical insights into the sayings and actions of the Prophet **Muhammad (peace be upon him)** and offer interpretations of the Quran that continue to influence Sunni practice and law to this day. Among these are the celebrated **Kutub al-Sittah (Six Books)** of Hadith, revered commentaries, and other fundamental works. Each text holds a unique place in Sunni scholarship, shaping the way millions of Muslims around the world engage with their faith.

Sahih al-Bukhari: The Pinnacle of Authentic Hadith Collection

Sahih al-Bukhari, compiled by **Imam Muhammad ibn Ismail al-Bukhari**, is universally regarded as one of the most **authentic collections** of Hadith in Sunni Islam. This compilation consists of thousands of narrations from the Prophet Muhammad (peace be upon him), meticulously authenticated through a rigorous process of verifying the reliability of the narrators and the chain of transmission.

What makes **Sahih al-Bukhari** particularly significant is its influence across Sunni jurisprudence and theology. The book is organized into multiple thematic sections, covering areas such as **faith, worship, morality**, and **social conduct**. Each Hadith is analyzed in the context of its reliability, leading scholars to cite Bukhari as the gold standard for **Sahih (authentic)** Hadith collections.

Sahih al-Bukhari is often memorized and studied by scholars and students of Islamic knowledge. Beyond being a text for **legal**

rulings (**fiqh**), it serves as a guide for personal conduct and understanding of the **Prophetic Sunnah**, making it a staple of Sunni Muslim religious practice.

Sahih Muslim: A Companion to Bukhari's Collection

Sahih Muslim, compiled by **Imam Muslim ibn al-Hajjaj**, is another cornerstone of Sunni Hadith literature, often paired with **Sahih al-Bukhari** due to its equally rigorous authentication process. **Imam Muslim** carefully scrutinized the chain of narrators (isnad) to ensure the Hadiths he included met the highest standards of authenticity.

What distinguishes **Sahih Muslim** from **Sahih al-Bukhari** is the format of its compilation. While Bukhari's collection is organized thematically with commentary, **Sahih Muslim** focuses more on preserving the **exact wording** and chain of each narration. The book's streamlined structure allows scholars to focus on precise language, contributing to its importance in jurisprudential debates.

The combination of **Sahih al-Bukhari** and **Sahih Muslim** is referred to as **Sahihayn** (the two Sahihs), and together they form the foundation of Sunni Hadith scholarship. Both texts are pivotal in legal discussions, ethics, and spiritual guidance, making them indispensable for Sunni scholars and laypeople alike.

The Kutub al-Sittah (Six Books): Expanding the Canon of Hadith

Beyond **Bukhari** and **Muslim**, four other significant Hadith collections complete the **Kutub al-Sittah**, or the **Six Books**, which are highly respected in Sunni Islam:

- **Sunan Abu Dawood:** Compiled by **Imam Abu Dawood**, this collection focuses on **legal matters**, making it a key resource for scholars developing **fiqh (Islamic jurisprudence)**. It includes many narrations that deal with everyday legal rulings on issues such as marriage, trade, and ritual purity.

● **Jami' at-Tirmidhi**: Compiled by **Imam Tirmidhi**, this work is distinctive for its detailed commentary on the authenticity and reliability of the Hadiths. **At-Tirmidhi** often includes the opinions of jurists regarding the narrations, which aids in scholarly discussions on legal interpretations and theological issues.

● **Sunan an-Nasa'i**: Known for its detailed examination of **Hadith narrators**, **Sunan an-Nasa'i** is one of the more compact collections but offers highly authentic Hadiths that focus on ritual worship and ethical conduct. It is particularly valued for its emphasis on correct practice in acts of worship, such as prayer and fasting.

● **Sunan Ibn Majah**: The final book in the **Kutub al-Sittah**, compiled by **Imam Ibn Majah**, includes Hadiths that are not found in the other five collections. Though some scholars have debated its inclusion in the canonical six books due to the variable reliability of some narrations, **Sunan Ibn Majah** remains an important source for legal rulings and historical insight into early Islamic practices.

These four books complement **Bukhari** and **Muslim** by providing broader context, additional narrations, and clarifications on various legal and ethical matters. Together, they form a comprehensive Hadith canon that informs **Sunni fiqh**, theological debates, and ethical considerations.

Tafsir al-Tabari: The Standard for Quranic Exegesis

In addition to the Hadith collections, **Tafsir al-Tabari** is one of the most respected works of **Quranic exegesis (tafsir)** in Sunni Islam. Written by **Imam Muhammad ibn Jarir al-Tabari**, this monumental work offers a comprehensive interpretation of the Quran, blending linguistic analysis, historical context, and Hadith references to explain the meanings of Quranic verses.

Tafsir al-Tabari is particularly valued for its methodical approach to interpreting each verse, where **al-Tabari** often presents **multiple interpretations** from earlier scholars before offering his own view. This allows readers and scholars to appreciate the richness of Islamic intellectual tradition and the diverse ways the Quran has been understood across generations. **Al-Tabari**'s work remains a foundational reference for any serious student of **tafsir**, influencing later scholars such as **Ibn Kathir** and **Jalaluddin al-Suyuti**.

Al-Tabari's ability to contextualize the Quranic verses within the **Prophet's life** and the **early Muslim community** makes his tafsir an essential resource for anyone seeking to deeply understand Islamic theology, law, and spirituality. His work also serves as a vital link between the Quran and Hadith, showcasing how the two sources of Islamic law complement each other.

Conclusion

The **Hadith collections** and **Quranic exegeses** in Sunni Islam form the backbone of the tradition's legal, ethical, and theological framework. Texts like **Sahih al-Bukhari** and **Sahih Muslim** set the highest standards for authenticity and are indispensable for understanding the **Sunnah** of the Prophet **Muhammad (peace be upon him)**. Meanwhile, the **Kutub al-Sittah** expands the range of Hadith sources, allowing scholars to address diverse legal and ethical questions with a wider body of knowledge. **Tafsir al-Tabari**, on the other hand, offers an essential guide for interpreting the Quran, blending historical, linguistic, and theological insights into a coherent and widely respected work.

These texts continue to guide Sunni Muslim life, shaping daily practices, legal rulings, and the pursuit of moral and spiritual excellence. They are the cornerstones of Islamic education and discourse, ensuring that the legacy of the **Prophet Muhammad (peace be upon him)** and the Quran remains central in every aspect of a Muslim's life.

The Four Pillars of Sunni Jurisprudence: A Detailed Look at the Major Schools of Thought

WITHIN **Sunni Islam**, the application and interpretation of **Sharia** law are guided by four major schools of jurisprudence, each offering a unique approach to legal reasoning and methodology. These schools—**Hanafi, Maliki, Shafi'i**, and **Hanbali**—are named after the founding scholars who developed their distinctive systems of legal thought. While they all share the core tenets of Sunni Islam, they differ in how they interpret **Hadith**, the **Quran**, and other sources of Islamic law, leading to various rulings on matters such as worship, personal conduct, and social justice.

These schools have developed authoritative texts that continue to serve as legal and theological references for scholars, students, and practitioners. Each school, or **madhab**, represents a deeply rooted intellectual tradition, and their influence extends to Muslim communities around the world. Here, we explore the primary texts and methodologies that define each school, providing a comprehensive understanding of their contribution to **fiqh** (Islamic jurisprudence).

Hanafi School: Flexibility and Rationalism in Legal Thought

The **Hanafi** school, founded by **Imam Abu Hanifa** (699–767 CE), is the largest and one of the earliest schools of thought in Sunni Islam. Known for its **rationalist approach** to jurisprudence, the Hanafi school emphasizes the use of **reason** and **analogy (qiyas)** when addressing legal issues. This flexibility has allowed Hanafi jurisprudence to adapt to various cultural contexts and legal systems, making it the dominant school in regions like **Turkey**, **India**, **Pakistan**, and parts of the **Middle East**.

The Hanafi school relies on a collection of key texts, which serve as foundational references for its legal interpretations:

- **Al-Hidayah**: One of the most well-known texts in Hanafi jurisprudence, **Al-Hidayah**, written by **Burhan al-Din al-Marghinani**, is a comprehensive guide to Hanafi fiqh. It presents a systematic overview of legal rulings on a wide range of topics, from **ritual worship** to **commercial transactions**. This text is often studied by students of Islamic law as it condenses the complex rulings of the Hanafi school into an accessible format.

- **Fath al-Qadir**: Authored by **Kamal al-Din ibn al-Humam**, **Fath al-Qadir** serves as a commentary on **Al-Hidayah**, providing further insight and expanding upon the original rulings. Ibn al-Humam's work is highly respected for its depth of scholarship and careful analysis of legal issues. It delves into the **principles of jurisprudence (usul al-fiqh)**, discussing the methods by which Islamic rulings are derived.

The Hanafi school is notable for its use of **istihsan (juristic preference)**, which allows jurists to prioritize a ruling that best serves the common good or promotes justice, even if it deviates from strict analogical reasoning. This approach has contributed to the Hanafi school's reputation for being adaptable to changing circumstances, a key factor in its widespread adoption.

Maliki School: Tradition and Practice in Medina

The **Maliki** school, founded by **Imam Malik ibn Anas** (711–795 CE), is rooted in the practices of the people of **Medina**, the city where the Prophet **Muhammad (peace be upon him)** established the first Muslim community. For the Maliki school, the **tradition (Sunnah)** of the people of Medina holds a special status, as Imam Malik believed their practices reflected the most authentic continuation of the Prophet's legacy.

Imam Malik's seminal work, the **Muwatta**, is both a **Hadith collection** and a **legal manual**:

- **The Muwatta of Imam Malik**: As one of the earliest collections of Hadith and legal rulings, the **Muwatta** remains a cornerstone of Maliki jurisprudence. Unlike later Hadith collections, which focus solely on the sayings of the Prophet, the **Muwatta** integrates legal discussions based on the actions and decisions of the **people of Medina**. This focus on local practice gives the Maliki school a unique approach to interpreting Islamic law, emphasizing communal tradition as a key source of legal authority.

In addition to the Quran and Hadith, the **amal (practice)** of the Medinan community plays a significant role in Maliki legal reasoning. This reliance on practice ensures that the legal rulings of the Maliki school are deeply connected to the social realities of the early Islamic period. The Maliki school also employs **maslaha (public interest)**, which allows for rulings that promote the welfare of the community, even if such rulings are not explicitly mentioned in the primary sources.

Shafi'i School: The Architect of Islamic Jurisprudence

Imam Muhammad ibn Idris al-Shafi'i (767–820 CE), the founder of the **Shafi'i** school, is often credited with developing the formal **principles of Islamic jurisprudence (usul al-fiqh)**. His approach to legal reasoning sought to standardize the use of the **Quran**, **Hadith**, **consensus (ijma)**, and **analogy (qiyas)** as the primary sources of law, providing a systematic methodology for deriving legal rulings.

One of Imam al-Shafi'i's most important contributions to Islamic jurisprudence is his foundational text:

- **Al-Risala**: In **Al-Risala**, Imam al-Shafi'i outlines the principles of Islamic legal theory. This text is groundbreaking in its articulation of how jurists should approach the interpretation of the Quran and Hadith, the process of deriving legal rulings, and the role of **human reasoning** in Islamic law. **Al-Risala** is considered a foundational text for all students of Islamic law and has shaped the development of fiqh across all Sunni schools of thought.

The Shafi'i school is particularly known for its emphasis on the **authenticity of Hadith** as the primary source of law, giving preference to sound narrations over local practices or juristic preferences. Shafi'i jurists are meticulous in their application of legal reasoning, ensuring that rulings are firmly grounded in the primary texts. This approach has made the Shafi'i school highly respected for its rigor and intellectual consistency, and it is widely followed in regions like **Southeast Asia** and **East Africa**.

Hanbali School: The Conservative Preservation of the Sunnah

The **Hanbali** school, founded by **Imam Ahmad ibn Hanbal** (780–855 CE), is the most **conservative** of the four Sunni schools, emphasizing strict adherence to the **Quran** and **Sunnah** with minimal reliance on human reasoning or analogy. Imam Ahmad's approach was deeply rooted in a literal interpretation of the sacred texts, making the Hanbali school known for its resistance to speculative theology and its rejection of excessive reliance on juristic preference.

Key texts in the Hanbali tradition include:

- **Musnad Ahmad ibn Hanbal**: This extensive Hadith collection compiled by **Imam Ahmad** contains over **30,000 Hadiths**, making it one of the largest collections in Sunni Islam. The **Musnad** is organized according to the narrators of the Hadith, providing a valuable resource for scholars seeking to derive legal rulings directly from the sayings and actions of the Prophet. Imam Ahmad's reliance on Hadith as the primary source of law reflects his commitment to preserving the purity of the **Prophetic Sunnah.**

The Hanbali school's strict adherence to the text has had a lasting influence on movements like **Wahhabism** and **Salafism**, which emphasize the importance of returning to the original sources of Islam and rejecting innovations in religious practice. Hanbali fiqh is dominant in **Saudi Arabia** and parts of the **Arabian Peninsula**, where its conservative legal rulings shape the judicial and social landscape.

Conclusion

The **four Sunni schools of thought** represent a rich intellectual tradition that has shaped Islamic law and practice for over a millennium. Each school offers a distinct approach to **jurisprudence**, rooted in the unique methodologies and texts of their founders. The **Hanafi school** is known for its flexibility and rationalism, while the **Maliki school** emphasizes the practice of the early Muslim community in Medina. The **Shafi'i school** is celebrated for its systematic approach to legal theory, and the **Hanbali school** is renowned for its strict adherence to the Quran and Hadith.

Together, these schools provide a comprehensive framework for understanding and applying Islamic law in diverse cultural and historical contexts. While they differ in their methods, the schools share a commitment to upholding the core principles of Islam, ensuring that the legal and ethical teachings of the faith remain relevant and accessible to Muslims around the world.

The Core Texts of Shia Islam: Foundations of Theological and Jurisprudential Authority

IN **Twelver Shia Islam**, alongside the **Quran**, there are several key texts that form the foundation of religious practice, jurisprudence, and theology. These texts, especially the **Hadith collections**, differ from those found in **Sunni Islam**, as they emphasize the sayings, actions, and teachings of both the **Prophet Muhammad (peace be upon him)** and the **Imams**—the divinely guided successors to the Prophet in Shia belief. These works shape Shia legal rulings, ethics, and religious guidance, with a deep focus on the unique role of the **Imamate**.

Among the most revered texts in Twelver Shia Islam are the collections compiled by eminent scholars such as **Al-Kulayni**, **Al-Saduq**, and **Shaykh Tusi**. These scholars are regarded as giants in Shia intellectual history, and their works remain central to the religious life of Shia Muslims worldwide. These books provide not only legal opinions but also valuable insights into Shia spiritual and theological teachings.

Al-Kafi: The Comprehensive Hadith Collection of Al-Kulayni

Al-Kafi, compiled by **Muhammad ibn Ya'qub al-Kulayni** (d. 941 CE), is one of the most important and authoritative Hadith collections in **Twelver Shia Islam**. The book is divided into three sections—**Usul al-Kafi** (dealing with theology), **Furu' al-Kafi** (legal rulings), and **Rawdat al-Kafi** (miscellaneous topics). This vast compilation contains over **16,000 Hadiths**, encompassing a wide range of topics such as **faith, ethics, worship**, and **social conduct**.

What sets **Al-Kafi** apart from Sunni Hadith collections is its emphasis on the teachings of the **Imams**, particularly the **Twelve Imams** who are believed to be the rightful spiritual and temporal successors to the Prophet Muhammad (peace be upon him). These Imams are considered infallible in Shia theology, and their teachings are seen as direct interpretations of divine will.

Usul al-Kafi focuses on theological issues, addressing topics such as **the nature of God**, **the Imamate**, and **divine justice**. It provides the philosophical and doctrinal framework for understanding the role of the Imams in guiding the community and upholding justice.

Furu' al-Kafi deals with legal matters, offering guidance on daily religious practices such as **prayer**, **fasting**, **marriage**, and **inheritance**. The rulings in **Furu' al-Kafi** are based on the interpretations and examples set by the Imams, making it a cornerstone of Shia jurisprudence.

Shia scholars regard **Al-Kafi** as an indispensable resource for deriving legal and theological rulings. Although not all Hadiths in **Al-Kafi** are considered equally reliable, the book's immense scope and depth make it one of the most studied and referenced texts in Shia Islam.

Man La Yahduruhu al-Faqih: Practical Legal Guidance for the Shia Community

Man La Yahduruhu al-Faqih, written by **Shaykh al-Saduq** (Ibn Babawayh), is another critical Hadith collection and legal manual within Twelver Shia Islam. The title translates to **"He Who Does Not Have a Jurist Present"**, reflecting its purpose as a practical guide for those who may not have immediate access to a learned scholar.

Unlike **Al-Kafi**, which includes a vast array of theological discussions, **Man La Yahduruhu al-Faqih** is more focused on **practical legal rulings** and everyday religious obligations. Shaykh al-Saduq's goal in compiling this work was to provide a concise and accessible legal text that could serve the needs of ordinary believers in matters of **worship**, **family life**, **commerce**, and **ethical conduct**.

Shaykh al-Saduq's approach is notable for its reliance on **Hadiths attributed to the Imams**, as well as his effort to simplify complex legal discussions for the layperson. The book covers a wide range of topics, including:

- **Ritual purity** (taharah)
- **Salah (prayer)**
- **Zakat** (almsgiving)
- **Fasting** (Sawm)
- **Marriage and divorce laws**

Man La Yahduruhu al-Faqih remains a key text in Shia jurisprudence, particularly for those seeking straightforward answers to common religious questions. It is highly respected for its clarity and practical application in daily life.

Tahdhib al-Ahkam and Al-Istibsar: Shaykh Tusi's Masterpieces of Shia Jurisprudence

The works of **Shaykh al-Tusi** (995–1067 CE), a towering figure in Twelver Shia scholarship, form another pillar of Shia jurisprudential literature. His two major contributions, **Tahdhib al-Ahkam** and **Al-Istibsar**, are among the **Four Books** of Shia Islam and are essential to the development of Shia fiqh.

- **Tahdhib al-Ahkam**: Compiled by Shaykh Tusi, **Tahdhib al-Ahkam** is a comprehensive collection of Hadiths that serve as the basis for Shia legal rulings. The book is notable for its systematic approach to organizing **jurisprudential issues**, covering everything from **personal obligations** (ibadat) to **social transactions** (muamalat). Shaykh Tusi's legal methodology involves presenting Hadiths from the **Imams** and then explaining how these narrations apply to practical legal issues. His detailed analysis helps clarify complex legal points, making the book a vital resource for students and scholars alike.

• **Al-Istibsar**: Shaykh Tusi's second major work, **Al-Istibsar**, focuses on resolving conflicting Hadiths. In Shia jurisprudence, it is not uncommon for different Hadiths to appear contradictory on certain legal matters. **Al-Istibsar** addresses this challenge by examining the chain of transmission, the context of each Hadith, and the authority of the narrators. Shaykh Tusi then provides clear rulings on which Hadiths should be followed in specific cases, offering a harmonized view of Shia law.

Both **Tahdhib al-Ahkam** and **Al-Istibsar** are revered for their depth of scholarship and their contribution to shaping **Shia fiqh**. Together, they provide a comprehensive framework for understanding Islamic law from a Shia perspective, ensuring that legal rulings are grounded in the teachings of the **Imams** while also addressing the complexities of contemporary life.

Conclusion

The **primary books in Shia Islam**—from **Al-Kafi** to **Tahdhib al-Ahkam**—serve as the foundation for the **theological**, **ethical**, and **jurisprudential** practices of **Twelver Shia Muslims**. These texts, deeply rooted in the teachings of the **Imams**, offer a distinct legal and spiritual framework that emphasizes the unique role of the **Imamate** in guiding the community.

The works of scholars such as **Al-Kulayni**, **Al-Saduq**, and **Shaykh Tusi** continue to shape the intellectual landscape of Shia Islam, providing detailed guidance on everything from **personal piety** to **complex legal disputes**. These books remain indispensable for scholars, students, and laypeople alike, ensuring that the teachings of **Shia Islam** are accessible, authoritative, and deeply connected to the **Prophet's family** and their legacy.

The Divine Role of the Twelve Imams in Shia Islam: Guardians of Knowledge and Justice

IN **Twelver Shia Islam**, the **Imams** are regarded as divinely appointed leaders, entrusted with the spiritual and temporal guidance of the Muslim community after the Prophet **Muhammad (peace be upon him)**. Beginning with **Imam Ali ibn Abi Talib (peace be upon him)**, the cousin and son-in-law of the Prophet, and continuing through a line of twelve successive Imams, each is considered to be infallible and uniquely chosen by God to preserve and protect the true interpretation of Islam.

For Twelver Shia Muslims, the Imams hold a crucial position not only as religious guides but also as the **interpreters of divine law** and the **guardians of spiritual knowledge**. Their teachings and sayings are meticulously preserved in **Hadith collections** and other religious texts, and they are seen as essential to understanding both the **Quran** and the **Sharia**.

The Imams play an indispensable role in shaping the theology, ethics, and jurisprudence of Shia Islam. Their guidance extends beyond merely religious duties, touching upon matters of **justice**, **leadership**, and **the struggle against oppression**. The concept of the **Imamate** (the leadership of the Imams) is central to Shia beliefs, distinguishing Shia thought from Sunni traditions, where the caliphs assumed leadership after the Prophet's death.

Imam Ali: The Foundation of the Imamate

The role of the **Imams** begins with **Imam Ali ibn Abi Talib (peace be upon him)**, whom Shia Muslims regard as the first rightful successor to the Prophet Muhammad (peace be upon him). **Imam Ali's** legacy is defined by his commitment to **justice**, **piety**, and **knowledge**. He is seen not only as a political leader but also as the **spiritual authority** entrusted by the Prophet himself. His sermons, letters, and sayings, particularly those compiled in the revered book **Nahjul Balagha (The Peak of Eloquence)**, form a cornerstone of Shia thought.

Imam Ali emphasized the importance of knowledge, wisdom, and justice in governance. His life exemplifies the Shia ideal of **resistance against oppression** and upholding divine justice, as seen in his conflicts with those who sought power through tyranny or manipulation of the faith. His leadership style and teachings continue to inspire Shia Muslims, especially in their pursuit of fairness and righteousness.

The Infallibility and Divine Knowledge of the Imams

A defining characteristic of the **Imams** in Shia Islam is their **infallibility**. Twelver Shia Muslims believe that the **Imams** are free from sin and error, both in their actions and their understanding of religion. This infallibility (Ismah) allows the **Imams** to act as perfect guides for the Muslim community, ensuring that their followers can rely on them for **divine knowledge** and the correct interpretation of the Quran and Hadith.

The **Imams** are also considered to have been given **divinely inspired knowledge** (Ilm al-Ladunni), which allows them to interpret the Quran and Islamic law in ways that are beyond the capacity of ordinary scholars. This unique connection to divine wisdom positions the **Imams** as the ultimate **interpreters of the Quran** and the custodians of the **Prophetic Sunnah**.

For example, the Hadith collections revered in Shia Islam, such as **Al-Kafi**, place significant emphasis on the sayings and interpretations of the **Imams**, especially when clarifying matters of law, theology, and ethics. Unlike Sunni Islam, which relies primarily on the sayings of the Prophet and the **companions**, Twelver Shia Muslims look to the teachings of the **Imams** for authoritative guidance.

Theological Contributions of the Twelve Imams

Each **Imam** contributed to the spiritual and theological development of Shia Islam in unique ways, offering teachings that addressed the challenges and crises of their time. Their lives were often marked by political turmoil, and many of the **Imams** suffered persecution at the hands of unjust rulers. Despite this, their contributions to Islamic thought have left an indelible mark on the Shia tradition.

- **Imam Hasan (peace be upon him)**, the second Imam, is remembered for his **peace treaty** with the Umayyad ruler **Mu'awiya**, which demonstrated his commitment to preserving the unity of the Muslim community while maintaining the principles of justice.

- **Imam Hussein (peace be upon him)**, the third Imam, is one of the most revered figures in Shia Islam due to his stand against the tyranny of the Umayyad caliph **Yazid**. His martyrdom at the **Battle of Karbala** became a symbol of resistance against injustice, inspiring Shia Muslims to value sacrifice in the pursuit of righteousness. **Ashura**, the day commemorating **Imam Hussein's** martyrdom, is central to Shia identity and is observed with great reverence.

- **Imam Zain al-Abidin (peace be upon him)**, the fourth Imam, lived in the aftermath of Karbala and contributed to Shia spirituality through his devotional prayers and supplications, which are compiled in the book **Sahifa Sajjadiya**. His writings emphasized the importance of piety, reflection, and the **moral development** of the soul.

Each subsequent **Imam** continued to guide the Shia community, offering wisdom and spiritual leadership in times of great hardship. **Imam Muhammad al-Baqir (peace be upon him)** and **Imam Ja'far al-Sadiq (peace be upon him)** were particularly instrumental in codifying Shia law and theology. **Imam Ja'far al-Sadiq** is credited with founding the **Ja'fari school of jurisprudence**, which remains the dominant legal system in Twelver Shia Islam.

The Hidden Imam: Al-Mahdi and the Doctrine of Occultation

The twelfth and final Imam, **Imam Muhammad al-Mahdi (peace be upon him)**, holds a special place in Twelver Shia belief. According to Shia tradition, the twelfth Imam entered into **occultation** (Ghaybah) in 874 CE. Shia Muslims believe that he is still alive but hidden from public view and that he will return at the end of times as **Al-Mahdi**, the divinely guided one, to restore justice and establish true Islamic governance.

This doctrine of occultation is a defining feature of **Twelver Shia Islam**. During the period of occultation, the Shia community looks to its scholars and religious leaders to interpret the teachings of the **Imams** and guide them in matters of religious practice and governance. The **return of the Mahdi** is anticipated as a time when the world will be purified of injustice, and God's law will be fully realized.

The Imams and Shia Tafsir (Exegesis)

The **Imams'** unique role as interpreters of divine knowledge is also reflected in **Shia tafsir (Quranic exegesis)**. In contrast to Sunni exegesis, which relies on the opinions of various scholars and companions of the Prophet, Shia tafsir often incorporates the **teachings of the Imams** as a primary source of interpretation.

Works such as **Tafsir al-Qummi** and **Tafsir al-Mizan** by **Allama Tabatabai** draw heavily on the insights provided by the **Imams**, offering a distinctly Shia understanding of Quranic verses. These exegeses emphasize the spiritual dimensions of the Quran and highlight the role of the **Imamate** as a means through which God's guidance is conveyed to humanity.

Shia tafsir provides both a **literal** and **esoteric** interpretation of the Quran, often delving into the deeper, symbolic meanings of verses. This approach reflects the belief that the **Imams**, through their divinely inspired knowledge, can uncover the **inner meanings** of the Quran that are not accessible to ordinary individuals.

Conclusion

In **Twelver Shia Islam**, the **Imams** are not merely successors to the Prophet Muhammad (peace be upon him) but are seen as **infallible guides** endowed with divine knowledge. Their teachings are preserved in **Hadith collections** and tafsir, making them the central authority for understanding the Quran, Islamic law, and spiritual practice. From **Imam Ali's** commitment to justice to **Imam Hussein's** sacrifice at Karbala, the **Twelve Imams** embody the principles of righteousness, courage, and divine leadership.

Their role in Shia Islam is unparalleled, shaping the community's theology, jurisprudence, and approach to governance. Through their teachings, the **Imams** provide a path to understanding God's will, offering both legal guidance and spiritual insight. The legacy of the **Imamate** continues to inspire Shia Muslims in their pursuit of justice and devotion to God, as they await the return of the twelfth Imam, **Al-Mahdi**, to restore peace and equity to the world.

Illuminating the Quran: Key Tafsir Texts in Shia Islam

IN **Shia Islam, tafsir** (Quranic exegesis) holds a central place in understanding the deeper meanings of the **Quran**. What distinguishes Shia tafsir from other interpretations is the incorporation of the teachings and insights of the **Imams**. For Shia scholars and believers, the Imams, particularly the **Twelve Imams** in **Twelver Shia Islam**, are considered the divinely inspired guides whose understanding of the Quran is unparalleled. Their insights are seen as essential to unlocking the full spiritual, ethical, and legal dimensions of the Quran.

Two of the most influential tafsir texts in Shia Islam are **Tafsir al-Qummi** and **Tafsir al-Mizan** by **Allama Tabatabai**. These works not only reflect a profound engagement with the Quran but also highlight the **Imams' wisdom**, providing both literal and esoteric interpretations of the sacred text. They continue to be pillars in Shia intellectual circles, guiding scholars and believers in their quest for a deeper understanding of God's message.

Tafsir al-Qummi: A Classical Foundation in Shia Exegesis

Tafsir al-Qummi, compiled by **Ali ibn Ibrahim al-Qummi** in the 9th century, is one of the earliest and most respected Shia Quranic exegeses. **Al-Qummi** was a prominent Shia scholar from **Qom**, and his tafsir draws heavily on the teachings of the **Imams**, particularly from **Imam Ja'far al-Sadiq (peace be upon him)**, the sixth Imam, and **Imam Muhammad al-Baqir (peace be upon him)**, the fifth Imam.

Tafsir al-Qummi is structured as a verse-by-verse explanation of the Quran, and it focuses on providing both a **literal interpretation** and the **context** in which the verses were revealed. Al-Qummi emphasizes the importance of the Imams' guidance in understanding the Quran and often quotes their sayings to explain the deeper meanings of the text. This approach reflects the Shia belief that the Imams have an intrinsic connection to the divine and are therefore capable of providing unparalleled insight into the Quran's teachings.

One of the key themes in **Tafsir al-Qummi** is the role of **justice** and **oppression**, especially as it relates to the **Ahl al-Bayt** (the family of the Prophet, including the Imams). Al-Qummi's tafsir often discusses the injustices faced by the **Imams** and their followers, highlighting the Quran's call for resistance against tyranny and the establishment of a just social order. This theme is central to Shia theology and resonates deeply with the historical experiences of the Shia community, particularly the martyrdom of **Imam Hussein (peace be upon him)** at **Karbala**.

Tafsir al-Qummi is regarded as an essential text for Shia scholars, particularly those who focus on the early development of Shia thought and the role of the **Imams** in guiding the Muslim community. Its incorporation of the **Imams' interpretations** makes it a unique and invaluable resource for understanding the Quran through a distinctly Shia lens.

Tafsir al-Mizan: A Masterpiece of Philosophical and Spiritual Exegesis

Tafsir al-Mizan, written by **Allama Muhammad Husayn Tabatabai** (1903–1981), is widely regarded as one of the most profound and comprehensive Quranic exegeses in the modern Shia tradition. **Allama Tabatabai** was an influential Shia philosopher and scholar whose works have had a lasting impact on Islamic thought, both within the Shia world and beyond.

Tafsir al-Mizan differs from earlier tafsirs like **Tafsir al-Qummi** in its approach. While it incorporates the sayings of the **Imams**, **Allama Tabatabai** also engages deeply with **philosophical reasoning**, **mysticism**, and **scientific principles** to offer a more holistic understanding of the Quran. His tafsir provides not only a literal explanation of the Quranic verses but also delves into their **esoteric** meanings, exploring the spiritual and metaphysical dimensions of the text.

One of the hallmarks of **Tafsir al-Mizan** is **Allama Tabatabai's** method of explaining the Quran through the Quran itself, a technique known as **Tafsir al-Quran bil-Quran**. This method involves using various Quranic verses to shed light on one another, providing a more interconnected and cohesive understanding of the text. In doing so, **Allama Tabatabai** shows how seemingly disparate verses of the Quran are, in fact, part of a larger divine message that can be understood when viewed in its entirety.

Allama Tabatabai also emphasizes the importance of the **Imams' spiritual guidance**, particularly in understanding the deeper, hidden meanings of the Quran. According to Shia belief, the **Imams** possess **inner knowledge** that allows them to interpret the esoteric aspects of the Quran, which are not always accessible to ordinary people. For instance, verses that deal with the nature of the soul, the afterlife, and the attributes of God are explored in **Tafsir al-Mizan** in light of the teachings of the Imams.

Another significant aspect of **Tafsir al-Mizan** is its engagement with **modern intellectual trends**. **Allama Tabatabai** addresses contemporary issues such as the relationship between **science and religion**, the nature of **human free will**, and the role of **social justice** in Islam. His tafsir provides answers to modern-day questions by drawing from both the Quran and the wisdom of the **Imams**, showing how Islamic teachings remain relevant in the face of new intellectual challenges.

Tafsir al-Mizan remains a monumental work in Shia intellectual history, widely studied in seminaries and universities. Its blend of **philosophy**, **mysticism**, and **Shia theology** offers a multifaceted understanding of the Quran that continues to inspire scholars and believers alike. **Allama Tabatabai's** ability to bridge traditional Islamic teachings with modern philosophical inquiry makes **Tafsir al-Mizan** one of the most important tafsirs for Shia Muslims today.

The Role of the Imams in Shia Tafsir

Both **Tafsir al-Qummi** and **Tafsir al-Mizan** exemplify the essential role that the **Imams** play in **Shia tafsir**. The **Imams**, particularly in **Twelver Shia Islam**, are viewed as the divinely guided interpreters of the Quran, whose understanding of the text is seen as both comprehensive and authoritative. Their teachings form the backbone of Shia exegesis, providing clarity and depth to the interpretation of complex Quranic themes such as **divine justice, the nature of God**, and the struggle between **good and evil**.

Shia tafsir is characterized by a strong emphasis on both the **literal** and **esoteric** meanings of the Quran. The **Imams' insights** allow Shia scholars to go beyond a surface-level understanding of the text, offering interpretations that speak to both the material and spiritual dimensions of life. This dual focus on the apparent and hidden meanings of the Quran is what distinguishes Shia exegesis from other traditions and underscores the importance of the **Imams** in guiding the community toward a fuller understanding of God's will.

Conclusion

The key tafsir texts of Shia Islam, such as **Tafsir al-Qummi** and **Tafsir al-Mizan**, highlight the deep connection between the Quran and the teachings of the **Imams**. These works provide both a literal explanation of Quranic verses and delve into the spiritual and philosophical aspects of the text, offering a uniquely Shia perspective on **Islamic thought**.

While **Tafsir al-Qummi** serves as a foundational text that draws directly from the **Imams' teachings**, **Tafsir al-Mizan** by **Allama Tabatabai** represents a more modern engagement with the Quran, blending traditional insights with contemporary philosophical inquiry. Both texts continue to be pillars of Shia scholarship, offering guidance to those seeking a deeper understanding of the Quran's divine message.

Essential Texts of Ibadi Islam: Foundations of Jurisprudence and Theology

IBADI ISLAM, A BRANCH of Islam distinct from both Sunni and Shia traditions, has its own unique theological and legal system. The Ibadis, primarily found in **Oman**, parts of **North Africa**, and **East Africa**, emphasize a strong commitment to **justice, moderation**, and **ethical governance**. Central to their understanding of Islam are a few foundational texts that shape Ibadi jurisprudence and theology, distinct from the Hadith collections and legal texts that dominate Sunni and Shia thought.

Among these texts, the **Jami Sahih, Al-Mudawwana**, and **Kitab al-Mabsut** are of primary importance. These works provide a rich insight into Ibadi law, ethics, and theology, reflecting the sect's early roots and its emphasis on a **rational** and **practical** approach to Islamic teachings. They guide the Ibadi community in interpreting the **Quran** and the **Sunnah**, offering rulings and perspectives that align with the core values of **justice, piety**, and **communal well-being**.

Jami Sahih: A Unique Compilation of Prophetic Traditions in Ibadi Islam

The **Jami Sahih**, compiled by **Al-Rabi bin Habib** in the 8th century, is considered one of the earliest Hadith collections in Islamic history. It stands as a fundamental text in Ibadi Islam, distinguishing itself from the more widely known Hadith collections in Sunni and Shia traditions, such as **Sahih al-Bukhari** or **Al-Kafi**. The **Jami Sahih** is highly regarded for its authenticity and focus on the **Prophetic traditions** that are most relevant to Ibadi theological and legal priorities.

The **Jami Sahih** differs from Sunni and Shia Hadith collections in that it is more selective, focusing on Hadiths that align with Ibadi principles, particularly those that emphasize **moderation**, **piety**, and the rejection of extremism. The Ibadis have a unique theological stance on issues like leadership, governance, and community justice, and the **Jami Sahih** reflects these values. It avoids some of the more controversial traditions found in other Hadith collections, focusing instead on Hadiths that promote **rational decision-making** and **ethical behavior**.

One of the key themes in the **Jami Sahih** is the emphasis on **individual responsibility** and **moral accountability**. The Hadiths selected by **Al-Rabi bin Habib** guide Ibadis in understanding how to live a life of **faith**, **justice**, and **personal integrity**. This focus on the moral and ethical dimensions of Islam is central to Ibadi thought, and the **Jami Sahih** continues to serve as a critical reference for scholars and believers in Ibadi communities.

Al-Mudawwana: The Legal Framework of Ibadi Jurisprudence

Al-Mudawwana is a significant Ibadi legal text that outlines the core principles of **Ibadi jurisprudence**. It provides a detailed analysis of the legal rulings that govern everyday life, covering topics such as **ritual worship**, **marriage**, **commerce**, and **inheritance**. Unlike Sunni schools of thought, which rely on the four major madhabs (Hanafi, Maliki, Shafi'i, and Hanbali), Ibadi jurisprudence developed independently, reflecting the distinct theological priorities of the Ibadi sect.

The **Al-Mudawwana** is known for its emphasis on **consensus** and **community consultation** in legal matters. Ibadi scholars believe that the **righteous community** has the authority to interpret Islamic law through reason and dialogue, as long as the rulings align with the **Quran** and **Sunnah**. This reflects the Ibadi rejection of hereditary leadership and dynastic rule, which they view as contrary to Islamic principles of justice and meritocracy.

One of the unique aspects of **Al-Mudawwana** is its approach to **ijtihad** (independent reasoning). Ibadi scholars are encouraged to engage in ijtihad when making legal decisions, allowing for flexibility and adaptability in the application of Islamic law. This pragmatic approach has enabled Ibadi jurisprudence to evolve in response to changing social and political circumstances, while still adhering to the fundamental principles of justice and fairness.

Al-Mudawwana also emphasizes the importance of **communal welfare** in legal rulings. Laws regarding **charity**, **social justice**, and **public interest** are given significant attention, reflecting the Ibadi commitment to promoting the well-being of the entire community. This focus on collective responsibility distinguishes Ibadi law from other Islamic legal systems, which often place greater emphasis on individual rights.

Kitab al-Mabsut: Ethical Practices and Legal Rulings in Ibadi Islam

Kitab al-Mabsut is another foundational text in Ibadi jurisprudence, focusing on **legal rulings** and **ethical practices**. It is a more comprehensive work that covers a wide range of topics, from personal obligations like **prayer** and **fasting** to broader issues of **social justice** and **economic fairness**. The **Kitab al-Mabsut** serves as a practical guide for both scholars and ordinary believers, helping them navigate the complexities of Islamic law in a manner that reflects Ibadi values.

One of the central themes in the **Kitab al-Mabsut** is the balance between **individual rights** and **community obligations**. Ibadi law places a strong emphasis on the **collective good**, and this is reflected in the rulings found in **Kitab al-Mabsut**. For example, the text provides detailed guidelines on the distribution of **zakat** (almsgiving), ensuring that the wealth of the community is used to support the poor, the orphaned, and the marginalized.

Another important aspect of **Kitab al-Mabsut** is its discussion of **governance** and the role of leadership in Islam. Ibadi thought rejects the concept of **dynastic rule** and instead promotes a system of governance based on **merit, piety**, and **justice**. The **Kitab al-Mabsut** outlines the qualities that a leader must possess, emphasizing that leadership should be based on one's ability to uphold justice and ensure the well-being of the community, rather than on familial or tribal connections.

The **Kitab al-Mabsut** also deals with issues of **business ethics**, providing rulings on **trade, contracts**, and **economic transactions**. Ibadi jurisprudence stresses the importance of **honesty, fair dealing**, and **transparency** in all economic activities. This focus on ethical behavior in both personal and professional life reflects the broader Ibadi commitment to living a life of **moral integrity**.

Conclusion

The primary texts of **Ibadi Islam**, including the **Jami Sahih**, **Al-Mudawwana**, and **Kitab al-Mabsut**, offer a unique perspective on **Islamic law, theology**, and **ethical practice**. These works, deeply rooted in the Ibadi tradition, emphasize values such as **justice**, **moderation**, and **collective responsibility**, setting Ibadi Islam apart from Sunni and Shia interpretations of Islam.

The **Jami Sahih**, with its careful selection of **Hadiths**, reflects the Ibadi focus on personal **moral accountability** and the promotion of **ethical behavior**. Meanwhile, **Al-Mudawwana** and **Kitab al-Mabsut** provide the legal framework that guides Ibadis in their daily lives, covering everything from ritual practice to issues of governance and social justice.

Together, these texts ensure that Ibadi communities continue to uphold the core principles of **justice**, **equity**, and **piety** in their pursuit of living a righteous life according to the teachings of **Islam**.

Returning to the Roots: The Ibadi Focus on

Early Islamic Sources

ONE OF THE DEFINING characteristics of **Ibadi Islam** is its emphasis on returning to the **pure practices** of the early Muslim community. Ibadis believe that after the death of the Prophet **Muhammad (peace be upon him)**, deviations began to emerge in how Islam was practiced and understood. Therefore, Ibadi scholars strive to restore the simplicity and authenticity of the early Islamic period, particularly the practices of the **Companions of the Prophet** and the first few generations of Muslims. This focus on **early Islamic sources** shapes their distinct approach to **governance**, **law**, and **ethics**, setting Ibadi thought apart from both Sunni and Shia traditions.

For Ibadis, the primary goal is to live in accordance with the principles exemplified by the Prophet and his closest companions, emphasizing **justice**, **moderation**, and **community welfare**. To achieve this, Ibadi scholars rely heavily on the **Quran** and **Sunnah** (traditions of the Prophet), as well as the teachings of the **early caliphs** and prominent companions, while rejecting practices and innovations that they believe were introduced later by both Sunni and Shia groups. This theological and legal approach has led Ibadis to develop a distinctive set of beliefs and practices, while also producing significant scholarly works that remain central to their community's religious life.

Emphasizing the Purity of Early Islamic Practice

Ibadis see the era of the **Rashidun Caliphs** (the first four rightly-guided caliphs) as the period when Islam was practiced in its purest form. They believe that the caliphs, especially **Abu Bakr** and **Umar**, governed according to the true principles of Islamic justice, equality, and community responsibility. For Ibadis, this era represents the ideal model for Islamic governance, and they seek to emulate the simplicity and fairness of that time in their own lives and communities.

A key part of this focus on the early community is the rejection of what they consider to be later **innovations (bid'ah)** that emerged in both Sunni and Shia practices. Ibadis reject the notion of **hereditary leadership**, as seen in both the **Umayyad** and **Abbasid dynasties** in Sunni history, as well as the concept of the **Imamate** in Shia Islam, where leadership is passed down through specific bloodlines. Instead, Ibadis emphasize the idea that leadership should be based on **merit**, **piety**, and the **ability to govern justly**, rather than on familial ties or political power.

This principle is reflected in Ibadi political thought, where they advocate for **shura** (consultation) and the **consensus** of the community in selecting leaders. Ibadis believe that the leader (Imam) should be chosen by the community based on his **competence** and commitment to **justice**. If the leader fails to uphold justice or deviates from Islamic principles, the community has the right to remove him. This idea of accountable leadership, rooted in the practices of the early caliphs, is a key tenet of Ibadi thought and is reflected in their legal and ethical writings.

Theological Works on Governance, Law, and Ethics

Ibadi scholars have produced an extensive body of literature that discusses **governance**, **law**, and **ethics** in ways that are distinct from both Sunni and Shia perspectives. Their focus is on ensuring that all aspects of life, from personal conduct to political leadership, align with the teachings of the Quran, the Sunnah, and the practices of the early Muslim community.

In the realm of **governance**, Ibadi scholars have written extensively on the qualifications and duties of the **Imam** (leader). In contrast to Sunni and Shia political thought, which often allows for dynastic or hereditary rule, Ibadi scholars argue that the Imam must be chosen through **consultation** and consensus. This ensures that the leader is accountable to the community and can be held responsible for upholding justice. If the Imam fails in his duties, he should be removed from office—a principle that underscores the Ibadi commitment to ethical leadership and the protection of the community from tyranny.

Al-Mudawwana, one of the primary Ibadi legal texts, discusses not only the legal rulings that govern daily life but also the principles of **justice** and **leadership**. It provides guidelines for how an Imam should govern, emphasizing that he must always act in the best interest of the people and uphold the values of **compassion**, **fairness**, and **equity**. This focus on ethical governance reflects the Ibadi belief that political authority should serve the community and reflect the just governance practiced by the early caliphs.

In terms of **law**, Ibadi jurisprudence places a strong emphasis on the use of **independent reasoning (ijtihad)** and the **consensus** of the community. Ibadi scholars encourage the use of **reason** and **consultation** when deriving legal rulings, ensuring that the law remains adaptable to changing circumstances while still adhering to the core principles of Islam. This pragmatic approach to law allows Ibadis to balance the teachings of the early Muslim community with the realities of contemporary life.

In **ethical matters**, Ibadi thought is characterized by its emphasis on **moderation** and **balance**. Ibadi scholars reject both extreme asceticism and excessive indulgence, advocating instead for a life of **moderate piety** and **responsibility**. They believe that Muslims should strive to live ethical lives that reflect the values of **honesty, compassion**, and **justice**, as taught by the Prophet and the early caliphs. This emphasis on personal integrity and ethical conduct is central to Ibadi identity and is reflected in their legal and theological writings.

Distinct from Sunni and Shia Perspectives

While Ibadis share certain theological beliefs with both Sunnis and Shias, they diverge on key issues related to **leadership, governance**, and **community responsibility**. Unlike Sunnis, who accept the legitimacy of the caliphs following the Rashidun period, Ibadis reject the later caliphates as corrupt and illegitimate, believing that these rulers strayed from the true path of Islam. Unlike Shias, who believe in the divine appointment of the Imams, Ibadis emphasize that leadership must be based on merit and consensus, rather than lineage.

Ibadi rejection of hereditary leadership aligns with their broader commitment to **justice** and **equality**. They believe that all members of the community should have a voice in the selection of their leaders and that power should never be concentrated in the hands of a privileged few. This commitment to communal responsibility and accountability sets Ibadis apart from both Sunni and Shia political thought.

Moreover, Ibadi theological works emphasize **rationality** and the importance of **independent reasoning** in understanding Islamic teachings. While Sunni and Shia scholars have developed their own methodologies for interpreting Islamic law, Ibadi scholars have long promoted the use of **ijtihad** to adapt Islamic principles to new challenges and circumstances. This flexible approach to legal reasoning ensures that Ibadi jurisprudence remains dynamic and responsive to the needs of the community.

Conclusion

The **Ibadi focus on early Islamic sources** reflects their commitment to preserving the purest form of Islamic practice as exemplified by the Prophet **Muhammad (peace be upon him)** and the **Rashidun Caliphs**. Their rejection of later innovations in both Sunni and Shia traditions has led to the development of a unique set of theological and legal principles, rooted in **justice, moderation, and community accountability**.

Through their extensive scholarly works, Ibadi thinkers have articulated a vision of **governance, law,** and **ethics** that emphasizes the importance of **merit-based leadership, rational**

decision-making, and the **collective good**. This approach has allowed Ibadis to maintain a distinct identity within the broader Islamic tradition while upholding the values of **justice** and **ethical governance** that they believe were central to the early Muslim community.

Foundational Texts of Ahmadiyya Islam: The Legacy of Mirza Ghulam Ahmad and His Successors

THE **Ahmadiyya Muslim Community**, founded in the late 19th century by **Mirza Ghulam Ahmad**, has developed a distinct theological framework within Islam. Central to Ahmadi belief is the understanding that **Mirza Ghulam Ahmad** was the **Mahdi** and **Messiah**, roles that many Muslims traditionally associate with a future leader who would appear to restore justice and faith in the world. As such, Ahmadis follow a unique interpretation of Islamic prophecy and the life of the Prophet **Muhammad (peace be upon him)**, guided by the writings of their founder and successive leaders.

Ahmadiyya theology is built upon two core pillars: the extensive writings of **Mirza Ghulam Ahmad**, which elaborate on his claims to spiritual leadership and his vision for the revival of Islam, and the **Quranic exegesis** of **Mirza Bashir-ud-Din Mahmud Ahmad**, the second caliph of the movement. These texts provide Ahmadis with the theological basis for their beliefs and practices, while also engaging with broader Islamic traditions in a way that sets them apart from mainstream Sunni and Shia interpretations.

The Writings of Mirza Ghulam Ahmad: A Messiah's Vision for Islam

As the central figure of the Ahmadiyya movement, **Mirza Ghulam Ahmad** (1835–1908) left behind an extensive body of work that is considered foundational to Ahmadi belief. His writings encompass a wide range of topics, including **Islamic theology, prophethood, the role of the Mahdi**, and the spiritual rejuvenation of Islam. Two of his most influential works are **Barahin-e-Ahmadiyya** and **The Philosophy of the Teachings of**

Islam, both of which outline his theological perspectives and claims to spiritual leadership.

Barahin-e-Ahmadiyya is perhaps the most significant work by **Mirza Ghulam Ahmad**, serving as a detailed defense of Islam against its critics and a declaration of his mission as the **Promised Messiah**. Written over several volumes, this book addresses the spiritual decline of the Muslim world and offers **Ghulam Ahmad's** vision for a renewed Islam that embraces both the **rational** and **spiritual** dimensions of the faith. He argues that Islam is the only true and universal religion, capable of addressing the moral and intellectual challenges of modernity.

In **Barahin-e-Ahmadiyya**, **Ghulam Ahmad** claims that God revealed to him that he was the **Messiah** and **Mahdi** foretold in both Islamic and non-Islamic scriptures. He uses **Quranic verses**, **Hadiths**, and theological reasoning to substantiate his claim, emphasizing that his mission is to **revive the true teachings of Islam** and unite humanity under the banner of peace. His approach combines **rational apologetics** with a strong emphasis on **spiritual experience**, arguing that true Islam must be based on direct communion with God.

Another key work is **The Philosophy of the Teachings of Islam**, which provides a comprehensive overview of Islamic teachings on subjects such as the nature of the human soul, the purpose of life, and the relationship between humanity and God. In this book, **Ghulam Ahmad** articulates a spiritual philosophy that emphasizes **moral purification**, **personal transformation**, and the pursuit of divine love. He argues that Islam offers a complete system for achieving spiritual and moral excellence, and that by following the teachings of the Quran, individuals can attain closeness to God and inner peace.

The Philosophy of the Teachings of Islam is particularly influential for its engagement with other religious traditions, as **Ghulam Ahmad** sought to present Islam as the culmination of all previous religious systems. His inclusive approach to interfaith dialogue, combined with his claim to being the universal **Messiah**, marks a significant departure from mainstream Islamic thought, which tends to focus more on the finality of **Prophethood** rather than the arrival of a new **spiritual guide**.

Through these and other writings, **Mirza Ghulam Ahmad** laid the theological foundation for the **Ahmadiyya community**, framing their beliefs around his role as a divinely appointed reformer. His works remain central to Ahmadi thought, studied by followers and scholars alike as key sources for understanding both the historical development of the movement and its contemporary relevance.

Tafsir al-Kabir: A Distinct Ahmadi Interpretation of the Quran

Tafsir al-Kabir, written by **Mirza Bashir-ud-Din Mahmud Ahmad** (1889–1965), the second caliph of the **Ahmadiyya community** and the son of **Mirza Ghulam Ahmad**, offers a unique Quranic exegesis that reflects the distinct theological principles of the Ahmadiyya movement. As a monumental work of tafsir (Quranic commentary), **Tafsir al-Kabir** spans several volumes and provides detailed interpretations of Quranic verses, often addressing both **spiritual** and **intellectual** concerns.

In **Tafsir al-Kabir, Mirza Bashir-ud-Din Mahmud Ahmad** follows his father's tradition of combining **rationalism** with **spiritual insight**. His approach to Quranic interpretation emphasizes the **universality** of Islam, arguing that the Quran provides timeless guidance that can address the moral and spiritual challenges of all ages. Like his father, he seeks to demonstrate the **compatibility** of Islam with modern science, philosophy, and ethics, while also affirming the Quran's **miraculous nature** and its divinely revealed wisdom.

One of the key features of **Tafsir al-Kabir** is its emphasis on the **role of the Promised Messiah** in interpreting the deeper meanings of the Quran. **Mirza Bashir-ud-Din Mahmud Ahmad** argues that his father, as the **Mahdi** and **Messiah**, was divinely inspired to reveal new insights into the Quran that had previously been hidden from the Muslim community. This belief in the continuing **guidance of the Messiah** is a central aspect of Ahmadi theology and distinguishes their approach to Quranic exegesis from mainstream interpretations.

In his commentary, **Mirza Bashir-ud-Din Mahmud Ahmad** also addresses contemporary social and political issues, offering interpretations of Quranic verses that promote **peace**, **justice**, and **tolerance**. He emphasizes that Islam is a religion of **universal peace**, and that the true jihad is the struggle for moral and spiritual reform, rather than physical warfare. This focus on **non-violence** and **interfaith dialogue** reflects the broader Ahmadi commitment to promoting global harmony and understanding.

Tafsir al-Kabir also engages with theological debates within the broader Muslim world, particularly regarding the status of **prophethood** and the finality of the **Prophet Muhammad (peace be upon him)**. While mainstream Sunni and Shia Islam maintain that Muhammad was the last prophet, the Ahmadi interpretation—based on the teachings of **Mirza Ghulam Ahmad**—argues that **non-law-bearing prophethood** continues, and that **Ghulam Ahmad** was a **subordinate prophet** sent to revive the true teachings of Islam.

This interpretation has been a source of significant controversy within the Muslim world, with many Muslim scholars rejecting the Ahmadiyya view as a deviation from orthodox Islamic beliefs. However, within the Ahmadi community, **Tafsir al-Kabir** is seen as a vital contribution to Islamic scholarship, offering a new lens through which to understand the Quran and its relevance in the modern era.

Conclusion

The **primary books in Ahmadiyya Islam**, including the writings of **Mirza Ghulam Ahmad** and **Tafsir al-Kabir** by **Mirza Bashir-ud-Din Mahmud Ahmad**, form the foundation of the Ahmadiyya community's distinct theological framework. **Mirza Ghulam Ahmad's** works, such as **Barahin-e-Ahmadiyya** and **The Philosophy of the Teachings of Islam**, outline his claims to be the **Promised Messiah** and provide a spiritual vision for the renewal of Islam. His writings emphasize the importance of **rationality, spiritual experience**, and the **universal truth** of Islam.

Similarly, **Tafsir al-Kabir** reflects the Ahmadi approach to **Quranic exegesis**, combining **rational interpretation** with a belief in the continuing **spiritual guidance** of the Messiah. Through these texts, the **Ahmadiyya movement** offers a unique perspective within the Islamic world, one that emphasizes **peace, justice**, and **spiritual revival**. Despite the controversies surrounding their beliefs, these works remain central to the identity and theological foundation of the Ahmadiyya Muslim Community, guiding its followers in both **faith** and **practice**.

Ahmadiyya Hadith Interpretation: Prophecies and Fulfillment through the Teachings of Mirza Ghulam Ahmad

IN **Ahmadiyya Islam**, the interpretation of **Hadith** plays a crucial role in shaping the community's understanding of **prophecies** and the mission of their founder, **Mirza Ghulam Ahmad**. While Ahmadis accept many of the same **Hadith collections** as mainstream Sunni Islam, including the revered works of **Sahih al-Bukhari** and **Sahih Muslim**, they approach these texts through a unique lens. For Ahmadis, many of the prophecies contained in the Hadith collections find their **fulfillment** in the life and teachings of

Mirza Ghulam Ahmad, who they believe was divinely appointed as the **Mahdi** and **Promised Messiah.**

This approach to Hadith interpretation sets Ahmadis apart from other Islamic groups, particularly in their understanding of **the end times, the coming of the Mahdi,** and the nature of **prophethood.** Ahmadis argue that **Mirza Ghulam Ahmad's** arrival fulfills key prophecies mentioned in the Hadith, reshaping traditional Islamic eschatology and offering a new vision for the spiritual revival of Islam.

The Role of Prophecy in Ahmadi Hadith Interpretation

A central focus of Ahmadiyya Hadith interpretation is the **prophetic traditions** concerning the **Mahdi** and **Messiah,** figures who are foretold in both Sunni and Shia traditions to appear at the end of times to restore justice and establish a true Islamic order. For mainstream Sunni Muslims, these figures are generally seen as distinct individuals, with the Mahdi expected to lead the Muslim community and the **second coming of Jesus** (Isa) heralding the final victory of truth over falsehood. However, in Ahmadiyya belief, **Mirza Ghulam Ahmad** claimed to fulfill both roles as the **Promised Messiah** and **Mahdi,** reinterpreting these prophecies in a symbolic rather than a literal sense.

For instance, one of the Hadiths often cited by Ahmadis refers to the **second coming of Jesus,** who will descend from heaven, break the cross, kill the swine, and end religious conflict. While mainstream interpretations expect a literal return of **Jesus (peace be upon him),** Ahmadis interpret this Hadith metaphorically. They believe that the **breaking of the cross** signifies the **defeat of Christianity's dominance,** and the **killing of swine** represents the **eradication of sinful practices.** In this view, **Mirza Ghulam Ahmad** fulfilled this prophecy not as the actual return of Jesus but as a spiritual **Messiah** sent to restore the true teachings of Islam and guide humanity toward peace.

Hadiths on the Mahdi's Emergence and the Ahmadi Interpretation

Another important Hadith tradition speaks about the **coming of the Mahdi**, who will appear in a time of widespread corruption and injustice to lead the Muslim community back to righteousness. Sunni Muslims traditionally believe that the Mahdi will be a descendant of the **Prophet Muhammad (peace be upon him)** and will arise as a political and spiritual leader to unite the ummah.

Ahmadis, however, interpret the role of the **Mahdi** in a **spiritual** rather than **political** sense. They believe that **Mirza Ghulam Ahmad** fulfilled this prophecy by providing spiritual leadership in an era marked by moral decline and the weakening of Islam. Ahmadis argue that the signs described in the Hadith regarding the appearance of the Mahdi—such as the rise of **false doctrines** and the **misuse of religion** for political gain—were evident in the late 19th century, when **Ghulam Ahmad** emerged to **reform** and **revitalize** Islam. His role, they contend, was not to lead a **physical jihad** but to engage in a **spiritual jihad** (jihad of the pen) to defend Islam from both internal and external threats.

Ahmadi Interpretations of Hadith on Jihad

The concept of **jihad** as mentioned in the Hadith is another area where Ahmadis offer a distinct interpretation. Many Hadiths discuss the importance of striving in the cause of Islam, with some referring to physical combat against oppression. However, **Mirza Ghulam Ahmad** reinterpreted the concept of **jihad** as a **spiritual struggle**, particularly relevant to the modern context in which Islam faces intellectual and ideological challenges rather than physical threats.

In his writings, **Mirza Ghulam Ahmad** argued that the time for violent jihad had ended, and that the true struggle of Muslims in the modern world should focus on **moral reform**, **spiritual purification**, and the **intellectual defense of Islam** through reasoned debate and dialogue. He pointed to Hadiths that emphasized the importance of the **greater jihad** (jihad al-akbar)—the struggle against one's inner desires and sins—as the primary form of jihad for contemporary Muslims. This interpretation was significant in shaping the Ahmadi community's pacifist stance and their emphasis on **non-violence** and **peaceful propagation** of Islam.

Hadith on the Signs of the End Times

Ahmadis also interpret the **signs of the end times**, as mentioned in the Hadith, in ways that align with **Mirza Ghulam Ahmad's** mission. Many Hadiths describe natural disasters, widespread injustice, and social chaos as precursors to the **Day of Judgment**. Ahmadis believe that many of these signs were already manifest during the late 19th century, including the **decline of moral values**, the rise of **materialism**, and the spread of **religious confusion**.

According to Ahmadi teachings, the advent of **Mirza Ghulam Ahmad** marked the **beginning of the final age**, during which humanity would be called back to the true teachings of Islam. His arrival, they argue, was a **mercy from God**, offering the world a chance to reform before the ultimate Day of Judgment. This understanding of the **end times** is central to Ahmadi eschatology, distinguishing their belief system from other Islamic interpretations that await a future Mahdi and Messiah.

Hadith as Evidence of Continuation of Prophethood

A particularly controversial aspect of **Ahmadi Hadith interpretation** relates to the concept of **prophethood**. Mainstream Sunni and Shia Islam hold that **Prophet Muhammad (peace be upon him)** was the **final prophet** (Khatam an-Nabiyyin), and that no prophets will come after him. Ahmadis accept the finality of Muhammad's **law-bearing prophethood**, but they argue that **non-law-bearing prophets** can still emerge, particularly those who act as spiritual reformers.

Ahmadis cite various Hadiths that speak of **the coming of a reformer** in every century or the **revival** of Islam in the latter days. They interpret these as indications that the **institution of prophethood**—in a **subordinate** and **reformist** capacity—can continue, with **Mirza Ghulam Ahmad** being the most significant example. Ahmadis maintain that **Ghulam Ahmad** was sent not to bring a new law but to restore the true spirit of Islam, fulfilling the prophecies found in both the Quran and Hadith.

This interpretation has been a major point of contention between **Ahmadi Muslims** and the broader Muslim community, leading to the **marginalization** of Ahmadis in some countries. Despite this, the **Ahmadiyya movement** remains firm in its belief that their founder's mission aligns with the **prophecies** outlined in the Hadith, and that his teachings provide the framework for **Islam's spiritual revival**.

Conclusion

Ahmadiyya interpretation of **Hadith** is deeply rooted in the belief that **Mirza Ghulam Ahmad** fulfilled key prophecies concerning the **Mahdi** and **Messiah**. Ahmadis accept many of the same Hadith collections as other Muslims but interpret these texts through the lens of **Ghulam Ahmad's mission**. They view his arrival as the realization of **prophecies** about the end times, the revival of Islam, and the spiritual leadership needed to guide the Muslim community in a time of moral decline.

Through their unique approach to Hadith interpretation, Ahmadis offer a **spiritual** and **metaphorical** understanding of traditional Islamic prophecies, emphasizing the importance of **peaceful reform, moral struggle**, and **intellectual defense** of Islam. This perspective continues to shape the identity of the **Ahmadiyya Muslim Community** and its commitment to promoting **justice, peace**, and **religious renewal** in the modern world.

Appendix: Key Concepts, Figures, and Texts in Islamic Doctrines

This appendix provides definitions and explanations of important terms, figures, and texts referenced throughout the book. These entries cover major Islamic sects, theological concepts, and foundational works, offering readers a comprehensive guide to the diverse beliefs and practices within **Islam.**

1. Quran

The central religious text of Islam, believed to be the literal word of God revealed to the Prophet **Muhammad (peace be upon him)** over 23 years. It serves as the primary source of Islamic theology, law, and spiritual guidance for all Muslims.

2. Hadith

A collection of sayings, actions, and approvals of the Prophet **Muhammad (peace be upon him).** Hadiths are used in conjunction with the Quran to guide Islamic law and practice. Different Islamic sects recognize various Hadith collections as authoritative.

3. Sharia

Islamic law derived from the Quran, Hadith, and other sources. It covers religious, ethical, and legal guidelines for how Muslims should live their lives.

4. Sunni Islam

The largest branch of Islam, Sunni Muslims recognize the first four caliphs as rightful successors to the Prophet **Muhammad** (**peace be upon him**). Sunni jurisprudence is based on four schools of thought: **Hanafi, Maliki, Shafi'i,** and **Hanbali.**

5. Shia Islam

A major branch of Islam that believes **Imam Ali (peace be upon him)**, the cousin and son-in-law of the Prophet, was the rightful successor. Shia Muslims emphasize the authority of the **Twelve Imams**, beginning with Imam Ali.

6. Imamate

In **Shia Islam**, the Imamate refers to the leadership of the Muslim community by a series of twelve divinely appointed Imams, starting with **Imam Ali (peace be upon him)**. These Imams are considered infallible and are responsible for guiding the community in both spiritual and temporal matters.

7. Twelver Shia

The largest sect of Shia Islam, which recognizes twelve Imams. **Twelvers** believe that the twelfth Imam, **Imam Muhammad al-Mahdi (peace be upon him)**, is in occultation and will return as the Mahdi to restore justice.

8. Sufism

The mystical dimension of Islam, focused on personal spiritual experience and the pursuit of divine union. Sufis often engage in practices like **Dhikr** (remembrance of God) and follow specific **Sufi orders.**

9. Wahhabism

A conservative Islamic reform movement that seeks to return to the original practices of Islam. It emphasizes **Tawhid** (the oneness of God) and rejects **Bid'ah** (innovations). Wahhabism originated in the 18th century in **Saudi Arabia.**

10. Salafism

An Islamic movement that advocates for a return to the practices of the early Muslim community (Salaf). Salafism shares some similarities with **Wahhabism** but has a broader scope and includes a variety of subgroups.

11. Ahmadiyya Movement

A reformist sect founded by **Mirza Ghulam Ahmad** in the late 19th century. Ahmadis believe that Ghulam Ahmad was the **Promised Messiah** and **Mahdi**. The movement emphasizes non-violence and peaceful propagation of Islam.

12. Ibadi Islam

A distinct branch of Islam that developed in **Oman** and parts of North Africa. Ibadis emphasize the early Islamic community's practices and have a unique approach to governance and law. They reject hereditary leadership and advocate for consensus-based rule.

13. Rashidun Caliphs

The first four caliphs after the death of the Prophet **Muhammad (peace be upon him)**: **Abu Bakr**, **Umar**, **Uthman**, and **Ali (peace be upon him)**. These caliphs are considered rightly guided by Sunni Muslims.

14. Mahdi

A prophesied figure in Islamic eschatology who is expected to appear at the end of times to restore justice and righteousness. The concept of the Mahdi varies across Islamic sects, with Shia Muslims expecting the return of the **12th Imam**, and Ahmadis believing that **Mirza Ghulam Ahmad** was the Mahdi.

15. Jihad

In Islamic theology, **jihad** means "struggle" or "striving," and can refer to both spiritual and physical efforts in the way of God. While jihad is sometimes associated with armed struggle, it primarily refers to personal efforts to improve one's faith and moral character.

16. Al-Kafi

A major Hadith collection compiled by **Al-Kulayni**, central to **Twelver Shia Islam**. It includes theological, legal, and ethical teachings attributed to the Prophet and the **Imams**.

17. Man La Yahduruhu al-Faqih

A Hadith collection compiled by **Al-Saduq**, an important source for **Twelver Shia** legal opinions. It provides practical legal rulings on worship, family life, and social obligations.

18. Tafsir al-Tabari

A widely respected Sunni Quranic exegesis by **Imam al-Tabari**. It offers detailed interpretations of Quranic verses and is a foundational text in Sunni tafsir (exegesis).

19. Barahin-e-Ahmadiyya

One of the most important works by **Mirza Ghulam Ahmad**, in which he defends the truth of Islam and outlines his claim to be the **Promised Messiah** and **Mahdi**.

20. Tafsir al-Kabir

A Quranic exegesis by **Mirza Bashir-ud-Din Mahmud Ahmad**, the second caliph of the **Ahmadiyya Muslim Community**. It offers a unique Ahmadi interpretation of Quranic verses, emphasizing **Mirza Ghulam Ahmad's** role as the fulfillment of prophecies.

21. Al-Mudawwana

A foundational legal text in **Ibadi Islam** that outlines the core principles of Ibadi jurisprudence and law, emphasizing justice, ethical governance, and consensus-based leadership.

22. Jami Sahih

A Hadith collection compiled by **Al-Rabi bin Habib**, which is an early and significant text in **Ibadi Islam**, reflecting the distinct theological priorities of the Ibadis.

23. Dhikr

A spiritual practice in **Sufism** that involves the **remembrance of God** through the recitation of His names, Quranic verses, or supplications. It is a key component of Sufi worship.

24. Fiqh

Islamic jurisprudence that governs the religious, social, and legal aspects of a Muslim's life. Different schools of thought, such as the **Hanafi, Shafi'i, Maliki**, and **Hanbali** schools in Sunni Islam, as well as the **Ja'fari** school in Shia Islam, have developed their own interpretations of fiqh.

25. Usul al-Fiqh

The principles or methodology of Islamic jurisprudence. **Usul al-Fiqh** is the framework that scholars use to derive legal rulings from the **Quran, Hadith, consensus (Ijma)**, and **analogy (Qiyas)**.

26. Ijtihad

The process of independent legal reasoning used by Islamic scholars to interpret **Sharia** and derive rulings. **Ijtihad** is essential for adapting Islamic teachings to new situations and challenges.

27. Shirk

In Islamic theology, **Shirk** refers to the sin of associating partners with God, which is considered the gravest sin. It involves attributing divine attributes to others besides God, and is strongly condemned in the **Quran**.

28. Tawhid

The belief in the absolute oneness of God. **Tawhid** is the most fundamental concept in Islam, affirming that God is unique, without partners or equals.

29. Bid'ah

Innovation in religious matters that is not supported by the Quran or **Sunnah. Bid'ah** is considered negative in Islamic theology, especially when it deviates from the established practices of the early Muslim community.

30. Fana

A key concept in **Sufism**, meaning "annihilation" or the loss of self in the divine presence. **Fana** is the process by which a Sufi attains unity with God, transcending individual ego.

31. Hajj

The annual pilgrimage to **Mecca**, which is one of the **Five Pillars of Islam**. All Muslims who are physically and financially able are required to perform **Hajj** at least once in their lifetime.

32. Zakat

The obligatory giving of alms, another of the **Five Pillars of Islam**. **Zakat** is typically 2.5% of a Muslim's savings and is distributed to those in need, promoting social equality and care for the less fortunate.

33. Kharijites

An early Islamic sect that split from both Sunni and Shia Islam, known for their strict interpretation of Islam and their belief that only the most pious could lead the Muslim community. Ibadis trace their roots to the **Kharijites** but developed a more moderate stance.

34. Ijma

The consensus of Islamic scholars on a particular legal or theological issue. **Ijma** is one of the key sources of Islamic jurisprudence, alongside the **Quran**, **Hadith**, and **Qiyas** (analogy).

35. Qiyas

A form of reasoning in Islamic jurisprudence where a ruling from the **Quran** or **Hadith** is extended to new situations by analogy. It is one of the methods used in **fiqh** to derive rulings for issues not explicitly mentioned in the primary sources.

36. Ja'fari School

The school of jurisprudence followed by most **Twelver Shia Muslims**. It is named after **Imam Ja'far al-Sadiq (peace be upon** him), the sixth Shia Imam, who is credited with developing this legal tradition.

37. Ibadism

A distinct branch of Islam that developed independently of Sunni and Shia Islam, primarily practiced in **Oman** and parts of **North Africa**. Ibadis emphasize early Islamic principles of simplicity, justice, and moderation.

38. Dhimmi

Non-Muslims living in an Islamic state who are granted protection and religious freedom in exchange for paying a tax known as **jizya**. The term refers to Jews, Christians, and sometimes others, living under Muslim rule.

39. Ashura

A day of mourning observed by Shia Muslims to commemorate the martyrdom of **Imam Hussein (peace be upon him)**, the grandson of the Prophet **Muhammad (peace be upon him)**, at the **Battle of Karbala**.

40. Ismaili Shia

A sect of **Shia Islam** that broke away from the **Twelver Shia** line of Imams after the death of the sixth Imam, **Ja'far al-Sadiq (peace be upon him)**. **Ismailis** follow a line of Imams descended from **Ismail**, the eldest son of **Ja'far**.

41. Occultation (Ghaybah)

In **Twelver Shia Islam**, the concept that the twelfth Imam, **Imam Muhammad al-Mahdi (peace be upon him)**, went into hiding (occultation) and will return as the **Mahdi** to bring justice to the world.

42. Zaydi Shia

A branch of **Shia Islam** that follows **Zayd ibn Ali**, the grandson of **Imam Hussein (peace be upon him)**. **Zaydis** differ from **Twelver**

Shia in their views on the Imamate and are more aligned with Sunni legal practices.

43. Riba

The prohibition of interest or usury in Islamic finance. **Riba** is considered exploitative and unjust, and Islamic law prohibits charging interest on loans.

44. Sawm

The practice of fasting during the month of **Ramadan**, one of the **Five Pillars of Islam**. Muslims abstain from food, drink, and other physical needs from dawn until sunset during this holy month.

45. Khalifa (Caliph)

The leader of the Muslim community, considered the successor to the Prophet **Muhammad (peace be upon him)**. The role of the **caliph** has been interpreted differently in Sunni and Shia traditions.

46. Shura

A principle in Islamic governance that emphasizes **consultation** among members of the community. It is often used in decision-making processes to ensure that leadership is based on consensus and the welfare of the community.

47. Barzakh

In Islamic theology, **Barzakh** refers to the intermediate state between death and resurrection, where souls await the **Day of Judgment**. It is seen as a period of reflection on one's deeds in life before the final judgment.

48. Jizya

A tax levied on non-Muslim subjects (primarily **dhimmis**) living in an Islamic state. In return for paying the **jizya**, non-Muslims are granted protection and the freedom to practice their religion under Islamic rule.

49. Istihsan

A principle in Islamic jurisprudence, particularly in the **Hanafi school**, which allows jurists to prioritize rulings that promote the **common good** or justice, even if they deviate from strict legal reasoning. **Istihsan** can be used to address practical needs while staying within the ethical boundaries of **Sharia**.

50. Taqiyya

A concept in Shia Islam that permits Muslims to conceal their faith or true beliefs when they face persecution or danger. **Taqiyya** is seen as a protective measure to preserve one's life or faith in times of hardship.